MW01252995

Journey Into Prayer

Journey Into Prayer

Bill Stewart

Copyright © 2010 by Bill Stewart.

Library of Congress Control Number:		2010909652
ISBN:	Hardcover	978-1-4535-3104-4
	Softcover	978-1-4535-3103-7
	Ebook	978-1-4535-3105-1

All rights reserved. No part of this book may be reproduced or transmitted in any form or by any means, electronic or mechanical, including photocopying, recording, or by any information storage and retrieval system, without permission in writing from the copyright owner.

This book was printed in the United States of America.

To order additional copies of this book, contact:
Xlibris Corporation
1-888-795-4274
www.Xlibris.com
Orders@Xlibris.com
82322

CONTENTS

To Rita

My wife, a great example of combining
her prayers with her actions.

INTRODUCTION

My name is Philip, and I am going on a journey. I would like to invite you to come with me as far as you wish to go. The journey I would like to make is a journey into prayer. I have not been a Christian very long, but since I started on the Christian way, I have heard many people talk about prayer. They say it is very important. They say I cannot expect to make much progress in my Christian life unless I learn to pray. Those who are trying to help me in my experience with God speak well of prayer. Prayer, they say, is an essential ingredient to my spiritual health and vitality. If I am to experience God in a real and rich way, then I must undertake this journey into prayer. It is through prayer, they explain to me, that my soul really gets into touch with the Divine. This is where my spirit contacts His Spirit. It is in prayer where I learn to commune with Him and hear His voice and receive His guidance. When it comes to prayer, they say, you have many exciting and wonderful things to learn.

Much to learn? This surprises me; I did not think it was that complicated. All you have to do is get on your knees (even that is not essential) and tell God all of the things you want and ask Him to help you get them. What could be simpler? When I say this to those who have experience and know better, they simply smile at me, shake their heads, and say, "No! No! Philip, if that is what you think, then you do indeed have a lot to learn. It is all the more important that you make the journey into prayer. And if you are successful in this journey, you will reach the City of Prayer. This is where the people who know how to pray well live out their lives. Life in the City of Prayer will teach you that there is a lot more to prayer than just getting from God what you think He ought to give you. The journey to the city will itself teach you many things, and when you live in the city for a while, you will find it a most rewarding and rich experience. As your prayer life develops, your soul will experience great satisfaction, and you will learn to draw closer and closer to Him. The sense of union will increase, and the understanding of His will and wishes for your life will become clearer.

"All through the ages, the great servants of God have understood that they needed, more and more, to learn how to pray. Even Jesus Himself spent much time in prayer. Often He would separate Himself from the crowds and from His disciples, in order to pray. He spent whole nights in prayer. His disciples watched this aspect of His life and realized how important it was to Him, so they asked Him to 'teach us also how to pray.' So we encourage you to join them, Philip, and find out how to pray. It will be an exciting and rewarding journey. It will bring you more spiritual reality and vividness than any other journey you could undertake."

I respected this advice from my spiritual mentors. They seemed to know what they were talking about, so I decided that I would start the journey of prayer that leads to the City of Prayer. They did warn me, however, that this will be a challenging journey but, nevertheless, well worth the effort. Like most worthwhile journeys, it will have its times of difficulty, but also its rewards and encouragements. So I am going to give it a try. I would like you to accompany me on this journey. If you are more advanced in your understanding of prayer than I am, I would certainly appreciate your help and support, and who knows, you too may learn some important things about the art of talking and communing with God. There seems no end to the potential for growth and development in the soul's quest for God.

Actually, at this early stage in my Christian life I have found that there are many people who are interested in learning more about prayer. Nearly everybody, it seems to me, tries to pray at some time or another, and in one form or another. Some enjoy it and get something out of it, while others seem disappointed with the results. There are others, I understand, who do it out of habit or duty, because they think it is the right thing to do, but beyond fulfilling their duty, they do not seem too interested in learning more, or developing it into a significant part of their Christian experience. Still others that I talked to said they had tried to pray but found, in spite of the many promises made about it, that prayer did not seem to work for them and they have become discouraged. They think the fault is with themselves, and they wonder just what it is that they are doing wrong. So I realize from all this that I am not the only one who has a lot to learn about prayer. There are many like I am, just beginning this journey. But I hope that others, in spite of the challenges and difficulties will make the journey into prayer. It is encouraging at this point to know that there is such a wide interest in prayer and that so many people, whether successfully or unsuccessfully, have at least tried to practice it.

Someone suggested to me that prayer may be a little like learning to play the piano. Most people would like to play the piano and think it is a good thing. Some have even gained an elementary knowledge of the piano and can sit down and pick out a simple tune or two, but not too many are willing to pay the price and go to the discipline of becoming really good at it. When it comes to prayer, I have a desire in my heart to become really good at it. I want to learn well how to talk to God and have God talk to me. I want to know how to fellowship with Him and absorb His Spirit into mine. Jesus, when He prayed near the end of His life, prayed for us, and He said in His prayer, "Father, just as you are in me and I am in you. May they also be in us so that the world may believe that you have sent me" (John 17:21). I am hungry for that kind of close fellowship with God. To be one with Him. To be in such harmony with Him that I am actually united to Him. Jesus also made the astounding promise, "If you remain in me, and my words remain in you, ask whatever you wish and it will be given you. This is to my Father's glory, that you bear much fruit, showing yourselves to be my disciples" (John 15:7-8). This seems away beyond my reach right now, but even if I could approximate to this kind of relationship with God I would be delighted.

I know I have a long way to go, and many lessons to learn, but I want to undertake the journey into prayer and arrive at the City of Prayer. I want to live there, experience its richness, enjoy its beauty, and live that close to God. I want to learn to pray better and to pray more like my Lord. Why not join me in the journey? My mentors in this matter advised me that the first step in the journey is to go to what they call the "Viewing Platform." From this platform you can catch a distant glimpse of the City of Prayer; see some of its features and even sense some of its atmosphere. Anyone seriously pursuing the matter of prayer should certainly start at the Viewing Platform. The wonder of the city will become a little clearer, and the value of actually going there will become more evident. It will also give you an idea of the type of journey that is before you if you really want to reach the city. The Viewing Platform is the place to start.

The Journey

CHAPTER ONE

EARLY INFORMATION

One of my prayer mentors told me that, in many ways, starting into prayer is like visiting one of our national parks. If you have ever visited any of our beautiful national parks, you will discover that there are different levels available for experiencing the parks. Most parks have a visitors' center. This level of park experience is usually very easily accessible. You can normally drive up to it, park your car, and enter a well constructed and commodious building. It is comfortable and interesting, with many conveniences. In the visitors' center a great deal of information about the park is made available to you. You are taught the purpose of the park; you can view presentations about some of its special features and values. Most visitors show interest in the displays that exhibit the specimens of the park, its fauna, flora, and natural features. These visitors' centers in the national parks are very popular. Great crowds of tourists visit the centers and enjoy this interesting but rather superficial experience of what the park is all about. Most people will drive through the park, walk around the visitors' center, see some of the exhibits, pick up some information pamphlets, and then move on, having "visited the park."

In addition to the visitors' center, however, most parks also urge people to experience the park in a deeper and more personal way. Usually there are trails on which you are encouraged to walk. The trails help you to experience the park in a much more realistic way than the rather artificial but easier experience of the visitors' center. On the trails you move right into, and interact with, the park in a more immediate way. Occasionally on the trails you can have the benefit of a guided tour by a park naturalist. Sometimes the trails have information markers spaced along the way that explain the features you are seeing and give you opportunity to observe and touch for yourself. The trails are designed to get you out into the park and experience in a direct way the sights, sounds, and atmosphere of the park. It is a much more vivid, personal, and rewarding park experience than is offered by just viewing the exhibits in the visitors' center. On the trails, you are not only hearing about the park and experiencing it from a distance but you are actually walking through it for yourself and becoming a part of it.

Beyond the trails, however, it is possible to have an even more intimate experience of the park. Some people want to get away from the visitors' center and the tourist trails and get right into the wilderness itself. They want to experience for themselves the wonder of communing with nature, by actually living in it, and for a short time at least, by being a part of it, with all its beauty, rewards, and demands. In some parks you can camp and live in the park for a few days. You can swim in its lakes, walk its trails, climb its mountains, and see its sights. Some people go even farther than that. They hike into the back country, or they canoe and portage into wilderness places. This way they experience the park and react to it in a much more personal way. They live in it and interact with it and learn from it at a depth they could never know if they only experienced the park from the visitors' center. They become part of the park and its ecosystem. They join the life of the park and become part of its existence. For some people, this is the real way to experience the national parks. It is often arduous and difficult. Sometimes they may even encounter significant personal dangers such as getting lost, falling, drowning, or crossing paths with aggressive animals. But to these people the excitement and wonder of becoming part of the park and its wilderness experience are well worth the costs and efforts involved. They, more than anyone else, experience and taste the wonders and features of the park.

In many ways, the journey into prayer is similar to experiencing the national parks. Like the parks, there are many different levels of experiencing prayer. The Viewing Platform is the visitors' center level. It is easy, interesting, and many are quite willing to experience prayer at this level. Just as many people become acquainted with the parks through the visitors' center but never go out on the trails or into the back country, so many receive only the cursory, superficial, and introductory benefits of prayer by visiting the Viewing Platform but never undertake a serious journey into the trails that lead to the City of Prayer. Each person has a very important decision to make. They must decide how deeply involved they will become in the life of prayer.

Nevertheless, for all who are interested in prayer, the Viewing Platform, I was told, is a good place to start. From there you can decide just how far you want to go and how involved you want to become in the life of prayer. So in keeping with the advice I had received, I made my way to the center that contains the

Viewing Platform. As I approached the center, I was rather surprised at the size and elegance of the place. There was a large and modern building, which not only housed the platform but many of the other exhibits that gave insights into the life of prayer. It is more like a facility than a platform. I am also amazed at the number of people here. I never realized that so many people had an interest in prayer and wanted to see the City of Prayer.

As I approached the building, I was met by a man who introduced himself as the gatekeeper for the Viewing Platform.

"Welcome to the Viewing Platform for the City of Prayer. Can I help you?"

"Yes!" I said, "I am interested in getting to the City of Prayer and living there, so I would appreciate any information and guidance that you can give me that will help me on that journey."

"Indeed," said the gatekeeper, "you will find many things here that will help you get to your destination. First, there is an information room. It contains an immense amount of information about prayer. You will find books, pamphlets, slide shows, and maps about the City of Prayer and how to get there. Most of this material has come from people who have actually been there and so have good authority when they speak about it. You should spend some time getting good information. Many neglect to do this and, in their enthusiasm, set out on the journey into prayer without proper guidance, but they soon find themselves in difficulty and making mistakes that they could have easily avoided if they had acquired better information and direction. So it is important that you get good, reliable information.

"Second, you should talk to some of the trail guides. They are people who have actually been to, and lived in, the City of Prayer. They have experienced it and are well acquainted with it. And since they have traveled the way, they know how to get there. They will give you great help for your journey to the city and also give you an idea what to expect when you arrive there.

"Third, there is the Viewing Platform itself. From the Viewing Platform, on a good day, you can actually get a glimpse of the City of Prayer. When you really see it, it will be a great encouragement to you. Many who see the city and catch a glimpse of its beauty, strength and grace, are moved and motivated to actually take the journey and get there. It is a very inspiring and moving sight to see the City of Prayer. If you can see it, you will want to go there.

"Lastly, we also have a prayer room. Here you can prepare your heart for the journey ahead and decide just how far you will commit yourself to go on the journey. In this prayer room you will likely meet others who are inspired by the same desire and hunger that you have to get to the City of Prayer. You might even find companions who will journey with you. After the prayer room, if you are interested, you will see arrows pointing you to the actual head of the trail that leads to the City of Prayer. If you follow the arrows you will get started on the journey."

I thanked the gatekeeper for his help and then asked him, "But why are there so many people here? I did not expect to find so many people who are interested in prayer and are seeking to journey to the City of Prayer? Are all these people going to undertake the journey into prayer?"

"Oh no! Many people know and sense that there is much more to prayer than they are presently experiencing, and that there is a pathway that leads them into a far greater understanding of prayer, but they do not make the effort that is necessary for them to get there. Many settle for a light, informal experience in prayer. They are content to experience it at a level that does not call for much commitment or time. They may want to read about it and know more about it. They will look at the city and wish they could go there but do not want to invest the effort and time that is necessary into actually getting there. After they have viewed the city, they may spend a little time in the prayer room and then leave to go about their own business. For them, prayer is just a casual experience that does not penetrate deeply into their heart or cause much change in their life.

"Others will go a little farther and find the head of the trail and may even journey along the pathway of prayer for a little distance, but decide that there is too much involved and come back. You must understand the journey to the City of Prayer is not easy and demands time, effort, and discipline, and many do not want to make this kind of investment. But the fact is that even the superficial experience of just viewing prayer and thinking about it seems to help them a little, and they go away feeling better than when they came. I think you will find when you look at the city from the Viewing Platform, even at this distance, that a little of the atmosphere and spirit of the city radiates out and can reach down here. Some people, who go no farther than the Viewing Platform, do indeed sense this and absorb it, and they are helped and strengthened by it, even though they will never get closer to the city than they are now. The City of Prayer is a very powerful place and exerts tremendous influence, so that even those who do nothing more than view it from a far distance can be touched by it. These people do gain an idea about how important and influential the city is, and know it would be good for them to live there, but they are not prepared or ready yet to undertake the demanding journey in that is required.

"Then there are those, like yourself, who are hungry enough for a closer relationship with God and a better interaction with God and will give themselves to discovering the blessings and secrets of prayer. As you explore the Viewing Platform, you will meet many people who are satisfied with a casual acquaintance with prayer. I hope, however, that you will also meet some others who are ready to undertake the journey to the City of Prayer with you."

I thanked the gatekeeper again for his help and moved into the building that housed the Viewing Platform for the City of Prayer. Following the advice of the gatekeeper, I thought the first place I should visit was the information room. This would give me some of the basic information that I needed. It would tell me more about what was involved in the journey into prayer. I would understand better its values and benefits as well as its responsibilities and duties. I would gain some information on the nature of the pathway that leads to the City of Prayer. I hoped to receive information about some of the difficulties and pitfalls of the journey. It was important, I thought, that I learn from those who have gone before and benefit from their experience and mistakes.

When I entered the information room and saw how large it was, I was once again surprised. It seemed to be more than just a place for quick information; it was a vast library suitable for study and reference. Obviously many people had written about prayer. This large library confirmed my growing impression that prayer was not just a little corner of human experience that was reserved only for a few select people, but it was a basic, fundamental interest and hunger of the human heart. Wherever you find people, you find some level of desire to communicate with the spiritual world that exists both in them and all around them. There is an innate need in the human heart that causes us to gravitate toward fellowship and communion with God, and prayer is understood to be an important expression of that fundamental hunger and need.

The vast amount of material in the room, however, somewhat overwhelmed me. In order to get the simple and basic information that I needed, I wondered where I would start to look in the midst of this wealth of material. In my uncertainty, I went up to the lady librarian who sat behind a desk in the middle of the information room.

"Can you help me?" I asked. "I am looking for some good reading material that will give me basic information about the City of Prayer and about the journey I have to undertake in order to get there."

"Well, certainly," she said, smiling. "Are you a Christian?"

"Yes," I said.

"Have you been a Christian for long?"

"No."

"Good," she said, "that is helpful. As you see there is a lot of fine material written about prayer by people from other religions as well as Christianity. It seems that prayer, in some form or another, is a vital part of all aspects of human spirituality. You, however, will want Christian books on prayer. Also, since you are a young Christian, you may not yet be ready for many of the books on prayer written by very advanced and specialized people. These books would not be appropriate for a beginner like yourself. You are looking for something very basic and simple to help you get started?"

"Yes," I replied.

She took out a piece of paper and started to write some things on it.

"There," she said, handing me the paper. "Here is a list of four books that will give you the basic information that you need. It is important that you keep it simple. I would start with these books." (**This list of books is given in the appendix.)

As she handed me the paper with the list on it, she said, "While these books will help you, it is important that you understand that the two best sources for improving your prayer life are not found in books written about prayer. The first best source is practice. You will learn much by the trial and error of faithfully practicing prayer in your life. Like developing any skill, prayer is best learned by faithful and intelligent participation. The other best source for learning about prayer is the Bible. Especially look at the prayers of Jesus and the things He said about prayer. There is no greater authority than this. Also, Christians down through the ages have used the book of Psalms as a devotional prayer book. The Psalms are mostly a book of prayer and worship. They express the heart desires and deep emotions of those who wrote them. And prayer should express our deepest heart desires and emotions. The Psalms will show you how other people expressed themselves to God. Some of these prayers are not appropriate for us today. Indeed you may find some of them objectionable and not very Christian in their desires. But they are honest and come from an earlier, pre-Christian time. The way to get the most benefit from the Psalms is not just to read them but to pray them. Make their prayers your prayers. Let the prayers in the Psalms express for you what is in your heart, and you will find them a very honest and real way to begin to talk with God. They are not all pretty, or even what we would consider Christian, but they do express the prayers and desires, even wrong and sinful desires, of the people who wrote them."

I thanked the lady for this good advice. From the shelves of the library I hunted down the books she had recommended and decided to peruse them right away. I happened to sit down at a table opposite a rather elderly and elegant-looking lady, who looked up and smiled as I sat down. She obviously wanted to strike up a conversation, so I said to her, "I see you are reading books about prayer?"

"Yes!" She said with enthusiasm. "I have been reading books about prayer all of my life. I find them so motivating and informative."

"That is good," I said. "You must be very knowledgeable about the whole matter of prayer. I am just starting out, so the books I have here are very simple."

"I am glad you are starting," she replied. "I have found the books so helpful and full of insights, it has given me a great understanding of prayer over the years. And they keep on inspiring me and exciting me even now. Prayer is such a wonderful thing."

"But," I asked doubtfully, "have you never actually made the journey to the City of Prayer?"

"Oh, no!" she said. "I just enjoy reading about it, and hearing all of the good things about it. I do of course pray, but I have never thought it necessary to go to the effort of actually going to the city. You can experience it in an indirect sort of a way by reading what others have done and said. I never tire of it."

I did not quite know how to respond to this, so I let her get back to her reading. I did think, however, about the words of Jesus who said, "Everyone who hears these words of mine and puts them into practice is like a wise man who built his house on the rock" (Matt. 7:24). It seemed to me that it was certainly a good thing to be inspired and motivated by gaining knowledge and insights about prayer, but the time had to come when you actually set out on the journey and put into practice the powerful and enlightening truths you had learned. While I wanted to gain more knowledge about prayer, the real hunger of my heart was not just to know about it in a substitutional sort of a way, but to be able to do it effectively and experience it meaningfully in my own life. It was a surprise to me to find out that there were fine people who were very knowledgeable and had great insights into prayer but were not practitioners in any significant way. I thought knowledge without practice was unsatisfactory, indeed dangerous.

I took some time surveying the books that I had been given and decided that they were just what I needed to help me on my journey. I would buy them from the lady at the desk and take them with me and refer to them as necessary on the journey that lay ahead.

By now I was anxious to take the next step suggested by the gatekeeper. I wanted to meet with the trail guides. They were people who had actually made the journey into prayer and had experienced its realities. Following the instructions of the gatekeeper, I found the room where the trail guides were.

The room was not large, and there were only a few of the trail guides present when I entered. Most of them were engaged in quiet conversation. My first impression was that they were a group of normal but good people. There was an atmosphere of friendliness amongst them, and this helped me overcome the shyness I felt. They possessed a sense of assurance and confidence that attracted me to them. *These are people I really want to know*, I thought, and approached one who was sitting by herself. She gladly welcomed me and introduced herself as Mary. I said, "Mary, I am interested in going to the City of Prayer. I believe that you have been there, and I thought you could help me with the journey and tell me a little about what to expect when I get there?" She was clearly delighted and anxious to talk about this. I sensed in Mary a personality that possessed a controlled power and energy.

"Let me tell you some things about the journey," she said, without more introduction. "I expect you will find the journey to be longer and more difficult than you think. There are no shortcuts or easy ways to get there. But the marvelous thing is that the journey itself is a wonderful and valuable experience. It is not just getting to the destination that counts. The journey itself is exciting and rewarding. So let me tell you four important things about the journey that I think will help you.

"First, take your time. Don't be in a hurry. Don't let your anxiety to reach the city blind you to the fact that the pathway that leads there should be enjoyed, savored, and valued. It is just as important to learn from the journey as it is to get to the destination. You will experience many powerful new insights as you travel the pathway toward the city. It is important that you take time to linger over these experiences of enlightenment. Linger and enjoy them. Give them time to take root and penetrate deeply into your soul. Let them become permanently ingrained in your consciousness and in your experience. You remember the story Jesus told about the sower who went out to sow seed? Some of the seed fell on rocky or shallow ground. It grew up quickly, but as the days got warmer, the heat of the sun soon dried up the new plants, and they withered and died because of the shallowness of the soil. The same thing can happen to many of the wonderful new insights and experiences that you have in prayer. God will give you an experience that thrills you. But if you do not take time to let it sink into your soul and become an essential part of your understanding about God and how He works, but you impatiently want to rush on and find what the next wonderful experience will be, then the value of this experience will wither and die and be forgotten.

"The voices of those who are proficient at prayer and at fellowship with God are unanimous in insisting upon this. Take your time. You cannot hurry this. You need time to absorb it, and let its full meaning impact your soul. To properly read a meaningful book, you cannot read and rush. You need to read, learn, and inwardly digest the material in the book. Likewise you need to read, learn, and inwardly digest the lessons of prayer. If you do not give the seeds of truth learned time to germinate, grow, and come to fruitfulness, then you will be ill-equipped to understand the future blessings and challenges of the journey into prayer, or adjust to life in the City of Prayer. So take your time, enjoy the journey, smell the roses, absorb the scenery, and be excited about the progress you are making. Remember, prayer is a skill that is learned. In learning any skill, you must take time to learn the fundamentals of the skill. If you neglect, forget, or carelessly hurry through the fundamentals, then you will never really master the skill. Even a very gifted person, who wants to learn to sing well, cannot rely only on his giftedness. He must learn and practice over and over and over again until the basic principles become second nature to him. And the better he masters the basics of vocal singing, then the greater are the possibilities he will develop into a proficient and distinguished singer. So if you rush through a lesson that you have learned about prayer and anxiously push on to the next, without really grasping the first, you will greatly handicap your final ability. Before a child can read an encyclopedia, he has to learn his ABCs. You cannot expect a student to understand advanced calculus who has not grasped the basics of algebra. So take your time. Don't be impatient. God will lead you on at your own pace. When you look at those who seem to be very advanced in prayer, remember they did not learn this skill in one day. They are simply reaping the harvest that comes after long and patient sowing and growing and nurturing. Don't be impatient for what is next or what is round the next corner of the journey. God will lead you at your own pace and at your own capacity. Just take your time.

"Second, be consistent. Persevere. Learning to pray will take a 'long commitment in the same direction.' There will be times when you will not feel like praying; when these times come, persevere, pray anyway. There will be days when you are so busy you don't want to take time to pray, but persevere, pray anyway. In the prayer experience, there will certainly be seasons when God seems so real and so present when you pray that prayer will come easily and naturally. At times like this, you will want to pray, and you will find prayer easy and very exciting and rewarding. But you must not expect it to be like this all the time. There will be other seasons when it seems that you are wasting your time. God is nowhere to be found. You find it hard to enter into the spirit and atmosphere of prayer. It will be much more difficult to pray at these times. But when these difficult times come, then you persevere. You pray anyway. If you pray only when you feel like it, or when you are in the spirit of prayer, then significant vacant gaps will develop in your life of prayer. Prayer should be done whether we feel like it or not. It is the ability to keep going, even when the way is tough that develops our faith and trust and ability in prayer. Remember that prayer is more a skill that is learned than a gift that is given. To be good at any skill takes time, experimentation, failure, and perseverance. When Jesus told the disciples the parable of the persistent widow, it was introduced by these words, 'Then Jesus told His disciples a parable to show them that they should always pray and not give up' (Luke 18:1.) The implication of this statement is that if they don't keep on faithfully praying, they will give up. So persevere.

"It is important that you set aside your time to pray each day and then consistently and faithfully enter into your prayer time. Do this even when it is inconvenient and when you do not feel like it, or especially when you are discouraged with the whole process. You must learn to overcome the ups and downs of your feelings and your day-by-day setbacks and discouragements, and develop the habit of reliably disciplining yourself to pray. That is why many consider prayer to be one of the disciplines of the Christian life. It is a discipline, but a blessed and rewarding discipline.

"Third, expect and accept changes in yourself. Prayer is a powerful thing. It releases forces and energies from God that you would not otherwise experience. When the power of prayer begins to be released in your life, you must expect that changes will begin to happen. I am especially talking about changes to yourself. Someone has said that prayer does not change things so much as prayer changes me. You will find that your prayers will begin to change you. The more you enter into the presence of God in prayer and fellowship with Him, the greater will be His influence on what you are and how you live. An obvious change will be the increasing selflessness of your prayers and the increasing sensitivity to God's will. Many start out on the journey wanting to be good at prayer because they want to learn how to get God to answer their prayers and do what they want Him to do and give them what they ask from Him. But as they mature their focus in prayer begins to change. As they grow their concerns begin to change from what God can do for them to what they can do for God. It changes from what they want to what God wants. It is a measure of growth and maturity when you become less concerned about 'how can I get God to move the way I think He ought to be moving?' to 'how can I learn to receive what God wants to give?" In fact, that is a good statement that defines the real essence of prayer. You ought to memorize it. You will hear it time and time again on your journey to the City of Prayer. **PRAYER IS LEARNING TO RECEIVE WHAT GOD WANTS TO GIVE.**

"As you grow in prayer, there will be more and more value placed on the fellowship and communion with God than on what He is answering and what He is giving. Prayer will become more relational than action, more interaction than transaction. There will be a change from 'my will to His will,' from 'my kingdom to His kingdom' from 'my way to His way.' As prayer leads you closer to God and into a more mature relationship with Him, you will find there is a strong call in your spirit to make some changes. You will begin to give up self-will and self-interest. You will be called upon to obey and follow in some new, and perhaps difficult, ways. You will be expected to trust when it would be easier to doubt. You will be asked to be strong enough to persevere and obey when disobedience would be much easier. There will be times of humbling yourself in His presence. There will be times of receiving new light that is painful and seems to sear and burn your conscience. It calls for confession and repentance. Getting closer to God will mean a holier life and a holier you. He is a holy God, and as you get closer to the heart of this holy God and absorb the spirit of His holiness, the desire of your own heart will be to reflect more and more His holiness. 'Be holy because I am holy,' becomes a meaningful relationship (1 Pet. 1:16). Are you ready for this? Do you really want this?

"As your relationship with God matures, then there will be growth in grace. If you are unwilling, along the way, to make the necessary changes in your life; in your attitudes, values, and priorities, then your journey into prayer will grind to a halt. Many of those who are disappointed in prayer are disappointed because they have not understood this growth principle or have been unwilling to make the changes that growth demands.

Growth also demands patient and consistent development. In prayer, people cannot jump easily from kindergarten to university level. They have not developed the skill of prayer but suddenly are faced with a difficult and complex situation that calls for advanced wisdom and strong faith, and they come up short. Their skill is not equal to the demands. Some do not pray much until a catastrophe strikes, and then they turn to God and hope He will deliver them. Some pay scant attention to fellowship with God until sickness comes to them, and then they suddenly pray and want God to heal them. Others consistently pursue their own will and their own ways until problems arise, then they want God to take over, rescue them and give them guidance. They are often disappointed. But if they had allowed themselves to grow and mature, they would have had the God-given resources to overcome these situations with victory.

"The last thing I want to tell you about the journey is that it is a journey of faith. You will undertake it because you believe in it. You believe that the experience of closer and intimate fellowship with God is infinitely worth the costs of getting there. You believe that the greatest thing for your soul is the presence of God. You believe that the dominant purpose in your life is to do God's will and that real satisfaction is found in being in the center of His will. You acquire the faith that Jesus talked about when he said, 'The kingdom of heaven is like a treasure hidden in a field. When a man found it, he hid it again, and then in his joy went and sold all he had and bought that field' (Matt. 13:44). That is faith. It is the faith that says 'the treasure is worth the cost.' It is the faith that says 'my relationship with God is worth paying the price.'

"There will be times when all that keeps you going onward is simple faith, that God's way is the best way, God's presence is the greatest thing, that God's fellowship and will are more valuable than your own ease and comfort. It is the simple faith that helps you accept that God's value system and priorities are best and should become your priorities and your value system. Even more fundamentally, it is the basic faith that believes God loves you, and because He loves you, then what He desires for you is your highest good. The loving God wants the very best for you. The greatest life for you is the life that God wishes for you. It is the belief that the most satisfying thing you can do is to establish a relationship with God that is so close and so unified that you begin to reflect his Spirit in your spirit; His values become your values; His focus becomes your focus; His desires become your desires. The expressions of His heart more and more become the expressions of your heart. This is the great objective of prayer. Jesus described it best when He prayed for us that "they may be one. Father, just as you are in me and I am in you. May they also be in us" (John 17:21). Remember, **prayer is learning to receive what God wants to give,** and what God wants to give more than anything else is Himself—His love, His Spirit, His values, and His priorities. What God wants to give you is the most meaningful and satisfying, fulfilling life that is possible. Jesus encouraged us to believe this when he said, 'I am come that they might have life and that they might have it to the full' (John 10:10). To believe that this is the greatest and best thing for you calls for great faith, but that is the basis of a real prayer life."

I was rather concerned after hearing this. I said to Mary, "I am afraid I am a long way from this. I am not sure that I will ever be that kind of person."

She answered, "Of course you are a long way from this. But believe me, you can develop this lifestyle, and if you reach the City of Prayer, this will be your experience. And it will be wonderful. The important thing right now is to get started. Begin the journey. The journey itself is exciting, rewarding, and you will keep on making progress that will bring you new joy and great victories. I think it is important that you go now to the Viewing Platform and see if you can catch a sight of the City of Prayer. This will encourage you and give you strength to start into the journey."

I thanked Mary for her guidance and her advice. I would have occasion to often remember some of the things she said and realize more and more the wisdom and truth of the direction she gave. I certainly understood that the journey ahead of me was going to be a real journey, and there were no easy ways or shortcuts. I decided to take her advice and move on to see the Viewing Platform itself.

TOPICS FOR DISCUSSION—CHAPTER ONE

1. In this chapter, different levels of experiencing a national park are compared to different levels of experiencing prayer:

   - Discuss the three levels of prayer experience.
   - In your prayer life, which level do you normally experience?

2. The gatekeeper said, "You should spend some time getting good information. Many neglect to do this and, in their enthusiasm, set out on the journey into prayer without proper guidance, but they soon find themselves in difficulty and making mistakes they could easily have avoided":

   - Is correct information about prayer important?
   - Can you explain some poor piece of information you received and how it hindered your prayer development?
   - Where would you go to receive good information about prayer?

3. The gatekeeper said, "The fact is that even the superficial experience of just viewing prayer and thinking about it seems to help them a little, and they go away feeling better than when they came."

   - Do you agree that even superficial prayer has some benefits? Discuss.

4. Discuss the statement, "Wherever you find people, you find some level of desire there to communicate with the spiritual world that is around them and in them."

   - Do only Christians pray?
   - Are the prayers of non-Christians meaningful and effective?

CHAPTER TWO

THE VIEWING PLATFORM

The Viewing Platform was actually outside of the building. It was constructed in such a way that it gave a good view of the mountains that towered around. Once again my first impression was one of surprise. I was surprised at how large the platform was and how many people were there. Clearly, people were interested in viewing the pathway to prayer and had a desire to see the city. I joined a group that was standing at the edge of the platform. They were looking up and pointing to something in the far distance that I assumed was the City of Prayer. I followed the direction of their gaze and caught my first view of the city. This first glimpse of the city was rather awesome. From where I stood on the platform I could see that the city was high up in the mountains. It was a long way from me and too distant for me to catch any of the details. But even at this distance, I was impressed by the size of the city and its beautiful location. At this moment the sun was shining on it and gave it an appearance of brightness and appealing warmth. As I gazed at it, it captivated me, and I felt a desire begin to grow in me that I wanted to be there and enter it. I wanted to walk its streets, see its sights, and enjoy its atmosphere. Although the city was a long way off and higher up than I had anticipated, I intuitively experienced a strange and beautiful quality coming from it. As I looked and sensed, rather than saw, this aura seemed to flow from the city and reach me. I felt drawn to it, like a weary wanderer feels drawn to home. There was a light that emanated from it, and the effects of that light seemed to shine out with a glowing warmth that even reached down here where we stood on the platform.

I looked around me on the platform and I could see that some of the other people were aware of the same atmosphere that I was sensing. They were clearly captivated by the appeal of the city. There were others, however, who did not share their interest and had little awareness of it. These people came, looked, passed a few comments, and then moved on. They had seen enough and had little concern in finding out any more. But a few of us continued to drink in the mystery and wonder of the distant city.

I felt my kinship was with the group of interested observers. I joined this group. Some were still standing while others were sitting down, but all were giving the city their full attention. One person in particular I noticed. He was a young man, tall and straight, with black wavy hair. He had a serious and earnest face, and was deeply absorbed in, and focused on, the city. I was drawn to him, as his attitude of earnest hunger seemed to reflect what I felt within my own spirit. I moved over and stood beside him. For a while neither of us spoke. Then he turned to me and without preamble said, "I want to go there. I want to be there." The earnestness and sincerity of his spirit shone from his eyes and were captured by the tone of his voice. I sensed a kindred spirit.

"Yes," I said, "so do I." That simple exchange was all it took. Our spirits seemed to join in mutual desire. We felt immediate comradeship. It was the most natural thing in the world for me to then say, "Why don't we make the journey together?"

His face lit up with a smile, and he said, "Yes, let's do it together." He extended his hand to me and said, "My name is John, and I want to learn to pray."

I took his hand firmly and said, "I am Philip, and I too want to learn to pray. We can help each other, learn from each other, and support one another." In this brief but poignant moment, our friendship was sealed. We would journey together to the City of Prayer.

We turned again and gave our attention to the faraway city. After a period of absorbed quietness, John said, "Tell me Philip, can it be my imagination, or do I really have an awareness of the presence of God coming from that place?"

"I certainly feel an appeal emanating from it," I replied. "It almost feels like home."

"Just think," John continued, "even this far away, on this Viewing Platform, which is meant only to give us a distant glimpse of the city, if we can sense His presence here, can you imagine what it will be like as we get closer to the city? And then how real and rich will His presence and fellowship be when we enter the city?"

"It is like hearing a distant echo," I replied. "It makes you want to trace the sound to its origin. I think the best thing is for us to get going. I am anxious to get started and begin to make some progress."

"Agreed," said John. "I have not yet been to the prayer room. Why don't we go there and pray together, and then we will find the head of the trail and get started?"

We soon found the prayer room. Already some others were using it, so we made our way to a quiet corner where we could pray together, and there we knelt in prayer. We prayed for each other. We prayed for God's help on our journey. We asked that He would accompany us with His presence and that His Spirit would guide us. As we rose from our prayers, we felt our spirits were even more united. There was in both of us a deep understanding and a desire to get started on the journey into prayer and learn better how to communicate with God.

The signs, pointing us to the beginning of the trail that led to the City of Prayer, were clear, and we followed them eagerly. I thought, *I am so glad I am here. I am so thankful that I have found a companion like John. I can hardly wait to get started.* As expected, we soon found the head of the trail. What we did not expect to find was a trail master sitting there ready to give us directions and instructions. "Congratulations!" he said as we came toward him. "I am glad you have found the beginning of the pathway into prayer. I am here to help you by giving you some equipment that you will need as you go on the journey to the City of Prayer."

I thought that perhaps he wanted an entry fee from us, so I asked him, "Does it cost anything to enter the trail?"

"Oh no!" he said. "The trail is free. It does not cost any money. Anyone can enter this pathway and follow it. Everyone can afford it. It is for anyone, rich or poor, humble and famous. There is a cost, but the cost is not in money. The costs will be in self-discipline, self-denial, perseverance, and a willingness to obey God and die out to selfish-interest. I am here to give you some essential pieces of equipment that will help you on your journey. It will be difficult to complete the journey without these tools. All who have reached the City of Prayer have found them quite essential. This equipment is available to everyone. You will not want to be without it."

When neither John nor I offered any response to this, the trail master continued, "The first piece of equipment is something you no doubt already possess—it is the Bible. Almost every Christian who has successfully learned to pray uses the Bible. Take your Bible with you when you go to pray. Read it quietly and thoughtfully. It has many encouraging promises. It gives insights into God's will and way. It gives illustrations of faithful men and women and how they learned to pray. It tells of many exciting answers to prayer. Read the Bible in your prayer time. Read it thoughtfully and prayerfully. Ask God to speak to you from the portion that you read that day. Don't hurry. Be sensitive to the Spirit of God. Listen in your heart to any impression that comes to you as you read. When God impresses some truth upon you from the Bible, take time to think about it and to pray over it.

"Many people make a practice of reading the Bible devotionally before they pray. This helps them to open up their spirit to God, to be sensitive to what God might want to say to them, and helps bring them into an atmosphere of prayer. Some make a practice of reading until a portion of the Bible impresses itself upon them. This, they feel, is God's Word and guidance to them for that day. This Word from God could be a promise to help them believe something that they are having trouble believing. It could be a word of encouragement to strengthen them. It could be a rebuke about something that is wrong in their life or attitude. It could be the revelation of a new truth that excites and enlightens them. It could be an old truth revisited with fresh vividness and power. One of the wonders that start to happen when you mature in prayer is that God begins to talk to you, as well as you talking to God. Often, God uses the Bible to speak to us.

"The second piece of equipment that I am going to give you is a key. You will need this key. You will not make it to the City of Prayer unless you use it often. All along the pathway to the city you will find many private prayer huts. They are there for your use and encouragement. This key opens the door to the prayer huts. You can go in and be alone in your prayers to God. Do you remember the basic instructions that Jesus gave about our prayer times? He said, 'When you pray, go into your room, close the door and pray to your Father, who is unseen, then your Father, who sees what is done is secret, will reward you' (Matt. 6:6).

"I am glad to see that you two are friends and will make this journey together. I hope you will pray together often, but Jesus tells us that there is also praying that needs to be done alone. These are times spent only between you and God. Public prayers and praying together in groups are good and should be practiced. But each individual must spend time in prayer alone with God. This private prayer is your own personal time with God. You will find many prayer huts along the way. Each of you should choose your own hut and use the key to get in so that you are alone with God. It is hard to express how vital this practice is for the development of your prayer life. It is during these times alone that you will develop your ability to sense God's presence, to speak to Him and hear Him speak to you. This is your time of communion and fellowship. It is the time when your soul rests in His presence, when He refreshes you and fills you again with His strength, when you open your heart and tell Him what is in there—even if what you see in there is not good. This is often the time when God reveals Himself.

"There will be occasions when these private sessions of communion with God are awesome and filled with worship and praise. On other occasions, you will experience a joyful wonder and amazement, and sometimes a quiet peacefulness as you rest in His presence. On the other hand, there will be times that are burdensome as you express to God the concerns that are on your heart. When properly done, this practice of private prayer is rewarding, rich, varied, and refreshing. If you are going to learn how to pray, this is where it will become real to you and bring you close to God. There will never be an end to what you experience and learn in private prayer. God comes to you in ever new and different ways that will thrill you and expand your soul. This is a feast for the soul. This is what your heart hungers for. This is when you meet with God and talk to Him and have Him talk to you. This is the home of the soul."

"But how often should we go into these private prayer huts?" asked John.

"They are set out all along the way," said the trail master. "You should use them as often as you need. Those who are most seasoned in prayer generally make it their habit to have a time each day when they withdraw from the journey and spent time alone with God in the prayer huts. Daily practice is essential. But you can also use them whenever you feel the need."

"We are in a hurry," I said. "We want to get to the City of Prayer as soon as possible. Can't we just save time by praying as we walk along?"

"No," said the trail master with great emphasis. "It is certainly good to pray as you walk along. Indeed you should also practice and participate in this kind of prayer. It is good to form the habit of learning to pray as you go about your daily business. As you become more and more a person of prayer, you will find that your mind and heart will rise to God more naturally even as you are engaged in the activities of the day. These spontaneous prayers have a useful and important place in the life of prayer, but they are not the same as the focused, concentrated, quiet waiting on God that happens in the private prayer times. The private prayer times are often too intense and vivid to be practiced effectively in the midst of other activities. There is special value in entering the prayer hut, closing the door, shutting everything and everyone else out, except you and God, and then spending time concentrating on Him, listening to Him without distraction or interruption, letting your soul open up in His presence, and getting in touch with him. This calls for concentration and focus and sensitivity that only aloneness can give you."

"So at least once a day, we should go into our private prayer hut for time alone with God?" I asked.

"Yes," replied the trail guide.

"How long then should be spend in these private prayer times?"

"It varies," said the guide. "To begin with, you may find ten to fifteen minutes is quite enough. As you develop, however, and as prayer becomes more meaningful to you, you will want to spend more time than that. Many will spend thirty minutes. Some will spend an hour. Some even spend more time than that. There can also be special times when you are able to devote more time to prayer and give attention to it for longer periods. Jesus, remember, would spend all night sometimes in prayer. Many find it helpful to go for a prayer retreat when they can have an extended period without distraction to give to God in prayer. Be sure of it, however, as prayer becomes more precious to you and its practice more vivid, you will want to spend more time alone with God. Always keep in mind you want to reach the City of Prayer. If you reach it and decide to live there, then the atmosphere of prayer and the spirit of communion with God will be part of your life and an essential part of your conscious living." The trail guide continued, "In addition to all of this, the prayer huts are also equipped with a sleeping bunk and eating facilities, which you can use for overnight camping."

"I have a third piece of equipment here for you," said the trail guide. "It is a notebook. Many find it very helpful to keep a record of their interactions with God. They write down their thoughts and feelings each day as they go along. This helps them to better define the processes that are going on in their soul. It reminds them about experiences that they tend to forget. It is a journal of their interaction with God."

"Yes," said John, "that is a good idea. Sometimes I have gone through an experience with God, and I thought it was so vivid and impressive that I would never forget it, only to find that next week, my mind had gone on to other things and the experience that I thought was so important and vivid had faded from my mind."

"Yes!" said the trail guide. "To keep a record of your walk with God can be a very helpful thing. It is your story. As you keep this daily journal and use it to look back over your story, it helps you to see with surprising clarity the way God has guided and directed you. To keep a record like this will also encourage you when you read back over it, and it brings to your attention some of the things that were difficult issues for you at one time, but now you have moved on and are able to handle them easily. Your journal will contain struggles that you have now found victory over. It will record answers to prayer that have taken a long time to happen, and without the memory of your journal, you may not have realized that the answer came. It is like a map of your journey. You can see all of the twists and turns of your experience; you become aware of the distance you have come and the general direction in which you are headed. It is a map that gives you the big picture.

"Your journal is also your own story. It can be intensely personal. You may want to write in it some things that should be kept only between you and God. So be sure you keep it private and have confidence that it will remain that way. If you become afraid that others may read it or have access to it, then you may begin to omit or modify some items and a lot of the honesty and value of the journal is lost.

"These are the three pieces of equipment that I think are essential. They are very simple and plain, but that is the way it should be. Prayer should be kept simple. It is not a complicated or intricate matter. It may not always be easy, but it should be kept simple.

"There are other things that you might want to take with you. While they are not essential, they could be helpful if you choose to take them. I notice, Philip, that you have some good books with you. Many find that good devotional books help them focus their mind on the things of God. Good books can enlighten and inspire as you learn to pray. Books are helpful to any student. You are becoming students of prayer, so good books on prayer will be helpful to you. Use books. Read books. Refer to books. They are helpers along the way.

"Some also find that a hymnbook is good to take into the place of prayer. They like to sing and worship in their prayer time. This is to be encouraged. Good hymns can help get us into the spirit. They often express for us, in a way that we could not do for ourselves, the deep yearnings and motions of our heart. So certainly sing songs that are appropriate to the state of your heart. Some people achieve the same effect if they begin their prayer time by playing or listening to sacred music. It all helps set the tone and atmosphere of worship and prayer. Be careful, however, to always remember that your main purpose is to pray and seek the face of God. These other things are only helps to smooth the way into His presence. They should not become the main feature that eats away all of your time and attention. Keep them as appetizers, not the main meal.

"Also, some people like to reserve a special place for their prayer time. It can be special room, or a special chair, or a particular corner of the house. But they reserve this place for prayer only. If possible, they do not use it for anything else. It becomes a sacred place for them. There develops a consciousness about the place, a sense of reverence towards it so that whenever they approach it, the sacred association helps them to enter into the spirit of prayer because they feel they are approaching holy ground. These things and others can be aids that help you enter the presence of God and enjoy fellowship with Him. Use them if they help, but do not feel bound that you must include all of this. The three essentials are the Bible, the key, and the notebook/journal

"Now you are ready to start," concluded the trail master. "Let me show you to the start of the pathway to the City of Prayer. Follow it all the way, and you will reach the city. The path is not always straight but follow it even if it seems to be taking you where you do not want to go. There will be hardships on the way, but there will also be encouragements. You will not have to go very far on the pathway until you come to the first real difficulty, which is the "Thicket of Distraction." Everyone must pass through this and learn to deal effectively with the distractions and wandering thoughts that disturb our prayer lives if we let them. The important thing is to persevere. Remember, when these difficult times come, and come they will, if you gain victory, then the rewards will be great. Be encouraged that countless numbers of people have gone this way before you and found rest and blessing for their souls. God bless you on your journey. Let me pray for you, and then you can be on your way."

TOPICS FOR DISCUSSION—CHAPTER TWO

1. From the Viewing Platform many people caught a glimpse of a deeper and better prayer life. Not all responded to this vision in the same way.

    - Discuss the various reactions to the glimpse of the City of Prayer.
    - What is your reaction?

2. Philip and John felt an immediate kinship in prayer.

    - Do you have a prayer partner?
    - Is there value in this kind of partnership?

3. What were the three pieces of experience the trail guide gave to Philip and John?

    - Discuss the importance of these three items.
    - How well are you presently using them in your prayer life?

CHAPTER THREE

THE THICKET

After thanking the trail master, John and I, without further delay, started to walk up the pathway that leads to the City of Prayer. The path itself was well constructed and easy to follow. It was a well-worn path, so we assumed that many had passed this way before us. It was encouraging for John and me to understand that we were not alone on this journey or that we were unusual or exceptional people because we wanted to reach the City of Prayer.

While the trail guide had warned us about the Thicket of Distraction, there was no indication of it in this early part of the trail. The way was pleasant and easy at this point, so I asked John a question, "Why do you think, John, you wanted to come on this journey? Why do you want to pray well?"

John thought of this for quite a while, and then with some hesitation he answered, "Well, I believe there are two or three reasons. First, I sense a real need in my own heart and soul to be close to God. I have a deep hunger to be on intimate terms with Him. There is in me a desire to feel that I am in contact with Him. I experience a spiritual need. I sense I will never really be satisfied or know real joy or satisfaction until I am in close fellowship with Him. Prayer seems to offer a pathway to that kind of fellowship. When I pray, I talk to Him, He talks to me. Even at this early stage in my prayer life, I still experience a level of communication and harmony, and it is a beautifully satisfying experience. But I know I can greatly improve and develop this interaction between myself and my God. That is first I think."

"Yes! I understand that," I said, "but do you think everyone has this deep desire to connect with God?"

"Yes, I do," said John, "but perhaps not everyone feels it so acutely. I believe there is a hunger in the human heart for God, and everybody has it, but some ignore it, never cultivate or recognize it, and so it does not develop and become a strong conscious need in their life. The desire for God needs to be recognized and cultivated, and prayer is a vital tool in this development of the human heart."

"Why is it then," I asked, "that many people who do not have this strong and cultivated desire for closeness to God still pray and still want to pray?"

"That," replied John, "brings me to the second reason I want to go on this journey into prayer. I do have some urgent personal needs that I want God to help me with. I have needs within my family, with my personal finances, and problems within myself that I want to effectively ask God to help me with. So I want to learn better how to pray so that God can intervene and solve these problems, or at least, help me to solve them."

"And you think that many people, who do not have a strong desire to know God better, still pray because they hope that God will give them help to deal with their problems?"

"Yes!" replied John. "But any attempted connection with God that is built only on the basis of having Him fix our problems and helping us get what we want in life is not a good foundation upon which to create an intimate and satisfying relationship."

"But suppose God does not want to give you what you are asking for?" I asked. "We keep on saying 'that God answers prayer,' but does God really answer selfish prayers that are outside of His will? I don't think so. I suspect we ask God to do all kinds of things that He does not want to do. Remember the essence of prayer the trail guide taught us was **prayer is learning to receive what God wants to give.** I would assume that if God does not want to give it, He won't, no matter how much I might pray about it. Getting my desires into harmony with His desires seems to me to be a vital matter in prayer. I know I tend to get very mixed up with what is my will and wish and what is God's will and wish. Especially in personal matters, it is difficult for me to know if what I want is in harmony with what God wants. I find that often my own selfish will, ambitions, desires, and wants clamor so loudly for attention that I spend much of my prayer time asking God to respond favorably to them, but I have very little idea whether He approves of the things I ask for or not. They are on my agenda, but I do not know if they are on His. I am not sure what to think about this. I hope we get help on this issue farther up the pathway of prayer"

"Well," said John, "you are by no means alone with that kind of problem. I am afraid that a lot of our prayers come from our own will and wish and not from God's will and plan for our lives. You remember what James said in his epistle? He said, 'When you ask you do not receive because you ask with the wrong motives, that you may spend what you get on your pleasures' (James 4:3). I guess a lot of my prayers were never answered because I was asking from the wrong motive. That makes **learning to receive what God wants to give** a principle in prayer that I need to give much more attention to. You are right, I think we need more teaching on this.

"That brings me to the third reason I want to go on this journey," said John. "I have a deep desire to serve God and do something for Him. I want to be used of God to extend His kingdom. I like action and achievement in my life. But I suspect when it comes to serving God and doing it effectively that my own enthusiasm and energy will not achieve very much. I need His power and blessing upon what I do for Him. I want to be a fruitful branch on the vine and see things accomplished for Him. But in order for this to happen, I realize that I cannot do much on the basis of my own strength and giftedness. I need Him to anoint and empower me for effectiveness in His service. I remember when Jesus was going away to leave His disciples and the future of the work would be left in their hands, He said to them, 'Do not leave Jerusalem, but wait for the gift my Father promised, which you have heard me speak about. For John baptized with water, but in a few days you will be baptized with the Holy Spirit' (Acts 1:4). It was this power of the Holy Spirit that enabled the early apostles to be so effective in their service for God. I want some of the power and anointing to come upon my work and ministry for God. So I need to learn to pray, so that I do not try to do it all in my own strength."

"That sounds great to me, John. I think we can be sure that this empowering for effective service is something that meets with God's favor. Didn't Jesus say that it was the fruitful branches on the vine that brought glory to His Father? He said, 'This is to my Father's glory, that you bear much fruit, showing yourselves to be my disciples' (John 15:8). I believe you will make a great servant of the Lord and bring glory to the Father, John, if you do it for His glory and not for your own."

"Yes!" said John. "I think in this respect God's will and my will are in harmony, as long as I am careful to do it for His glory and not for my own."

"While we agree in what we think about God's will, John, I have another question that I would like you to respond to. I met some people who had the strange and, I think, rather perverted notion that if they want something, then God must be against it. They think God only wants them to have hard and difficult stuff. They are afraid that His will calls on them to give up all pleasure and happiness and embrace all that is dreadful and hard. They think that if they surrender to His will, He will impose a regime on them that consists only of extreme difficulty and attendance to duty. In addition, they feel they must deny themselves all pleasure in life. They assume that if they really enjoy something and get a lot of pleasure out of it, it must therefore be wrong or sinful in some way and that God disapproves."

"What a strange notion," said John. "I have never thought like that. I just believe that God loves me, and so only wants what is absolutely good for me. His plans for me are only for the best. These people must think that God does not love them and that His main purpose is to impose a joyless and burdensome way of life. How can they think like that?" John seemed genuinely mystified.

"It is indeed a strange way of thinking and very contrary to the spirit and purpose of God. I can, however, imagine that sometimes something may come up that I think is very important for me, and I really want to have it, but God, with His superior wisdom and foresight, understands that in the long run, this would not be good for me and may do me or others harm. So although I want it deeply, God does not grant it, for He knows better than give it."

"I suppose," said John, "that in many ways it is like a parent and a child. The child may badly want something that the parent knows is bad for him/her to have and says no to the child's request—like too many candies and cookies, or a venturesome game that is dangerous. When the child grows up, he/she begins to understand the reason behind these restrictions, but at the time, it may seem that the parent is just being mean and unreasonable instead of loving and generous."

I pursued this thought of John's by saying, "I suppose it gets down to a matter of faith and trust in God. If you believe in Him and His loving and good intentions toward you, then you will believe that what He wants is best for you, even if, at the moment, it seems to be frustrating your own desires. If you do not trust and believe in God's love and good intentions, then you will be inclined to rebel against Him or resist His will in favor of your own."

"Well," said John, who obviously found this attitude difficult to understand, "those people should read what Jesus said, 'I have come that they may have life and have it to the full' (John 10:10). I just believe the best life is the life lived in the center of God's will. The only way to find real soul satisfaction and joy is to be in harmony with God. If this calls for me to give up some selfish things, then I will be glad to do it."

"Good for you, John. I am glad you also feel that way, but sometimes I still find it difficult to give up my own way for God's way. I certainly believe God's way is the best way, but it is not always the easiest way, especially when it conflicts with something I want for myself."

"Well," said John humbly, "I guess if I am honest, I still have a struggle with that too sometimes. I expect we are going to have to deal with this question again as we progress along the pathway of prayer. I look forward to having someone who can lead us and guide us in some of these issues."

I replied, "I have to keep on coming back to what the trail guide said to me when I asked her about the journey to the City of Prayer, and she described the essence of prayer as **learning to receive what God wants to give.** If what she said is true, and what you say is true, then an important part of what we have to understand about prayer is for us to learn what it is that God wants to give us. If that is the case, my friend John, you and I have to start listening a lot more to God. I have to confess that in my prayers, I have done nearly all the talking. I have told God all the things I want and all the things I need from Him. It seems to me that I will have to start to learn how to listen to God, so that He can begin to tell me what He wants to give and what He wants to do."

"Yes," said John rather remorsefully. "I have a rather long prayer list, and it includes all the things I want God to help me with and do for me. Not all of these things are bad, in fact, I think most of them are good, but now that we talk about it in this way, it does seem rather one-sided. We have a lot to learn."

This conversation came to a halt when we encountered another traveler on the pathway. He was not walking along the path but had seated himself to the side, and he was looking very dejected and unhappy.

"Good day to you, sir," I said. "I gather that you too are journeying to the City of Prayer?"

"I was," said the gentleman, "but I am too discouraged and disappointed to go on. I am thinking of giving up on this matter of prayer."

"That is a serious thing to say," I said. "Why are you so discouraged?"

The fellow traveler stood up and pointed around the next corner on the pathway and said, "You will find out very quickly for yourself. Just around this corner you will come to a very dense thicket. It is a wild and prolific growth of trees, weeds, and bushes. It is so confusing and distracting, that when you get in there, you lose track of where you are going. Trying to find your way through it takes up so much of your time and attention that you cannot concentrate on the pathway to prayer, you keep on straying and getting lost in a labyrinth of bushes and weeds. I have tried a number of times to get through this thicket, but each time I have failed. Yet I know I cannot make progress in prayer unless I conquer it and get through it and advance up the pathway to new and better things."

"This sounds serious, but this may be the very Thicket of Distraction that the trail guide warned us about," I said with a little alarm. If this traveler could not get through this distracting thicket, how could we expect to do so?

"Well," said John, "we were well warned that there would be difficult and trying times on the pathway. This would appear to be the first of those obstacles. The trail guide certainly did tell us that one of the first difficulties we would encounter in prayer is that of dealing with wandering thoughts and distractions. It seems to me this Thicket of Distraction you describe is just that. It tries to obliterate the path of prayer by getting our thoughts to wander off in all kinds of trivial ways, and it sidetracks us by presenting all kinds of incidental and tempting distractions. But others have come this way before us, and they would have had to pass through this thicket, so there must be a way through."

"Why don't you join us?" I asked the man. "Perhaps together, we can find our way through this. We can help each other."

"I have tried so hard to stay on the pathway of prayer, but when I get into that thicket, my mind and thoughts keep on wandering off in all kinds of directions. I find I spend more time trying to solve the irrelevant problems and worries that my mind presents, than I do concentrating on my prayers. Even when I pray about things that are of great importance to me, I find that my mind wanders off, and I do not concentrate. You would think that when I pray about simple things, like praying for my loved ones and my family, that I would be able to focus on what I am saying, but even in those elementary things, my thoughts are constantly deflected, and I begin to daydream. It is even more of a problem when I try to concentrate on worship and the greatness of God. But perhaps if you go with me, I will give it another try. I really do want to get farther along the pathway of prayer."

So it was agreed that we would go on together, and hopefully, with each other's help and encouragement, we would get through the Thicket of Distraction. When we walked around the corner in the pathway and got our first glimpse of the thicket, I realized that this was going to be a far more difficult obstacle that I had imagined. The thicket blocked the pathway. It was indeed a wild, unruly growth of heavy and undisciplined bushes, shrubs, and low-lying trees. There was no pattern to their growth. They were haphazard and intertwined. To get through, this would indeed call for strong effort and discipline. We stopped to see if there was an easier way to get around this obstacle. But although we looked diligently, we realized that the only way was to tackle it head-on.

I said, "If we want to make progress and get to the City of Prayer we are going to have to get through this. There is no other way to deal with it except to tackle it straight on. Let's keep together, and we can encourage and strengthen each other."

With that I stepped forward with John and the gentleman close behind. We entered the thicket. I realized immediately that our new companion had not exaggerated the difficulty. I found it almost impossible to keep on the path. The dense brush kept presenting obstacles that diverted us. I was in the lead, and I became so confused looking for the best way through the underbrush, that I kept losing the pathway. It was only with laborious effort that we were able to find our way back on to the prayer path again. The growth was so prolific and the distractions were so many that I feared we were not making much progress at all. The denseness of the growth certainly blocked out all sense of direction. I could not see clearly and wondered if perhaps we had indeed lost the path of prayer. I also found the constant struggle with this disorganized jungle to be very tiring. Soon I was weary of the struggle. I was beginning to feel the discouragement that the other traveler had expressed. Perhaps we, like him, would not successfully conquer this.

I became so scratched and bruised that I let John move up and take the lead for a little while. It was not long before he too became as weary, disorientated, and discouraged as I was. But we struggled on, determined not to give up. I remember what the advisor at the head of the trail had said to me, "Above all persevere." So I determined to persevere.

When it seemed like the thicket was going to win the battle and there was nothing for us to do but to give up and try to retrace our steps, we, surprisingly, came upon a number of the small private prayer huts that we had been told could be found all along the way. I immediately suggested that we make use of these huts and spend some time in prayer. John agreed, but our fellow traveler disputed the decision. He said, "I am too anxious to tolerate a delay here. I cannot concentrate on prayer, so going into one of these prayer huts will not help. I want to get on with the journey and get past this thicket. It seems to me that it is a waste of time trying to pray with all of this brush ensnaring us and entangling us. This is not the time to pray. There are too many distractions and too many other issues to be dealt with, I cannot concentrate on prayers at this time. Let's get through this thicket and when things are clear and open, and our minds are free, then we can spend time in prayer."

This did not seem the correct decision. John and I tried our hardest to get him not to panic or let the confusion destroy his determination to keep on the way of prayer. But he was adamant that real, concentrated prayer was not possible under these conditions, and it was not worth spending time at it. Better to get on with the attempt to find our way through the thicket and then pray when the spirit and mind were free and in the mood for prayer.

"But," I said, "that may be the very reason you have never been able to find your way through this confusion. You have let the distractions discourage you from prayer. You have allowed the thicket to stop you doing the very thing that you needed to do. In spite of the distractions and difficulties, we need to continue to pray and seek God's help. Yes, it is difficult to concentrate. I know it is hard to discipline our minds while we are surrounded by all of this confusion. But we were told, even in the demanding times, we must persevere in prayer. You, my friend, must do what you will, but I am going to discipline myself and take time to persevere in prayer, even though it is very difficult to pray under these circumstances." John agreed and using the keys the trail master had given us as one of the tools, we each opened a door and withdrew into our personal prayer huts. Regretfully we never saw the discouraged traveler again.

The inside of the prayer hut was very simple and unadorned. All the prayer huts we were to encounter along the way were designed in much the same way. There was a hard chair to sit on, and an altar to kneel at. A simple bunk for sleeping, if you were going to stay in the hut overnight and a plain table for eating. There was no other decoration or furniture. As I settled into my prayers, I found that our fellow traveler was correct. Even in the prayer hut, it was very difficult to concentrate on my prayers. My mind kept wandering off in various directions, but especially to the confusion outside. I decided it might help if I prayed about something that was heavy on my heart at that time. One of my brothers was facing some difficult times in life, and needed wisdom and guidance or he could make some very wrong decisions. I began to commit this matter to God, but soon, without quite realizing what was happening, I began to worry that my brother might make a bad decision. If he did, what would happen? Where would he end up? From there my mind wandered to the other members of my family, and I began to remember incidents in our lives and some of the good times we had together as a family. While I was enjoying some of these very nice and good thoughts, I realized with a jolt that I had wandered off in my prayers and was no longer praying for the need of my brother. *Well*, I said to myself, *this is not good. I will try to change the subject. I will think about God and worship Him.* But before long, in spite of my efforts, my thoughts again quietly slipped away to other subjects. Even as I tried to worship, I found that my mind insisted on trying to figure out the best way out of this terrible thicket. It was difficult to discipline myself and focus on what I was praying about. I continued to struggle to bring my thoughts under control, but all the time they kept straying away from me. I did, however, persevere. I have to confess it was not the best time of prayer I had ever had. I did not particularly sense God's presence. My heart seemed not to be in it. Prayer seemed a useless effort under these circumstances, but still I persevered.

This must be what they mean when they talk about prayer not going higher than the ceiling. I thought. And it certainly seemed that way. I felt no emotional response within myself. The thicket seemed to smother all spiritual sensitivity. I felt undisciplined and uncontrolled in heart and in mind. The thought then invaded my mind that perhaps this kind of prayer really was a useless waste of time? I asked God to help me. I asked Him to help me concentrate and discipline my mind and to focus it on Him. In my desperation, I allowed my mind to wander in the direction that it wanted to go. I confessed this to God and told Him what my thoughts were. I then committed them to Him and prayed about the very things that my mind was pulling me toward. This I found gave me some relief. I also found that it helped me if I talked out loud. This kept my mind more focused, and it did not wander so readily. Especially when I tried to worship, I found that singing a song of praise kept my mind on what I was doing. But in spite of all this, my thoughts still kept on wandering. I just was not able to stay focused on God, and I could not sense His presence. He did not seem to be listening. But still I persevered.

After a while I decided to go outside and see how John was getting on. He had already come out of his private prayer hut and was waiting for me.

"How did you get on?" I asked.

"Not very well." he replied. "I found it very difficult to pray. My mind was not on it. I keep worrying and being anxious about things in my own life and how you and I were going to get out of this thicket. It was hard to concentrate or to feel any spirit of prayer at all."

"I was the same," I said. "But we were told in times like this to persevere and to pray anyway, so I prayed even though I did not feel any response, either from God or in my own heart."

"Yes," said John. "I persevered in prayer too."

"I wonder if we should pray together before we go on and try to get out of this place? I discovered while I was praying in the prayer hut, that it helped me to talk out loud."

"Yes," said John, "that's a good idea, let's give that a try." And immediately he sank to his knees where he was and I joined him. We prayed out loud one after the other. We prayed for God's help and God's strength to get out of this difficult place. Hearing one another's voice and listening to one another, we found, immediately helped us to concentrate better than we had been able to do on our own. Being in one another's presence gave us encouragement and strengthened our spirits, so that we absorbed confidence from one another. I concluded that it really helped, when praying in these difficult and distracting places, to have a companion to pray with you and for you.

Feeling better from our prayer time, we renewed our struggle to get through the Thicket of Distraction. For a time it seemed just as discouraging, and progress continued to be frustrating until John, who was in the lead at this time, shouted, "I think I see the end." I looked in the direction that he was pointing, and sure enough it appeared that the thicket was not quite as dense and the bushes were a little farther apart. More light penetrated through the foliage. We were encouraged and continued on with renewed energy. It was not long after that, that the pathway became clear again, and we soon found our way out of the thicket into the clear light and beauty of the path to the City of Prayer.

Once out of the thicket, because both of us were exhausted, we threw ourselves down at the side of the path. After we had rested for a while we began to discuss the meaning of what had happened to us in the thicket.

"You know," I said, "all of the books I read about prayer warned me that there would be experiences like that. They said everyone struggles with this kind of thing. There are times in prayer when it is very difficult to keep our minds focused and to concentrate. Our thoughts want to wander. Our mind plays tricks on us and keeps diverting our attention from the prayer. It is a battle to stay focused and put our hearts into our prayers. But always they say when these times come, you must persevere. Don't give up on prayer, but discipline yourself and do the best you can. Persevere. At the end, if you haven't prayed very well, you can apologize to God and tell Him you will try to do better the next time, but you must persevere. You must not let these distractions deflect you from the discipline of prayer or cause you to cut back on your prayer time."

"Right," agreed John. "I found too that it was not just that I had trouble with wandering thoughts and a distracted mind, but I also felt that I was wasting my time. I had no sense of God's presence. No inner feeling of contact with Him. My own spirit felt dead and unresponsive. It felt like my prayers were not going anywhere and that it was not worthwhile to continue. But I did not yield to these negative thoughts. I continued and made the best out of the prayer time that I could. But at the end, it did not seem like it was very satisfactory. I questioned whether I was wasting my time or not. But I too persevered. I think that is the thing to do under these circumstances."

"It is encouraging to know," I said, "that we are not the only ones who have had this experience. Everyone who wishes to make prayer meaningful and effective in their lives will go through times like this. Even mature people of prayer have times when their thoughts wander and their hearts do not seem to be in it. The masters of prayer themselves describe these things happening to them. So if they struggled with it, how much more should two novices like we are find it a battle? The important thing is not to let it discourage us from developing our prayer life. These times will pass, and we will once again find prayer rich and rewarding. Just look around us now. Isn't this a beautiful spot? We have come through this difficult time, but now that it has passed, we are once again experiencing a warm glow and a peaceful sense of the presence of God. God was with us, even though to all appearances He had left us. He was there even though our feeling and our sensitivities told us that He was nowhere to be found and that He was not listening to us."

"We cannot accept our feelings as a reliable guide in prayer," John said. "Prayer is easy when we feel good and responsive, but we must also understand there will be times when these feelings will not be there. We simply believe that God is there and interested, even though we do not feel like praying or sensing His presence."

"I guess that is where faith comes in." I said. "We believe that God is there and interested even though we do not at the moment feel Him or are aware of His presence. I remember the statement of Jesus when He said 'Blessed are those who have not seen and yet believe' (John 20:29). Sometimes we cannot go by sight or by feelings, we simply have to proceed on the faith that God is there even though to all appearances it seems that He is not."

"One other thing this experience in the Thicket of Distraction taught me," continued John. "It really helped me to have a companion like you to pray with. This was one time when praying with someone else did me more good than praying on my own. I guess that in this case, listening to another voice and being in someone else's presence helps us to concentrate better than we can on our own."

"Yes," I said, "and even the simple matter of speaking out loud, rather than within ourselves, helps focus our attention. When distractions are a problem, some people find it helps to stand or walk while they pray. Others are helped by concentrating their attention on a sacred object like a cross or a painting. Anything to try to keep our minds on what we are doing."

"One sad thing about this experience," I observed, "is that our discouraged friend did not make it through the thicket. I am afraid he will not make much more progress up the pathway of prayer until he learns to deal with these wandering thoughts and distractions of the mind. If he allows his feelings to so dominate that he cannot get past the times when his mind wanders and his heart is unresponsive, then he will not develop the prayer life that he wants. He cannot let this conquer him. I am grateful that we have learned some lessons from this. If it happens again, as I imagine it will, we will be prepared for it and better equipped to handle it."

After this evaluation, we continued along the trail for a while until we came upon some more prayer huts. They were situated in a very beautiful part of the path. Since we were both tired from our experience in the Thicket of Distraction, we decided to stay there for the night.

THE JOURNAL: That night after I retired, I wrote in my journal. "*Well, I have started on the journey. After my first day I feel content and peaceful. I am glad to be on the way. The day has been eventful. I have learned a number of things. First, I can see that the path to prayer is not going to be all roses and sunshine. It calls for discipline, application, and stamina. It is not for the fainthearted or those who are concerned mainly about their own comfort and ease. Second, I am grateful to have the company of John. The companionship of having a fellow traveler is a great encouragement and strength. Third, I learned some practical things in the Thicket of Distraction. To persevere was the important lesson. Some simple and practical ways to deal with wandering thoughts is to pray aloud: if possible, to pray in the company of others: walk or change position as you pray; have sacred items that help focus your attention. I add to these a suggestion that I tried and found helpful. When I was dealing with wild thoughts in the prayer hut, and could not seem to harness them, I simply brought them before God and said, 'This is what I am thinking about,' and I actually talked to Him about them. The very fact that we are actually praying about these thoughts seems to help satisfy the mind that its concerns have been addressed and it is now free to return and concentrate on the matter of prayer. It fits the old adage 'if you can't lick 'em, join 'em.' I must not forget these things. It has been a good day. I have made progress."*

TOPICS FOR DISCUSSION—CHAPTER THREE

1. What do you think "the Thicket" describes in our prayer life?
2. Philip asked John, "Why do you think you want to come on this journey?-Why do you want to pray well?"

   - What were John's answers to this question?
   - What would your answer be if you were asked the same questions?

3. How did Philip and John successfully deal with "the Thicket?"

CHAPTER FOUR

THE PINNACLE

After a time of prayer and Bible reading in the morning, John and I started out again on our journey. The pathway to the City of Prayer passed through some very beautiful country at this stage. The way was pleasant and easy, and John and I were enjoying the walk. I found our conversation as we went along to be stimulating and uplifting.

"I am glad we are on this journey," I said to John. "I feel we are making good progress, although we, no doubt, still have a long way to go. I remember the trail master telling me that while it is important for us to reach the City of Prayer, nevertheless, the journey itself is very meaningful and significant."

"Yes!" said John, "I am enjoying the journey. The important thing is to keep on making progress toward the city and not get diverted or discouraged and give up before you get there."

In this warm and companionable spirit, John and I continued up the trail, making good progress. After a while, we saw ahead of us a small group of people who were standing at the side of the pathway. They stood together in a fairly tight circle. They seemed to be a very happy and joyful lot, so we looked forward to meeting with them. When we got close enough, we could tell they were singing hymns of praise and thanksgiving, and singing with their whole hearts. Even as they sang, they swayed their bodies back and forward in rhythm with the songs they sang. They raised their heads and clapped their hands. They gave every appearance of being very victorious and joyful.

When John and I arrived to where they stood, I saw that they were at the bottom of a side trail that left the main pathway and climbed up to a high pinnacle of rock. The pinnacle looked difficult to access, but if you could get up there, it would afford a splendid view.

"Greetings," I said, "you look a very joyful and happy group of people. Why so happy?"

"We have just come down from the Pinnacle up there," said their spokesman, pointing to the high pinnacle of rock. "It is wonderful on the top. The atmosphere is so bright and clear, it made it easy to sense the presence of God. We found being there made God's nearness very real to us. The beauty and wonder of the place filled us with a deep sense of peace and joy. In addition to that, we also had a clearer prospective of the City of Prayer. The clean, fresh air gives you a much sharper view of the city. It seems much closer up there and very desirable. This improved sight of our destination encouraged us, and we were glad and thankful that we came on this journey.

"Adding to these rich spiritual experiences," continued the man, "we also had some encouraging answers to prayer. One of our number"—he pointed to a woman who was standing with the group—"has been laboring under a great personal burden. It was a weight from which she was unable to free herself. It troubled her so consistently that it overshadowed her whole life of prayer and was wearing her spirit down. It has handicapped her on her journey so much that it started to interrupt her fellowship with God. She has struggled with it, and prayed much about it, but has never seemed to quite get victory over it. But up there on the Pinnacle, we all gathered round her and prayed that she would find relief. God answered our prayers, and she experienced a wonderful and powerful deliverance. Oh what joy. She now feels free, so liberated, we can hardly contain ourselves for the blessing of it all.

"Another of our group had a besetting sin." This time he pointed to a man. "Although he struggled to overcome it, it seemed to have a power over him, and in spite of his best efforts, it kept on defeating him. He felt hopeless and was constantly guilty, feeling that he was failing God. Again, we all gathered around him to pray, and the power and atmosphere of God was so near up there that our friend felt a great sense of God's power flow into him, he felt his hopelessness lift, and his guilt vanish, and we believe God has given him power to conquer this besetting sin. It was a great victory. So you see we have a lot to rejoice over. Wasn't it the apostle Peter who talked about rejoicing with an 'inexpressible and glorious joy'? (1 Pet. 1:8). Well, praise God, that is just what we are doing right now."

John and I joined with them in their rejoicing. It was a time of great and uplifting fellowship. *Could prayer*, I thought, *be this good? Could it really have power enough to provide such times of unalloyed blessing and victory?* This exuberant group certainly seemed to think so.

The spokesman for the group spoke up and said, "I hope you two are going to take in the side trip up to the top of the Pinnacle?"

"Well," I said doubtfully, "we are anxious to get on with the journey and reach the City of Prayer. The Pinnacle certainly sounds good, but I do not want us to get diverted from the task at hand or be detained on our journey."

"Oh, but didn't the trail guide tell you to enjoy the journey? Did he not tell you to stop and enjoy the scenery, drink in the atmosphere, smell the roses? If you are going to arrive at the City of Prayer in good spiritual health, you need to take time to enjoy the blessings and pleasures of the journey."

I looked at John, and he seemed convinced. "If visiting the Pinnacle does for us what it seems to have done for you, then I would not miss it for anything," said John.

"Good!" said the man. "You will find the atmosphere and the blessings of the Pinnacle well worth the effort and time you put into it. And it will refresh you and renew you so that you will be stronger for the journey ahead."

It seemed that the decision was made. John and I would climb up to the top of the Pinnacle. As we started out, I looked up and said, "It doesn't look easy."

"No," agreed John, "but we want to take in all of the experiences that we can. I certainly don't want to miss this."

The way up to the Pinnacle was indeed steep and difficult. It took a great deal of effort and persevering discipline for us to get there. But when we got to the top and had a chance to catch our breath and look around, it was well worth the effort. The Pinnacle was only a part of a great high meadow, green with grass and strewn with alpine like flowers. The scenery was breathtaking. The mountains towered over us; the valleys stretched out below. It was a grand, vast vista of beauty and wonder. John and I stood quiet and motionless, lost in our own thoughts. After some time John turned and looked in the other direction. He nudged me and quietly whispered, "Look! Over there you can see the City of Prayer."

I looked in the direction he pointed, and there, sure enough, lay the City of Prayer. From up here it was nearer than I had seen it from the Viewing Platform. In the sharpness of this cool air, its beauty, size, and structure were much clearer. The city was large, much larger than I imagined. It had some magnificent buildings, which stood out boldly. The layout and design of the city were also more evident here. It was obviously well planned and structured. Lying in a valley of the mountains with the sky above it blue and warm, and the sun shining, it seems a very inviting and desirable place to live. The city seemed to be growing. It was not old and deteriorating. Even from up here, we could tell that it was a prosperous and developing place. We could almost feel its energy and power. It looked peaceful and strong. John and I stood looking at it in wonder. John expressed the feelings of our hearts when he said, "I'm glad we're going there. I want to be there."

I sat down so that I could more comfortably absorb the beauty of the scene before me. John wandered around to different viewpoints so that he could take in the whole panorama. As I sat there, I remembered a line from a hymn "Lost in wonder, love and praise." That is how I felt. To be here. To drink in this atmosphere. To relax in this peaceful and beautiful place. I felt a quietness and restfulness seep into my soul. God was here. This was His world. I sensed He was close and nearby, and His presence brought peace and joy to my soul. How wonderful to be close to Him. How refreshing to sense His nearness. It seemed that His love and strength embraced me. His majesty and holiness thrilled me. The sense of harmony between Him and me was so beautiful that great rivers of warmth and happiness flowed through my soul. I do not know how long I sat there, glorying in His presence and His greatness and being united with Him. But after a period of time, John came back and sat by my side. I said, "John, I want to stay here for a while. I am not ready to leave. This is too enriching and marvelous. My soul and spirit are at home here."

"This is what they meant," John said, "when they said the journey itself is important. I just feel nearer God and more blessed than ever before. Who could have imagined such harmony of spirit?"

So we stayed. There were prayer huts up here on the Pinnacle for us to lodge in. We used our keys and spent time in the privacy of the prayer huts. Sometimes we came out and prayed and praised together. Sometimes we just sat and talked. Sometimes other travelers came up, and we joined with them in singing songs of praise and worship. Always joyful and always meaningful. At other times we sat alone in order to allow our spirits the opportunity to absorb the spiritual feast that was spread around for us. There was one spot that became my own private retreat place. I often sat there alone, watching, thinking, praying, praising. It became a very sacred spot for me. John, understanding my need to be alone, never disturbed me when I withdrew into this spot. Here in this private place, I seemed to commune with God in a unity beyond anything I had known before. My soul opened up to Him. I let my whole being expose itself to His presence. Nothing in my heart was hidden or held back. In turn I felt filled with His Spirit. I was a humble recipient as His grace and love flowed into my soul. Sometimes I stood here with arms raised and face uplifted and sang my heart out in gratitude and praise. It was an intense and overwhelming experience of God and His presence. I knew that the intensity could not last indefinitely. But during my stay on the Pinnacle, I was swept along through many different moods and emotions. There were times when my feelings moderated and I simply rested in quietness and peace. Then there were other times when the fervent joy and unsurpassed blessedness of God invaded my soul.

John, on the other hand, seemed to react differently to the close presence of God that was felt on the Pinnacle. Although normally exuberant and demonstrative in personality, he became very quiet and thoughtful. *Peace* and *serenity*, *harmony* and *fellowship* were the words he used to describe that period of intimate interaction with God. He was not as intense as I was, but no less blessed and consumed in wonder. In fact, we noticed among the other travelers who came up to the Pinnacle while we were there that each responded differently. Some were like I was, and responded with loud singing and praise. Some quietly worshiped. Some seemed to draw inward and commune with God in a state of deep personal awareness. Some wept. Some were broken and repentant. The responses to the presence of God were very varied, and I expect these reactions were orchestrated by the Spirit of God in such a way that they fitted into the needs and personality of each individual.

John and I stayed up there on the Pinnacle for more than two full days. The time did not seem important. But eventually we knew that it was time to go. We had experienced an extended period of focused and vivid communion with God, but we understood that we had to continue with our journey. We slowly wound our way back down the trail until we came again to the pathway that leads to the City of Prayer. We sat down there to debrief and explore the meaning of the experience that we had on the Pinnacle.

"That was incredible," said John.

"Now I know why prayer is so important in the lives of the saints of God. They experience with God a joy that is literally out of this world. I have never tasted joy like that," I said.

"God was so vivid I felt like I could almost reach out and touch Him."

"It was so real, time seemed either to stand still or flash by."

"It was so peaceful and comforting."

"But I couldn't live like that all the time."

"No," replied John. "It is too intense. If it had carried on, I think I would have blown a fuse or burst a blood vessel."

I laughed at this, but agreed. "In a strange way I feel completely exhausted, as if I couldn't take any more of that."

"But beautifully satisfied in heart and spirit."

"It is like I have had a great feast of the spirit. I know it has done me good. I know my soul is full and satisfied, but I could not eat another thing."

"So, Philip," asked John, "what do you think? Why did we have to climb the Pinnacle to receive that experience? Could it not have happened while we were walking up the path? Will we ever have it again? Are their other pinnacles on the way?"

"Well, John," I responded, "I am not sure what the answer is to all of these questions, but I certainly think we can know the joy of the Lord and sense His presence as we journey along the pathway of prayer. We do not need to climb up the Pinnacle to experience these things. They should be regular parts of our walk with God. But in some ways I think the Pinnacle was something special. We placed ourselves in a particular position to receive great blessings from God. On the Pinnacle, we were in touch with God in a special way because it was out of the way, we had to go to a great deal of effort to get there, there were no distractions, and we were treated to a wealth of spiritual stimuli, and we took plenty of time. It is when all of these things come together that a great and extended experience of God is possible. It was very real to us because we took the time to make the special effort to get to a place that provided great inspiration for us, and we did not hurry past it but stayed to enjoy it, and let the spiritual streams flow over us."

"I have talked to some people who went on special prayer retreats or spiritual getaways," said John. "From what they say, it would appear that often these extra times spent apart, when they are able to focus and concentrate on spiritual things, and be relatively free from distraction, can provide them with the same opportunity."

"Yes," I said, "I have heard of these retreats. I think they would be good. In many ways our time up on the Pinnacle was like a specialized retreat.

"But going on a spiritual retreat is a little different to attending religious conventions where there are usually lots of meetings and activities, classes and services."

"Yes!" I said, "I have not been to many of these kinds of conventions and gatherings, but I imagine they could be useful and helpful, but in a prayer retreat, you need to spend time alone. If our time on the Pinnacle was like a prayer retreat, then you listen more for the voice of God than listen to the voice of teachers and preachers. A prayer retreat becomes very personal. It is you and God. It is your soul seeking God in its own way and at its own pace. And God will respond in a way that is fitting and relevant to you and in a way that is suitable to where you are in your spiritual life."

"Did you notice," John continued, "that different people on the Pinnacle responded to the presence of God differently? You, Philip, felt joy. I felt, more predominantly, a spirit of peace. Some people were exuberant and boisterous and full of praise. Others were filled with remorse and brokenness."

"Yes, I noticed that. And when you are on a retreat like that, you are free to respond to God in a way that is appropriate for you and expresses where you are right now in your spiritual experience. The benefit of the retreat is that you are alone with God and so can respond as you wish. When you get into public services and communal worship, there are more restraints placed on you. The decorum and practices of the group limit highly individualized responses to God."

"So you would advise anyone who is seeking to develop their prayer life, like we are, that a retreat setting, when they can focus for a longer period of time, and are free from distractions, and have spiritual stimulus around them, is a good thing?"

"Absolutely," I said. "You only need to look at the lives of those who have learned to pray, to see that it was an essential part of their practice to take time and get apart for a season and focus on prayer and spiritual development. I remember reading a story from the life of St. Francis of Assisi, whose prayer life and communion with God were unparalleled. He had a hunger for a season of undisturbed fellowship with God. He asked his friends to row him over in a boat to an island in a lake. All he took with him were some loaves of bread. He told his friends to come back and get him in forty days. He remembered that Jesus prayed and fasted in the wilderness for forty days. He then gave himself to fellowship with God. He said his communion with God was such that he lost all sense of time and place and was actually surprised to see his friends coming to get him at the end of the time. The bread was untouched. He had been so absorbed in his fellowship that the time had passed almost unnoticed. But that season of retreat for Francis strengthened and empowered his soul, and he launched into one of the most effective and fruitful phases of his ministry."

"Forty days," cried John. "I know I just could not do that."

"No, nor could I. But Frances had had a lifetime of practice and development. Most of us could not do that, but we can all, in addition to our regular daily prayer times, arrange for a day, or an afternoon, or an hour, or even on occasion two or three days when we retreat and spend special time focusing on God."

"Well, Jesus did it, didn't He," said John. "There was the forty days in the wilderness before his ministry started. And we read that he often withdrew by himself to spend time, sometimes whole nights in prayer. So Jesus practiced prayer retreats."

"Yes," I said, "and don't forget the Mount of Transfiguration. That was like a pinnacle experience for Jesus. He and the disciples that were with Him experienced a spiritual high that fortified Him with strength for the ordeals that were soon to come."

"That's right," enthused John. "When you think about it, so many of the great men of God in the Bible had times of focused aloneness when they communed with God. Paul in the deserts of Arabia, John the Baptist in the wilderness, Moses in Midian, Elijah by the brook Kidron—he didn't even have to cook his own meals. Yes, I get the message, if I really want to develop my prayer life, it will be helpful to me to take time for retreats in addition to my regular prayer times and fellowship times. Even short, brief retreats are good."

"I believe that is right," I said. "In fact for beginners like we are, I think short retreats are quite enough. I could not stay focused for long periods of time or for days on end. Perhaps as I grow in prayer I may be able to undertake longer retreats, but right now, at the beginning. I think I would have to keep them shorter."

"Nevertheless," said John. "God Himself has a choice in all of this. When He decides to come and meet with us in a special way, we can have pinnacle experiences at any time."

"And," I added, "if He chooses to withdraw His presence, we could climb a hundred pinnacles and not experience what we experienced."

"Well, this has been a great discussion," said John. "Do you think everybody who is walking up the path to the City of Prayer realizes the importance of retreat experiences and of taking time and effort to climb up to the Pinnacle?" We were soon to find the answer to that question, for we noticed a gentleman laboring up the path toward us. He seemed loaded down with burdens. His back was bent, his head was bowed, and when he came closer, we could see that he had a long face, frozen into a permanent frown, unmodified by any suggestion of a smile. His brow was creased with the wrinkles of seriousness and care.

"Greetings, friend!" I cried.

"Greetings!" he said. "This is a long and arduous pathway to prayer."

"Well, I suppose it is," said John doubtfully. And then pointing to the side trail up the Pinnacle, he said, "Have you climbed the Pinnacle?"

The gentleman looked up the trail very suspiciously. "Where does that go?"

"Why, up to the top of the Pinnacle," exclaimed John.

"Why should I go up there?" asked the gentleman.

"Oh! It is wonderful," enthused John. "It is an experience of great joy, praise, and refreshment. It will make your journey a lot easier."

"Easier!" exclaimed the gentleman. "Easier! I do not view prayer as something that is meant to be easy. It is a solemn responsibility and duty that I am fulfilling with great seriousness and sacrifice. God has laid this burden on me, and I execute my duties out of obedience and with undaunted faithfulness."

John was incredulous. "But don't you ever get any joy or pleasure out of your prayers?"

"Pleasure!" cried the man. "Pleasure! How can you talk of pleasure when the world is so full of sadness, and sin? How can you talk of pleasure and joy when you are surrounded by lost and broken people? My heart is heavy with burden. My soul is bowed down with grief over the state of the world. Didn't Jesus weep when he prayed over Jerusalem? Didn't He sweat great drops of blood during the agonizing prayer in the Garden of Gethsemane?" He glanced up the Pinnacle trail. "I have no time for spiritual frivolities. Now if you will excuse me I must get on and carry out my duties with fortitude and discipline." With that, and without another glance up at the Pinnacle, he labored on up the pathway of prayer.

"Oh my!" said John, feeling as if he had been scolded and put down. "What do you make of that? Joy and peace have been eliminated from his list of the fruits of the Spirit."

We continued to walk slowly up the pathway of prayer, thinking seriously about what the man had said.

"He is partly correct," I said. "There is an aspect to prayer that calls for deep intercession and burden for others and for the cause of the Kingdom of God. There is no doubt that Jesus Himself prayed and interceded with great burden. Even the apostle Paul tells us that 'we do not know what we ought to pray for, but the Spirit himself intercedes for us with groans that words cannot express' (Rom. 8:26). So there are times when the Holy Spirit Himself expresses His burdens through us in prayer with 'groans that words cannot express.' This would seem to indicate great burden of soul. Remember too, the apostle Paul wrote to the Philippians and stated what his great ambition was 'I want to know Christ and the power of his resurrection and the fellowship of sharing in his sufferings' (Phil. 3:10). Part of getting to know Christ and fellowshipping with Him is to get to share in His sufferings. So there is a part of our prayer lives in which we share in the Spirit of Christ and help to shoulder the burdens that He carries. We should pray for the lost souls of men and women. We should pray for the pain and suffering in the world. We should pray for the needs and losses of our fellow Christians. There is no doubt that if we are going to learn to pray, we must also learn to carry a burden and feel the urgency of the spiritual battles that are being waged all around us. I think, John, I have not yet learned very well how to do this. While I do not agree with our gentleman friend who seems to think that prayer is all burden, duty, and responsibility, and no joy or blessing, I cannot help but agree with him that there is an element in prayer that calls on us to bear one another's burdens and to pray for the needs of other men and women. And sometimes, when the burden is great and our awareness of the suffering of other people is very vivid, it may cause our spirits to cry out to God in urgent painful prayer. I have to confess, John, that I have not yet learned this aspect of prayer very well, but if learning to pray properly calls for this, then I am willing to accept the responsibility and be burdened and concerned for others." I did not realize as I said this that these sentiments were to grow in me and at a later date blossom and become an essential part of my work and ministry for God.

John was quiet and thoughtful and did not respond to what I had said, so I continued, "On the other hand, as we have just experienced, there are seasons of great joy, praise, peace, and fellowship to be found in prayer. We will have to learn to experience both in our times of fellowship with God."

"I can see the truth in what you are saying," John at last replied. "I just have not been very good at responding to this part of prayer. I wanted to enjoy all of the good things but have been reluctant to accept the burdens and responsibilities. But in a real life of prayer I guess they both exist." He looked at me and sighed. "I have a lot to learn, dear brother, a lot to learn."

As we continued to walk up the pathway to the City of Prayer, I said to John, "You know, that gentleman was a good brother. He was very earnest and serious about his prayer life. And he taught me something about prayer that I was a little reluctant to learn. But I think it would be very good for him and for his experience of prayer if he could learn to enjoy God's presence and experience some happiness and comfort in prayer. We learned from him, but he too needs to learn how to rejoice in the Lord. I think, John, that we should stop and pray for that brother, that he will begin to experience the joy of the Lord in his prayer life, as well as the burden of the Lord."

"You're right," said John. "Let's do it right now." So we stopped on our journey, got on our knees, and prayed for this good brother who seemed to be needlessly burdened and joyless. We prayed that this good and earnest soul would experience happiness in walking the way of prayer. We even prayed that, God willing, we would meet up with him again and be able to see if God had answered our prayers.

That evening John and I found suitable prayer huts and retired early, as we were both tired after the demanding expenditure of spiritual energy that we had had on the Pinnacle. I took out my notebook and brought my journal up to date.

THE JOURNAL: "Being on the Pinnacle was an unparalleled experience. But my thoughts go to Jesus and the Mount of Transfiguration. That must have been an extraordinary and refreshing experience for Him, when He recaptured for a while some of the glory of Heaven. But when that mountaintop experience was over, He came down the mountain to find a crowd of people with their pain and suffering waiting for Him. Being on the mountain did Him good, but He could not stay there all the time. So when we came down from the Pinnacle, it was like a rude awakening to meet up with the gentleman who seemed to think that prayer was all burden and pain. The lesson I have learned from this is that I must seek to have a balance in my prayer life. It cannot be all blessing and joy. It cannot all be burden and sorrow. There needs to be a balance. I need to embrace both and see both as valuable elements in a well-rounded prayer life. There will be seasons of joy and blessings. There will be seasons of burden and care. I have been guilty of wanting one and neglecting the other. I need to change. I keep on learning."

TOPICS FOR DISCUSSION—CHAPTER FOUR

1. The Pinnacle represents a high point in the experience of prayer. It is vivid in its emotional content and magnificent in its view of God:

   - Do you have "Pinnacle" experiences in prayer?
   - What factors helped Philip and John to enjoy this experience?

2. People responded differently to the Pinnacle experience:

   - Why do you think this is?
   - How do you respond to God during your Pinnacle experiences?

3. Discuss how you would answer John's question to Philip as they came down from the Pinnacle. "So, Philip, what do you think? Why did we have to climb the Pinnacle to receive that experience? Could it not have happened while we were walking up the path? Will we ever have it again? Are there other pinnacles along the way?"
4. Discuss the two views of prayer experienced by John and the serious pilgrim—one view emphasizing joy, blessing, and fellowship; the other burden, care, and faithfulness:

   - Which of the two is correct?
   - To which one does your prayer life approximate?

CHAPTER FIVE

THE LORD'S PRAYER—OUR FATHER

John and I continued our journey along the pathway to the City of Prayer. We frequently used our keys to enter some of the prayer huts that we encountered as we went along. In the prayer huts, as we had been advised by the trail guide, we took time to pray, read the Bible, and update our journals. We were not in a great rush. We enjoyed these pleasant and leisurely days of the journey. While we were progressing along the pathway, we were learning many lessons about prayer. On the way, we occasionally got a glimpse of the city, and we knew that we were making progress, and it was now much closer than when we had started out from the Viewing Platform. We also took occasion now and then to stop and look back from where we had come, and we realized that we had indeed progressed a long way.

One morning, John, who was in the lead pointed ahead and cried, "Look, Philip, there is a building coming up." I could see the building he was pointing to. It was not a large building and clearly not someone's home. It was rustic. Built with logs and seemed to be constructed as a meeting hall to accommodate small groups of people. John was excited. "I am sure that must be one of the schools of prayer that the trail master told us about. We must go in and learn some things from the school. Maybe they will be able to answer some of the questions we have about prayer."

As we approached the school building, we could see other people were already gathering there. They appeared to be fellow travelers. Some of them were talking and discussing together in small clusters. It looked like they had gathered for a purpose. We assumed that they were there to receive some instruction on prayer and were waiting for a class to start. John and I entered the building. It was set up like a regular classroom. Desks were set out in rows with a teacher's table at the front along with a chalkboard, projection screen and other teaching helps. We noticed that the teacher was sitting at her desk, so we went up to her to inquire about the school. She seemed friendly and open to us, so we told her about our journey and explained some of the discussions and questions about prayer that we had been having. Especially, we indicated to her that we were anxious to know more about what we should say to God in prayer and also how to hear from Him when we prayed.

She listened carefully to what we were saying and responded by saying, "We are just going to begin a class on 'Important Things that We Should Pray About.' I think that if you take the class, it will help and give you guidance about what to say to God when you pray, and what the content of your prayer time should be. We will not cover the question of 'How to Listen to God.' You will receive instruction on that later on when you arrive at the Second School of Prayer, just before you enter the City of Prayer. But right now, why don't you attend this class? We are ready to begin, and then after we have finished, if you still have questions about the content of your prayer life, we can talk about it then?"

We were very happy to do this, and as the other travelers were gathering in for the class, John and I found desks near the center and settled down for the instruction. I was rather surprised and pleased, however, to notice that one of the travelers who came in to take the class was the serious friend that we met at the bottom of the Pinnacle who considered prayer only to be a burdensome duty. He sat just in front of John and me but did not recognize our presence. I leaned over and whispered to John, "I notice our serious friend is here, perhaps God is going to answer our prayers for him."

The teacher called us together and introduced herself to the class. Her name was Joyce. She seemed a very pleasant and relaxed person, and I thought we would enjoy listening to her talk about prayer. She then had each person in the group introduce themselves. There were about fifteen of us in the class. I took special note that the name of our serious friend was Alvin. I said a quick prayer for Alvin, asking that the class be of help to him as well as to us.

The teacher began. "Among the common and early questions that arise about prayer are 'What do I say? I am not sure what to say to God when I talk to Him? What is He interested in? What should be the content and makeup of my prayer time?' These are good and often-asked questions. In fact the disciples of Jesus asked Him a very similar question. They noticed how often

He prayed and how important prayer seemed to be to Him. They observed how frequently He withdrew from the crowds and the work of ministry in order to spend time alone in prayer. Some of these prayer times of Jesus were long and lasted the whole night. So the disciples wondered, 'What does He say? How can He spend all of that time in prayer? I would be tired and run out of things to say long before that.' So the disciples came to Him one day and asked Him to teach them how to pray."

Taking up her Bible, Joyce opened it and said, "The story is found in the Gospel according to Luke, chapter 11, verses 1 to 4. These verses say 'One day Jesus was praying in a certain place. When he finished, one of his disciples said to him, "Lord teach us to pray, just as John taught his disciples." He said to them "When you pray say:

> 'Our Father which art in heaven,
> hallowed be your name,
> Your kingdom come,
> Your will be done, as in heaven so on earth,
> Give us day by day our daily bread,
> Forgive us our sins, for we forgive everyone that is indebted to us
> And lead us not into temptation.
> But deliver us from evil. '

"Jesus is giving us a clear answer to the question, 'What do we say when we pray?' He said 'When you pray say . . . This is what to say when you pray.' He then goes on and recites what is commonly called the Lord's Prayer. So in answer to the simple question, 'What is the content of our prayer time?' Jesus would say, 'This is the content. This is what you say. This should form the subject matter of what you primarily talk to God about. When you pray say . . . '

"Now," continued the teacher, "most often, when we say the Lord's Prayer, we simply recite it straight through. It does not take long, we can say it all in less than a minute. And of course to recite it from memory is good. We use the Lord's Prayer this way in church and public gatherings. It is probably the most commonly quoted portion of scripture. This is good, and I would certainly encourage its use in this way. Jesus, however, had more in mind than just simply a straight recital of the words. He meant for each statement to be a foundational starting point, which we build upon and expand in a way that is meaningful and appropriate to us. Each statement of the prayer introduces us to a subject that we take time to think about, develop, and pray over.

"Think of the Lord's Prayer as a house in which there are a number of rooms. Each room has a different function and purpose. Each petition in the Lord's Prayer is like a doorway that leads into a room. In that room, different things are done and spoken about. In a house, the door that leads into the kitchen introduces us to activities and subjects that have to do with kitchens. The door to the sitting room introduces us into a room that is prepared for something very different to what the kitchen is set up to do. The doors to the bedroom, the washroom, the study, all introduce us to important but different aspects of life and living. Each room is designed to fulfill a different function and purpose. But each room is necessary for a full and comfortable life. So in the Lord's Prayer, each statement is like a door that introduces us to a very different aspect of the spiritual life. We are not meant to simply pass by the door and take note of what the room is all about. We are meant to open the door, enter the room, and say and do the things that pertain to living in that room.

"When you live in the house, then you use all of the rooms. They are important to the success and quality of your life. There are times when some rooms are more important than others. You may never think of the bedroom all day until night comes and you are tired and need a night's sleep. Then the bedroom is important. The dining room may sit untouched until evening when all of the family comes home and wants to sit down for a meal, then the dining room is vital. But each room adds some quality and meaning to the successful life and activities of the household. So each of the statements in the Lord's Prayer is like a room in the house, it has a particular function and needs to be entered into and lived in, in order for it to fulfill its purpose."

One of the students raised his hand and said, "The Lord's Prayer then is like the bones of the skeleton, it gives the basic shape and outline for our prayers, but we must fill in the muscle, flesh, and skin?"

"Exactly," said Joyce.

"Or," another young man said, catching the idea with excitement, "each statement is like the icon on a computer, it symbolizes something, and if you press it, it opens up a whole array of options."

"Yes," agreed Joyce, smiling, "you have got the right idea."

"Or," one man in a business suite spoke up, "it is like an agenda in a business meeting. It simply introduces a subject, but all kinds of discussion, debate, and decisions follow."

Joyce laughed. "I can tell you have all grasped the concept."

"So what we will do," continued Joyce, "is to explore each one of the statements in the Lord's Prayer and enlarge on its meaning. After we have completed these discussions, I think you will discover that you will have no difficulty in finding things to say, and your prayer time will not lack for variety and interesting subject matter. Indeed it is likely that you will soon have so much to cover that you will need to start spending more time in prayer. Having something to say will not be a problem."

Alvin, our serious friend, spoke up and said, "Is it necessary to cover all of the statements every time we pray?"

"Normally it is good to cover all of the statements. Clearly, in the various stages of your life, and as your walk with God develops, some things will be more important than others. Just like in a house, if you are preparing for a party, then the kitchen becomes very important and gets a lot of time and activity. Or if someone is sick, then the bedroom becomes the center of attention. So at different seasons of life, or as your circumstances change, some aspects of the Lord's Prayer will need more attention and time than others, but you should nevertheless cover them all. The reason for this is that it will keep you balanced in your prayer time. It is easy for us to get so consumed in some of the urgent issues of life that they take up all of our time and attention in prayer, and then other important matters are neglected." Nodding toward the businessman, Joyce said, "Our business friend here knows that in a board meeting, some items on the agenda take more time and seem more urgent than others, but if the chairperson allows all of the time and attention to be consumed by one item, then many other important areas will be neglected. A good chairperson does allow ample time and attention to be given to the important items but still disciplines the meeting to make sure that all items on the agenda are covered. So when you pray, there will be some items in your life that are important and urgent at the moment, and you will want to give good attention and time to them. You will, however, need to be disciplined and make sure that all the other items are covered, because the situations in your life will change, and some of the issues that are less important now may rise to become vitally important to you, and when that time comes, you will not want to discover that they are in a state of neglect and disrepair. When you pray over all of the statements in the Lord's Prayer, then it keeps you on track. Nothing important is being missed. You are covering all that is necessary for a healthy, growing, and enriching spiritual experience.

"Now let's look at the eight statements in the Lord's Prayer so that we understand just what Jesus meant. Notice that four of these statements are directed toward God:

Our Father who art in Heaven.
Hallowed be Thy name.
Your kingdom come.

Your will be done on earth as it is in heaven.

The other four have to do with ourselves and our needs:

Give us day by day our daily bread.
Forgive us our sins as we forgive every one that is indebted to us.
Lead us not into temptation.
Deliver us from evil.

"You can see the balance right away. The prayer is not just about us and our needs. The first portion of the prayer directs our attention to God and expresses to Him our thoughts and desires for His glory and the success of His kingdom. In the second part of the prayer, we turn attention on ourselves and the practical and spiritual needs that develop in our own lives. It is often the case in prayer that we get so engrossed on our own needs and the happenings in our own lives that our prayers become rather self-centered and selfishly focused. It can also happen, but not so commonly, that we can become so enamored by our fellowship with God that we neglect the practical and urgent needs of our own everyday life. That is why it is important that we pray the whole of the Lord's Prayer, to keep us balanced.

"Note too that not all of the statements are necessarily petitions. Some are expressions of worship towards God, such as 'Our Father who art in heaven.' Some express care towards others, such as 'forgive us our sins as we forgive everyone who is indebted towards us.' The Lord's Prayer involves us in a style of prayer that is more than just asking God for things. It also includes time for worship and reverence, time for praying for others, time for fellowship and interaction with God. You will see all of these features become important elements as we discuss the meaning of the eight statements in the prayer.

"Jesus opens the prayer with the words 'Our Father who art in heaven.' This is a statement of relationship. It sets the stage, creates the atmosphere. It prepares our hearts and spirits for the important matter of interacting and communing with God. It is an approach to God. It creates an awareness of the correct relationship between us and God. He is our Heavenly Father. Prayer is seldom successful when we rush in from the world all breathless and distracted and start urgently demanding that God help us take care of our problems or hear us when we have burdens. Meaningful prayer starts with developing a right relationship with God. We quieten our minds, still our soul, prepare our spirit. We humbly say, 'Our Father.'

"The words are carefully chosen. When we say 'Our Father' with thoughtfulness and sincerity, we are establishing an atmosphere of intimate belonging and trust. He is 'my Father.' I belong to Him. I am in the family. He is the one who cares and shows interest in me. He is 'my Father.' But on the other hand, it is not so familiar that it becomes cheap and easy. He is 'my Father who art in heaven.' He is above all. He is in heaven. He is to be respected and honored for His position of greatness and authority high above us all. So the relationship that we try to establish when we approach the time of prayer is one of trusting intimacy and humble reverence. When you open this door in the house of prayer and enter this room, time should be taken to help your spirit move into a humble awareness of God and His presence.

"The furniture in this room is designed to help establish a good relationship with God. When you enter this room, there are many options available for you that will help you establish the right connection with God. When you close this door, the room ensures privacy. It is constructed so that it reduces distractions and interruptions to a minimum. There is a comfortable chair to sit on or kneel by. Those who prefer to kneel do so, because they think the bodily language of kneeling speaks of a humble, submissive attitude before God. Many bring their Bible with them into this room. To read the Bible or some other devotional book helps settle the mind and get us into the groove of communing with God and listening to His voice. There is a hymnbook in here for those who find it helpful. Many find it prepares their spirit for fellowship with God to sing a hymn of worship or devotion. Many enjoy taking time to simply sit and quieten their spirit and consciously still their mind and relax their body before they approach God. However you wish to use it, there are many different features in this room. Each person should explore a variety of methods and then practice the ones which they find most effective for them.

"What is important is that we enter this room at the beginning of our prayer time and use it to help us lay aside the pressures and cares of life, still our minds and hearts, and reverently seek to enter into the presence of God. It creates atmosphere. It develops awareness of God's presence. It quietens our spirit. It opens our soul to an awareness of God and enters into the reality of the spiritual world. Take time here. Do not rush. Let your spirit become acclimatized to the wonder of God. Allow yourself time to reach out and touch the presence of God. Let your spirit and mind become aware of Him. Humble yourself before Him. Time and effort here can make the rest of the prayer time much richer and blessed. When you pray, say, 'Our Father, who art in heaven.'

"When your spirit has been prepared and contact has been made with God, you are ready to move on to the next room in the house of prayer and say, 'Hallowed be thy name.' In this room, we seek to worship Him. "Hallowed be thy name" means 'Father, I reverence you. I honor you. You are worthy of praise and worship.' In this part of the prayer, the focus is on God, His greatness, His holiness, His majesty. Your spirit opens up in praise and worship. Your soul rises on the wings of thanksgiving. When you pray, linger here. There is no rush. Express to Him your gratitude. This can develop into some delightful moments for the soul. The joy and wonder of His greatness may flood your being. The experience of being genuinely lost in the wonder and the worship of God is a delight to the soul. Why rush? Why hurry? Take time to enjoy His presence and let your soul drink in the marvel of who He is.

"When the soul gets lost in the worship of God, it is the most satisfying experience that the human heart can experience in this world. The opening words of the catechism state this truth very well when they say, 'The chief end of man is to love God and enjoy Him forever.' In this portion of your prayer life, you are loving God and enjoying Him. These seasons of being caught up into His presence will enrich and influence your whole life. When we read about the saints being able to spend long extended times in prayer to God and finding great joy and fulfillment in these times, this aspect of prayer often features prominently in their prayer time. They learned to spend time feasting their soul on His presence and majesty. Here the soul and God are joined. Here they are one, and it is a delightful experience. This is the joy of the saints. Bernard of Clairvaux stated it well when he sang,

> Jesus Thou joy of loving hearts,
> Thou fount of life, Thou light of men,
> From the best bliss that earth imparts,
> We turn unfilled to Thee again.[1]

"This experience of worship, we understand, will be one of the great joys of heaven. The book of Revelation describes a great multitude that gather around His throne in heaven and with all eyes on Him and all attention focused on Him, they sing in a mighty chorus of praise 'Blessing and honor and glory and power be unto Him that sitteth upon the throne and unto the lamb' (Rev. 5:13). This room in the prayer life can be the most delightful and enriching place. It can almost be like the gate of Heaven. I hope you are able to taste this experience. I hope you know what I am talking about. I hope you cultivate and expand this function of prayer.

"Now let me pause here, for this is a very important moment. I want you to think on what has been said, and then give you opportunity to ask any questions that you may have."

Immediately a hand went up. "This sounds wonderful. Are you supposed to feel this way every time you pray?"

"It is wonderful," said Joyce. "But no, you will not feel this way every time you pray. You must not expect that. But what is called for is that you cultivate this spirit, so that you begin to understand it better and experience it more regularly. There will be days when this attitude of worship seems to escape you, but there will be other days when your soul flows into it easily and basks in the light of His presence. On other days you will have to work at cultivating this relationship, and it may not seem to be so easy or as intense as it is at other times. Like all emotions, your ability to experience this attitude of reverent worship will fluctuate. What is important is that you make this time a regular part of your prayer life, that you cultivate the spirit of praise and worship. As you develop the ability and the skill to experience this, it will become more natural and more delightful."

Another hand went up. "How long should you spend at this aspect of your prayer life?"

"I do not want to put any artificial time restrictions on this," said Joyce. "There will be some days that you feel a worshipful relationship with God is just not happening. Since you are not able to make connection, you may wish to move on to other parts of the Lord's Prayer rather quickly. On other days your soul hungers for this experience and is able to move right into the close presence of God. At these times He is very real, and His presence is very vivid. Then you should not rush this. Do not feel that you have to move on to pray about other things. Linger here. Enjoy it. Stay as long as you like. The fact is that many of the saints and the masters of prayer spend great amounts of time here. This is the home of the soul. This is a breath of heaven, and they learn to maintain and increase this blessed fellowship over long periods of time. At first you may not be able to do this, but remember again, this is a spiritual skill that is learned. It is an experience that can be cultivated, and so the more you work with it and experience it, the more natural it will become. Once you have opened this door and enjoyed this room, you will find in the future that the door opens more easily and your enjoyment increases."

I was pleased to see our dutiful friend Alvin put up his hand. "I have a question," he said.

"Yes," said Joyce.

"I have always viewed prayer as my Christian duty," said Alvin. "Prayer is a means by which we can meet our responsibilities to God, our family, and friends and to a needy world. Prayer is a Christian duty that calls for discipline and self-sacrificing perseverance. You do not pray for pleasure and for joy, you pray because God commands it, and the needs of the world demand that we come before God with these burdens and concerns. All this joy and pleasure that you speak about seems to me to be rather selfish and rather frivolous when you are confronted with the massive needs of the lost souls of men and women What is needed is not for us to be sitting around enjoying ourselves but for us to be burdened and anxious over the way the world is going"

Since John and I had been praying over this very thing about Alvin, I was interested in the response that Joyce would make to him. Joyce did not hurry. She gave some thought to her answer and then carefully said, "You are, of course, partially correct, Alvin. There are aspects of prayer in which God wants us to share with Him our burdens and cares. He wants us to seek His help in caring for our friends and family. He needs us to enter into His passion for the needs and lost souls of men and women. This is certainly part of prayer, and as we explore the other rooms and aspects of the Lord's Prayer, there will be ample opportunity for this kind of praying. You remember what the apostle Paul said when he expressed the primary desire of his heart? He said, 'I want to know Christ and the power of his resurrection and the fellowship of sharing in his suffering, becoming like him in his death' (Phil. 3:10). Paul is saying that to get to know Christ means that we participate in his resurrection. That is a glorious, victorious, and joyful experience in which we share in the power and might of His resurrection. He wants us to do that. But Paul goes on to say that knowing Christ also means that we share in the fellowship of His sufferings. And Christ is burdened. He longs for the world. He grieves over men's sins and yearns for their lost souls. So knowing Christ has those two seemingly opposite features to it, 'the power of his resurrection and the fellowship of his sufferings.' But to really know Him, we should experience joy and burden, glory and grieving. And all these should be experienced in our prayer life. So, Alvin, I think there is a necessary place for both in your prayer life. If you only experience prayer as burden, grieving, discipline, and dogged perseverance, then you will find it very hard to maintain. You will soon get bored, empty, and resistant to it. Prayer will become a dry, arid, unrewarding duty. But if you include in it the glory of fellowship, the wonder of experiencing His presence, the joy and praise of participating in the victory of His resurrection, then your prayer time will not only become rewarding, rich, and blessed, and will be something to be sought after, it will also become more effective and fruitful as you pray for others. It will be something to be enjoyed, not endured. You are definitely correct when you say there is an element of discipline in prayer. We need to be disciplined to set time aside each day to do it. It takes discipline to pray even when we do not feel like it. Prayer always calls for a purposeful and focused concentration. But also, as the soul gets to know God and experience him, prayer will also become a time when you soar to the heights."

I could tell that Alvin was affected by this instruction from Joyce. He turned around and glanced at me, and I think I might even have seen a small smile break the seriousness of his face, but he certainly did give me a little approving nod of his head.

Joyce continued her talk. "The next two statements in the Lord's prayer could easily be combined into one subject. They belong together and one supports and follows the other. When you pray, say, 'Thy kingdom come, Thy will be done on earth as it is in Heaven.' This part of the prayer sets the priorities. It gets first things first. The focus is still on God, but now it moves to His will. The Kingdom of God was a frequent concern in the ministry of Jesus. He often referred to it. The Kingdom of God is the place where God rules. It is the place where His authority is accepted as supreme. It is the place where His commands and wishes are carried out. He is the king of the kingdom.

"This petition in the Lord's Prayer is all-inclusive. It has meaning for the whole world. 'Thy will be done on earth as it is in heaven.' Clearly there are a lot of things happening on earth that are not the will of God. The Kingdom of God has not yet come to the whole earth. Men and women, leaders and nations, are still pursuing their own will and their own interests and remain quite neglectful of the commands of God. We are being asked to pray that His rule will be accepted by the nations, leaders, and peoples of the world. We are instructed by the apostle Paul to pray for those in authority over us. He says, 'I urge, then, first of all, that requests, prayers, intercession and thanksgiving be made for everyone—for kings and all those in authority, that we may live peaceful and quiet lives in all godliness and holiness. This is good and pleases God our Savior' (1 Tim. 2:1-3). It is important that God's people pray and work so that the reign of God will increase in the world and that the reign of evil and sin will diminish. We work and pray for the day when finally,

> Jesus shall reign where 'er the sun,
> Does his successive journeys run;
> His kingdom spread from shore to shore,
> 'Till moons shall wax and wane no more.[2]

"This is the great objective of God. This is the final hope for the world and mankind, and God invites us to be part of the great struggle to overcome evil and cause righteousness to prevail. Just what influence the prayers of God's people are having on the affairs of the world cannot be assessed, but we believe that it is the prayers of God's people that enable the Holy Spirit to restrain evil and frustrate many of the purposes of sinful and selfish men. There is a great battle being waged right now around the world. A battle between good and evil, between God and Satan, and we can each one have an influence in helping righteousness prevail. In praying this prayer, we become part of this grand scheme and cooperate with Him in His great purposes for the world and for humanity.

"You could also, in a more personal way, include your prayers for other people in this section of the Lord's Prayer. You can pray that God's kingdom come and God's will be done in the lives and hearts of the people for whom you are praying. Indeed I heard of one great prayer master who had a long list of people that he prayed for regularly and his prayer for them consisted simply of repeating these words and adding the name of the person for whom he is praying. Thus he prayed 'Thy kingdom come, Thy will be done in the life of . . .' This is a very simple but effective way to pray for others. Pray that in their lives God's will should be done and God's kingdom should come. What could be more important? What is a greater priority than this? So certainly pray for others here, but pray that God's kingdom will come and God's will be done in their lives. Whatever other concerns you may have for them, whether career, health, relationships, nothing is a greater priority than this, that God's kingdom come and His will be done in their lives.

"But the prayer that God's kingdom come and God's will be done becomes even more personal. We need to make part of the prayer the realization that we want God's kingdom to come and God's will to be done in our own hearts and in our lives. It is rather insincere to pray that God's will be done in the lives of everyone else, but reserve the right to deny God's will and resist the coming of His kingdom in our own lives. So we pray 'Thy kingdom come, Thy will be done' in my life and in my heart. And this again is setting the priorities in the right order. Before we pray about ourselves. Before we ask for the things that are of interest to us, we humbly and willingly bow before Him and yield ourselves to Him and say, 'Thy will be done in my life.' When we pray like this, we are accepting the statement of Jesus to be true for us, 'But seek first his kingdom and his righteousness, and all these things will be given to you as well' (Matt. 6:33). In this room in the house of prayer we humbly kneel before God. Lift our eyes to Him and say, 'Not my will but Thine. Not my will but Thy will be done Lord in me.' We are saying to God 'Your will, your wishes, your plans and purposes come first.' This humble, broken submission to the sovereignty of God introduces us to an essential part of the atmosphere, spirit, and faith that is basic to prayer. This yielding of ourselves and our wills to the will and purposes of God is very difficult for most of us, but it is an exercise that we should regularly go through in our relationship with God. The relationship establishes that He is the Lord, and we are the subjects. He is the master, and we are the servants. To establish this submissive attitude at the beginning can strip much of the selfishness, worldliness, and pride from our prayers."

After a period of solemn silence, hands went up around the classroom. "But what if I have some things in my heart and life that I do not want to submit to God?" someone asked.

"Then you have an important issue that is between you and God." answered Joyce. "As long as you are aware of something in your life that is not in the will of God, then you need to bring it out and talk to God about it. Do not hide it, or suppress it, or make excuses about it. This is serious, and you need to openly and honestly talk to God about it. He will listen. You may need to confess. You may need to repent. You may need to ask for His help so that you do submit to His will. This thing, whatever it is, will disturb not only your ability to pray with sincerity, but it will also disturb your whole relationship with God. You cannot maintain a good relationship and fellowship with Him, as long as you acknowledge sin and disobedience in your life. But let's be true here. Whatever it is that you are having difficulty submitting to God, or obeying Him about, you can gain victory over it. God has the power and the grace to help you. The Bible promises 'Where sin increased, grace increased all the more' (Rom. 5:20). Be sure of it, since God has brought your attention to something in your life where you are uncommitted or disobedient, He is bringing it to your attention because it has now become a significant factor in your Christian walk. But whatever it is, there is power and grace in God to help you overcome it. We are promised that 'if we confess our sins, he is faithful and just and will forgive us our sins and purify us from all unrighteousness' (1 John 1:9). There is no reason why unyieldedness or disobedience should continue to reign and reside in the Christian's heart and life, and an important part of this prayer is to uncover such things. Once they are revealed, then God has power and grace to help you deal with them, but your willing confession and faith are necessary. For you to continue to acknowledge disobedience in your heart will eventually, not only adversely, affect the rest of your prayer life, it will also destroy your relationship with God."

Someone else spoke up and asked, "But suppose I do not know what the will of God is?"

"That is a difficult but very important question," said Joyce. "I will not attempt to answer all of it right now. But when you get close to the City of Prayer, you will come across the Second School of Prayer. If you attend that school, you will hear a great deal about the will of God. If you are going to live in the City of Prayer, then understanding what God's will is, is very necessary, and you need to develop the skill of learning to listen to God so that He can tell you what His will is. Right now, let me say three things to you that are important for you to know about the will of God.

"First, I remember, sometime ago hearing someone say, 'The problem I have with the will of God is not the bits of it I don't know, but the bits I do know.' No one knows all of the will of God for all of their life. Fortunately, that is hidden information. But God does reveal enough of His will to enable us to take the next step in our walk with Him. He reveals enough for us to move ahead into the next phase of our fellowship with Him. The real issue we have with the will of God is not getting Him to tell us all the things we don't know about it, but in our willingness to do something about what we already do know.

"I think God understands it could be very harmful for us to know everything about His will and His plans for the rest of our lives. To have that knowledge may satisfy our curiosity, or save us from the responsibility of making difficult decisions, but the truth is that to continually be adding more and more understanding of His will while we still have not acted on the things that we already know is His will could be very harmful for us. To keep on adding more and more knowledge and understanding about the will of God for us, while we have not yet acted on pending items that we know are His will, will suffocate our conscience and harden our hearts. We need to clear up the unfinished business of doing what we presently know is the will of God before He reveals what is next for us.

"The apostle John wrote a very important verse that deals with this issue in his epistle. He said, 'But if we walk in the light, as he is in the light, we have fellowship with one another, and the blood of Jesus, his Son, purifies us from all sin' (1 John 1:7). The important thing is to walk in the light that we have. It is like driving a car on a dark road at night. The headlights of the car illuminate the next fifty yards or so of the road. They do not light up the miles and miles of the entire road that we still have to travel. All you see is the next fifty yards. Your job is to drive into the next fifty yards. Once you move ahead and drive into the part of the road you can see, then new parts of the road light up for you. But if you stop and say, I can only see for fifty yards, and I want to see the whole road ahead. I will not move until more of the road is revealed to me. 'After all,' you may reason, 'if I do not know all that lies ahead of me on this road, then I may encounter all kinds of dangers, hazards, and hardships that I know nothing about.' If your fear of what you cannot see makes you pull over and stop driving until more is revealed, then you will cease to make any progress, and you will never get to your destination. The essential thing is to drive into the portion of the road that your lights are revealing to you right now. Once you do that, then more and more of the road will light up before you. So it is with walking in the light of God. God has revealed to you what He wants you to do right now. If you are obedient and walk in the light that you have received, then He will continue to reveal more and more, and if you continue to obey, you will make progress and newer and greater things will be revealed to you, but if you become disobedient or unsubmissive, then progress will stop.

"There is a second thing I want to say about the will of God right now. There is so much about our future lives that is presently unknown. Since large portions of the future are unseen today, we need to presently make a commitment to obey Him and do His will, whatever that will may be in the unknown future. People used to talk about 'yielding the unknown bundle.' By that they simply were saying, I do not know what God has in store for me up ahead. I do not know where He will lead me, or what He will ask me to do. There are a lot of things out there that are unknown. But I yield that unknown bundle to Him. Provisionally I will follow Him and obey him and submit to His will whatever it is. This is a general commitment to obey God whatever circumstances arise. It is a pledge to be His servant in whatever capacity He wants me to serve. The hymn writer expresses this spirit of commitment well, when he writes,

> It may not be on the mountain height,
> Or over the stormy sea;
> `It may not be at the battle's front
> My Lord will have need of me.
> But if by a still small voice He calls
> To paths that I do not know,
> I'll answer dear Lord, with my hand in Thine,
> "I'll go where You want me to go"
>
> I'll go where You want me to go, dear Lord,
> Over mountain, or plain, or sea.
> I'll say what You want me to say, dear Lord,
> I'll be what You want me to be.[3]

"This is a general commitment. You are saying, 'In the big picture of my future, whatever God's will is, I will trust Him and follow. But nevertheless, this general commitment narrows itself down to a day-by-day willingness to obey what I know to be His will for me right now. The general commitment for your whole future narrows down to a specific commitment, which says I will do what I know I am supposed to do today. You are agreeing that in this instance, and for this occasion I will obey God and follow His will. Sometimes it is easier to make grand commitments about unknown guidance that is going to occur sometime in the future, than it is to make a particular commitment to be obedient in special guidance over an issue that occurs today. But step by step, as you obey these specific things, then the next portion of His will is revealed. So step by step, you 'walk in the light.'

"Third, to obey and submit to the will of God like this takes a certain amount of faith and trust. Now this aspect of doing God's will will be expanded upon in more detail later on if you reach the City of Prayer. Although some of what I am about to say will be repeated at that time, I need to say it now to complete my thoughts on this matter. Faith is built on the solid foundation that you really believe that God loves you and wants the very best for you. Do you really believe that God knows better than you do? Do you really believe that God has a spirit of goodwill toward you? If you can trust in the basic love and goodwill of God, then you will believe that what He plans and wishes for you are the very best. It takes simple faith to believe that the greatest life you can live is the life that is lived in the center of God's will. Faith believes that the greatest person you can be is the person God wants you to be. It takes a simple faith to believe that God, as your heavenly Father, is working for your highest good.

"While this is a simple faith, it is not always an easy faith. We are always tempted to believe that we know what is best for us. There is an assumption in human nature that says if we want it, it must be good for us. If we strongly want it, then it must be necessary for our satisfaction and well-being. This assumption is by no means trustworthy. To act on this assumption can create in us a false belief that our way is the best way. It can make us imagine that God's will is fine, as long as it coincides with our will. It takes a strong faith and commitment when there is a division of will between what we want and what God wants, between our wisdom and God's wisdom, between our wishes and God's wishes, to bow the heart and say 'your will be done.' Faith in the goodwill and wise planning of God helps us to say to God day by day, 'Your kingdom come, Your will be done in my life.'

"Do you remember what you were taught by the trail guide in the Viewing Platform? The trail guide said that '**prayer is learning to receive what God**

wants to give.' To receive what God wants to give is not always easy, there are times when His priorities are different to our priorities, and what is important to Him is not what is important to us. But simple faith can rise up in these times of conflict and say, 'what He wills is best.'

"You can see," said Joyce, "that there is plenty to say to God and explore with God when you open this door and enter this room of prayer. 'Thy kingdom come, Thy will be done.'

"I believe that is enough for you to think and meditate about right now, let's dismiss for a break, and then we will come back and talk about the other statements in the Lord's Prayer."

I was very pleased when the class dismissed that Alvin made his way over to John and me to speak to us. "I want to thank you two," he said. "What you said to me about prayer being joyful and exciting did not make much sense to me at that time. I felt then that prayer was largely a duty and a responsibility that I had to fulfill, while to feel joy and happiness in prayer was rather shallow and frivolous and was not treating the matter with appropriate seriousness. But listening to Joyce has convinced me that prayer can also be very exciting, joyful, and satisfying. That to be in the presence of God is a soul-refreshing experience. I want to thank you both for seeing what I did not see and for trying to help me. I am going to try and enjoy God and find glory in His presence."

"This is wonderful," I said to Alvin. "You know John and I prayed for you that this very thing would happen. You are such a sincere and dedicated brother that we wanted your load to be lightened a little bit. I guess God has answered our prayers. But you must know, Alvin, that you taught John and me something as well. We understand better now, after listening to you, that there is an element in prayer where we carry burdens and have deep concerns for others, and we must learn to develop that aspect of our prayer lives. We have learned from each other."

"Yes," said John, "God has answered our prayers. But let's not forget to thank Him for the answers." So the three of us, bowed our heads, joined our hands, and thanked God for his mercy and for His faithfulness in answering this prayer.

"For sure," I said, "on this occasion we **asked for something that God wanted to give,** and He quickly and effectively answered our prayers."

TOPICS FOR DISCUSSION—CHAPTER FIVE

1. Discuss the concept that "each petition in the Lord's Prayer is like a doorway that leads into a room."
2. Why is it important to begin our prayers with the words and attitude of "Our Father?"
3. How do we make personal the petition "Thy will be done"?
4. How would you deal with the question, "But what if I am aware of some things in my life that I do not want to submit to God?"

CHAPTER SIX

THE LORD'S PRAYER—
DAILY BREAD

The break in the lesson gave John and me an opportunity to mix and mingle with the other members of the class. It was an encouragement for me to talk to some of the others about their experience with prayer and to hear from them how they were progressing in their prayer life. There was one aspect of our experience about which there seemed to be general agreement. Each one, as they progressed in prayer, was discovering more value and excitement in simply being in the presence of God and enjoying His fellowship. Prayer was developing into a time of interaction with God, and not just a time of presenting our petitions to Him. We were all learning, to our satisfaction, to give more time and attention to worship and fellowship. One of the fellow students said, "If the essence of prayer is **learning to receive what God wants to give,** then I am beginning to learn how to pay more attention to what God wants to give, than to what I want to get from Him."

Another added to this thought by saying, "I can understand now what the psalmist meant when he said, 'One thing I ask of the Lord, this is what I seek; that I may dwell in the house of the Lord all the days of my life, to gaze upon the beauty of the Lord and to seek him in his temple' (Ps. 27:4). It seems that the primary desire of the psalmist was to be in the presence of God and enjoy His fellowship. This awareness of the presence of God is developing in my own heart now."

It was clearly the unanimous opinion among those that I talked with that the growing edge of prayer was in the area of developing a relationship with God and experiencing His love and greatness. While they still had things that they asked God for, there was an increasing value placed in the relationship with God, enjoying His presence and rejoicing in His fellowship. Prayer was becoming more relational and not just transactional. This agreed with what John and I were experiencing, and it encouraged us to think that we were moving in the right direction. We were all also stimulated by what we had heard from Joyce about the content of the Lord's Prayer. What we were experiencing for ourselves in our own private prayer times was harmonizing with what Joyce was telling us about the balance and content of the Lord's Prayer.

One lady, however, did bring up a question that made me think. She said that she was praying for her son. This boy had made a number of bad decisions in life. The path that he had chosen had led him far from God and was very different to the style of life that his mother wanted and wished for him. She was greatly burdened for her son and prayed with great anguish of heart for his reclamation and his salvation. "But," she wondered, "I acknowledge that he has a free will of his own. God has given him the responsibility of making his own moral and salvation choices. I believe God will not overrule my son's free will, even if his choices are wrong and grieve God as much as they grieve me. My question is, since my son has his own free will, and God will not overrule his free will, can my prayers make any difference to the choices that he makes?" I imagined that many a concerned mother and father, who have wrestled with God in prayer for their family, have asked the same question. We discussed this in our group and concluded that 'yes! The ultimate responsibility for the moral and salvation choices that we make lie on the shoulders of the individual, and God will respect this and will not overrule those choices.' It is, however, very urgent, that we pray for these individuals, because, while God will not force them to make the correct decisions, He can and does bring influences to bear upon them that encourage them to make the right choices. He does this in answer to the prayers of concerned people. He can, for example, through the work of the Holy Spirit, bring a sense of guilt into their life. He can make them increasingly dissatisfied with their present way of living. He can create in them a hunger for something better and something different. He can impress them with the desirable way of life that they see godly people living. He can bring them into contact with the right people who can influence them in the right direction. There are many ways in which God, in response to the prayers of His people, will bring influences to bear on those who are going in the wrong direction. These influences can restrain them from going too far; they can motivate them to change their way of life; they can convict them into repenting and turn them to God for salvation; they can impress upon them the greatness of God's love for them. This is the work of the Holy Spirit, and He does it in response to the prayers of His people. So we should continue to pray for those we love, because we do not know whether the very thing that will make the difference in their ultimate decisions and destinies are the prayers of God's people.

We can be sure that God will respond to our prayers and work effectively in the lives of those for whom we are praying. Our responsibility is to pray fervently for them. God will respond to this, but we must accept, just as God accepts, that the final decisions and responsibilities lie with the individual. They can, in spite of many influences, still decide to reject the way of Salvation and grieve the Holy Spirit. But our responsibility has been fulfilled in that we prayed for them and seek to encompass their salvation.

This serious discussion went on for quite some time. One person contributed to the discussion by pointing out that Jesus encouraged us to pray, not for the harvest fields of the world, which are ripe and ready, but rather He said, 'Ask the Lord of harvest, therefore, to send out workers into his harvest field' (Matt. 9:38). "So," he continued, "I feel that I have said and done all I can for my children, so now I pray that the Lord of harvests will bring them into contact with good Christian people who will be able to have an influence in their lives."

Another lady added to this, by saying, "I have discovered that I like to pray for those I love and who need salvation by asking that they will be overcome by His love, and surprised by the impact of it." These discussions were very helpful and encouraging to those of us who had loved ones who still needed salvation. Clearly this was a matter of great concern to many of our group as most of us seemed to have someone whom we loved dearly who needed salvation.

I remarked to John, "I hope this subject will be dealt with in greater detail when we get to the City of Prayer."

"Right," answered John. "It is an important part of our prayer life, and I think we need more instruction on it."

At Joyce's request, we all gathered into the class again for the next session. We were anxious to hear from her about the next section of the Lord's Prayer.

When we were all settled, she began, "The next statement in the prayer is a petition. It asks, 'Give us this day our daily bread.' With this petition, the focus of the prayer changes from God to us. We begin to pray now for our own personal needs, and the first of these is our daily bread. As you can imagine, daily bread stands for more than just two or three slices of a whole wheat loaf each day. Daily bread stands for all of the basic necessities of life. In praying for your daily bread, you are praying that God will help you provide the basic necessities for sustaining and enjoying life. It covers more than just having enough to eat, it also includes all of the other things that are essential for a comfortable life, including shelter, warmth, and safety. And the wonder is that God will work with us and help us to provide these necessary things. Jesus included this promise in His statement about seeking first the Kingdom of God. He said, 'But seek first his kingdom and his righteousness, and all these things will be given to you as well' (Matt. 6:33). The promise is there, if you give priority to the development of the Kingdom of God within you, these other things will be taken care of as well.

"Jesus understood that we have a strong sense of urgency and responsibility to provide for ourselves and for our families. God is willing to help us take care of this important responsibility. He also knew how these affairs can become so pressing and demanding that we can easily slip into the way of life where they become the predominant value. So a promise and a caution are expressed in His Sermon on the Mount where He said, 'And why do you worry about clothes? See how the lilies of the field grow. They do not weave or spin. Yet I tell you that not even Solomon in all his splendor was dressed like one of these. If that is how God clothes the grass of the field, which is here today and tomorrow is thrown into the fire, will he not much more clothe you, O you of little faith? So do not worry, saying 'What shall we eat?' or 'What shall we drink?' or 'What shall we wear?' For the pagans run after all these things, and your heavenly Father knows that you need them. But seek first his kingdom and his righteousness, and all these things will be given to you as well. Therefore do not worry about tomorrow, for tomorrow will worry about itself. Each day has enough trouble of its own' (Matt. 6:28-34).

"These verses contain some beautiful promises and also some very real cautions. The promise is that our heavenly Father knows and understands that we have life needs that must be met. In fact He created us this way. We must eat, we must drink, we must have shelter. These things are the necessities of life. We cannot live a comfortable and satisfying life without them. We have a responsibility to provide these things for ourselves and for our family. And God will help us. He has given us a world that is fertile and can produce food. He has given us intelligence so that we can work and earn the necessities of life. For most of us, He has given us the strength and the desire to work so that these things can be provided. We are urged to pray about these matters, and this is accompanied with the promise that gives us the comfortable assurance that if we ask, God will help us to provide these things. It is a proper and correct prayer to daily pray that the necessities of life will be provided for you and those for whom you are responsible. In addition to this, we should not neglect to give thanks when we are able to provide them.

"Now," continued Joyce, "there are one or two things that we need to understand about this promise and the cautions that accompany it. First, what is considered the necessities of life, or daily bread, will vary from culture to culture. A stone age Indian living in the jungle and a university student living in a large metropolitan city can both pray this prayer. But both will have a very different concept of what daily bread is. To the Indian, providing daily bread would be a successful hunt, or a fertile, cultivated garden. The university student in the metropolitan city cannot hunt for his food or farm it for himself. He needs enough money to buy the food that others have farmed and produced. Both of these men need transportation. But transportation for the Indian means strong legs and tough feet in order to track and hunt the prey. For the university student it means an automobile, or a bike or public transportation. Clothing needs are different. Shelter needs are different. So when we pray 'Give us this day our daily bread,' we need to pray the prayer out of the culture and society in which we live. What appears to be embarrassing luxury for one may seem a necessity for the other. Daily bread applies to both cultures, but the meaning of daily bread is very different. The petition is that God would help us make provision for a comfortable life in the society in which we live.

"Second, the promise means that God will help by providing the processes by which the needs of daily bread are met. Jesus used the lily of the field as an illustration. They are beautifully clothed, but they went through necessary processes to achieve this. God provided some things—the sun, the rain, the fertile soil, but the lily also had a contribution to make if the system was to work. The lily had to grow, absorb the nourishment, develop a root system. Cooperation between God and the lily was necessary if the lily was to bloom and become fruitful. People, of course, are different to lilies. The processes which people have to go through in order to cloth themselves are different to lilies of the field. We have to spin and labor. God has provided the raw material and given us the intelligence and the skills whereby we can obtain, refine, and develop the material, but we ourselves must do the spinning and the weaving. Farmers produce food, but only if they go about the business of plowing, sowing, and reaping. God provides the raw materials, the sun, the earth, the rain, but the farmer cooperates in all of this by developing the skills and doing the work of farming. So the promise does not mean that God will provide while we sit in indolence and do nothing, or waste our lives and opportunities in laziness. Providing for our needs is usually a cooperative effort which includes God and us. With diligence and effort we work with God in order to provide.

This principle is enforced by the apostle Paul when he wrote to the church in Corinth. Some of the new Christians in Corinth were convinced that the second coming of Jesus was so immanent that they gave up their employment and spent their time eagerly awaiting the Lord's coming. These Christians, who had given up their source of income, became a burden on the rest of the congregation. Although these people may have considered themselves to be ultraspiritual the Apostle Paul leaves us in no doubt that this kind of behavior is unacceptable for a Christian. He puts it rather bluntly, 'For even when we were with you we gave you this rule: "If a man will not work, he shall not eat." We hear that some among you are idle. They are not busy; they are busy bodies. Such people we command and urge in the Lord Jesus Christ to settle down and earn the bread they eat' (2 Thess. 3:10-13). So the promise that our Heavenly Father will provide is not an invitation to laziness or sloppiness, in the hope that God, or others, will provide while we waste our time in trivialities and laziness. The petition is to be made sincerely by those who are industriously using the gifts, talents, strengths, and time that God has provided for them.

"Jesus also made some other very clear cautions about our attitude to the means of life. He was well aware how easily we can fall into the trap of becoming over-enamored and captivated by the desires for more and more of the things of the world. This is a spiritual deathtrap. This is especially the case for those who live in the kind of culture in which the amount of possessions you have determines your status and standing in the community. It is certainly a well-timed caution for us in our affluent and complicated society, where there seems to be an insatiable desire for more and more material possessions. We are warned continually, in the Bible, about being captivated into the value system of the world. This is a value system which tells us that our position and influence in society is determined by how rich we are. The way of the world gives the implicit suggestion that real happiness is found in possessing more and more things. And the more you have, the happier you will be. This is a spiritual fallacy. But it is very easy for us to be caught up in the system that urges us to possess more and more and more, on the false basis that more is better, and much more is happier. This is contradictory to all that the Bible teaches. The apostle Paul urges rejection of the system and pattern of worldly values in Romans 12:2, 'Do not conform any longer to the pattern of this world, but be transformed in the renewing of your mind.' I like the way J. B. Philips translates this verse. He says, 'Don't let the world around you squeeze you into its own mold, but let God remold your minds from within, so that you may prove in practice that the plan of God for you is good.' In spite of all of the trumpeting and advertising of the world's way of life, Christians are convinced that happiness and satisfaction are not found in the things we possess but rather in a soul-satisfying fellowship and communion with God. Ultimate reality is not found in things but in the spiritual experience for which the human soul is built."

A young lady raised her hand. "I have a question," she said. Joyce nodded her acceptance. The young lady asked, "Does that mean that God is not necessarily going to give me all that I ask for.?"

"That is correct," Joyce responded. "If you have learned anything about prayer so far on your journey, it is that God will answer only in accordance with His will. God is a good and loving heavenly father and wants only the very best for His children. To trust in Him is to believe that His will is always the best. So for Him to answer all and every request, whether it is good for us or not, would be very unwise, and it could be harmful for us in the long run, even though we think we just have to have it right now. Some requests that we make," Joyce continued, "are made out of poor and unwise motives, such as greed, selfish ambition, and pride. God is not likely to respond to these petitions."

The young lady was clearly unhappy with this response. She said with a touch of annoyance in her voice, "So what you really mean to say is that God's attitude is 'It is my will or nothing. It is my way or the highway.'"

Joyce thought for a moment and then replied, "When you stop to think about it, since God's highway is by far the best way to travel, and you will get along much better on it than on any other way, and when following His way will guarantee that you will arrive at the best destination, then I think God is quite correct when He insists that His way is the best way. On the other hand, since some of the other ways that we may choose for ourselves will lead us astray, bring us to a halt in a dead end, or cause us to end up in an empty wilderness, then clearly God wants us to go His way. He does not want us to go His way because His ego demands that He be in control. He wants us to go His way because He knows it is the best way for us. So when we pray He is not going to give us things that will harm us, or push us in directions that will get us lost or into trouble. So He will not respond to these kinds of requests. Remember the essence of prayer is **learning to receive what God wants to give.** If God does not want to give it, you are not likely to receive it from Him."

The girl was still not satisfied. "But I thought if we just had faith and prayed long enough and earnestly enough, God would answer. Is that not what He promised? Didn't He say 'Ask what you wish, and it will be given to you'?

"Well, no!" said Joyce, "what He really said was 'If you remain in me and my words remain in you, ask, whatever you wish, and it will be given you' (John 15:7). The conditions of the promise are that we remain in Him and His words remain in us. That means that we are in such close fellowship with Him and our hearts are so in tune with Him that we desire what He desires, and wish what He wishes. When His words remain in us, that means that on our part there will be a willing obedience to what we know is His will and direction for our lives."

The young lady was clearly not accepting this. So Joyce added rather sternly, "Why do you want something that is not God's will anyway?"

There was silence. Joyce waited. When there was no response from the girl or from anyone else, Joyce decided to continue with her lesson on the Lord's Prayer. "The correct use of this petition, 'give us this day our daily bread,' is to trust God, not that He will satisfy all of our selfish ambitions and worldly, greedy desires, but that He will help us provide for the necessities of life.

"When God answers this petition in our lives. There are three results or fruits that begin to blossom in our hearts. First, there develops an atmosphere of comfortable and conscious relaxation. God will support and help me to provide all that is enough for life in this society. This is contrary to the worry, and fretful anxiety that comes from not trusting this petition. Second, there comes a spirit of simple contentment. I have enough. I do not need more than I have for happiness. I have found my joy and fulfillment in other ways and in other values. I do not need to be restlessly striving to possess more and more. Third there is a spirit of balance. We must work to provide. We must trust that God will endorse our efforts with His help. We look to our spiritual as well as our physical life to satisfy the longings of our hearts. This gives us a good balance between living in this body and taking care of its needs, and also being, at the same time, a living soul that needs spiritual food and nourishment. The outcome of all of this is a simple, contented industrious way of life. It is described by the apostle Paul as 'Godliness with contentment is great gain. For we brought nothing into the world, and we can take nothing out of it. But if we have food and clothing, we will be content with that. People who want to get rich fall into temptation and a trap and into many foolish and harmful desires that plunge men into ruin and destruction. For the love of money is a root of all kinds of evil, some people eager for money have wandered from the faith and pierced themselves with many griefs'" (1 Tim. 6:6-10).

Joyce paused here. "I have taken a long time over this petition. Not only because it is so important, but also because some people find their prayer lives are disappointing. They are not getting out of prayer what they thought they would. One of the common reasons for this is that so much of their attention is taken up in asking God for temporal blessings and help that they become unbalanced and neglect the spiritual aspects of prayer. As a result, they feel disappointed in the results they get when God seemed largely silent in response to their requests. They find themselves in the unpleasant place that is described by James in his epistle when he says, 'You do not have because you do not ask God. When you ask, you do not receive because you ask with wrong motives, that you may spend what you get on your pleasures' (James

4:2-3). I am anxious that your prayer time become a rewarding, satisfying, and encouraging time for you, not a time of frustration when you keep on asking for things that you will not get. Remember the statement, prayer **is learning to receive what God wants to give.** God wants to give us enough material things for a comfortable and effective life, but He does not want to encourage greed and worldliness.

"So as you go through this house of prayer, be sure to spend some time in this room. God, your heavenly Father, wants to help provide enough for you to live comfortably and with a simple contentment. Do not feel reticent to express to Him the needs that come up in your life from time to time. And trust Him. He really loves you and knows you and wants to help provide all that is necessary for you.

On this encouraging note, Joyce suggested that we take another break, and then we would come back for the last section of the Lord's Prayer. We welcomed this break in the discussions. The class gathered into small groups to talk about the lesson. It seemed that John, Alvin, and I naturally gravitated to one another, and we began to comment about the teaching we had just received. As we talked, however, I noticed that two young ladies were talking to Joyce in a very earnest conversation. One of these young ladies was the one who had rather heatedly asked questions during the session. They seemed very animated as they exchanged their ideas. In fact they seemed a little frustrated. Joyce was obviously trying to explain something to them, but they were not accepting what she was saying. I was very curious to know what this was about, and so, taking John and Alvin along with me, I quietly moved over to this group to listen to their conversation. Joyce was pleased to see us and urged us to join in the exchange of ideas. She introduced us to the two women. "This is Janet and Helen," she said.

"I am happy to meet you," I responded. "My name is Philip." I turned to my two friends and introduced them. "This is John and Alvin."

After the introductions were complete, Joyce said, "Janet and Helen have some questions about prayer. Especially about the type of praying that I outlined in the Lord's Prayer where we say, 'Thy will be done on earth as it is in heaven.'"

"I really don't think I can go on with this," said Janet. "This is just not what I thought prayer was all about." Janet seemed to be the outspoken one of the two. She did most of the talking, while her companion, Helen, listened thoughtfully. "I wanted to learn how to pray better, because I thought that that way, I could get God's help in what I want to do. I did not really bargain for the idea that I was to start doing what God wanted me to do. I am afraid of that. What if God wants me to do something that I don't want to do? I have a good job, with really good prospects. I thought I would ask God to help me do the right things so that I could move forward in my position at work. But now, if I do His will, who knows but that He may ask me to give up my job and prospects and go away to some far corner of the globe and be a missionary. I am just not ready for that. I am hoping soon to buy a nice new home. I thought I would ask God to help me move in and make it comfortable and help me pay for it. I really planned on being a good neighbor and using my house as a hospitality center, opening it up to help and minister to other people. I don't think I am being greedy or selfish. I want to use my position and my home to be a blessing to others. I can't see that as being wrong. But now, if I say 'your will be done,' He might tell me to sell my house and give all my money to the poor. I am just not ready for that. Not only that, but suppose I meet a nice young man and we decide to get married? I would gladly ask God to bless our marriage and our home and our family and make us a blessing in our lives. But now, God might ask me to give all of that up. I am afraid to yield all to God. I am aghast at what He might ask me to do. I have my plans and my purposes in life all set out. It looks great and exciting to me. I certainly want to include God in my plans and make Him an important part of what I do in life, but I don't seem to be ready to turn it all over to God and say, if you want me to make other plans or do others things, I will do it. Who knows where I might end up and what I will have to start doing?"

I listened to Janet and felt like I wanted to kindly smile at her and pat her comfortingly on the back and assure her that God would not ask her to do all of these outrageous things. But I looked at Joyce, and Joyce was not smiling, nor was she patting Janet on the back. In fact, by the look on her face, it did not seem to me that she was going to give Janet any comfort at all.

"Janet," she said, "if you yield your life to God and commit yourself to doing His will, I have no idea what God might ask you to do. But let me ask you some questions. Do you believe that God loves you?"

"Of course," said Janet.

"If God loves you, do you not believe that He will, therefore, out of love, only want the very best for you?"

"Yes."

"Do you believe, Janet, that God is also wise? Perhaps even wiser than you are?"

Janet was a very smart and intelligent woman. She could see where this was going, so she rather reluctantly replied, "Yes."

"So if God loves you wisely, He will know what kind of life is the best for you. He will know where you can be most effective and useful. He knows exactly what a young lady with your gifts and abilities should become and what you should do with your life. A wise and loving God will not ask you to foolishly throw your life away. He will not ask you to become or do something that you are clearly not fitted for or gifted in. He does not want to waste you. What I am saying, Janet, is that God's will is the best way for you. You will end up being more satisfied, thrilled, and fulfilled by doing His will than following your own plans."

"I know what you are saying," said Janet. "But I am afraid to do that. It scares me. I want to be in control. I want to be in charge of my own life. I don't mind God coming along. I would be glad for Him to do that. In fact I keep asking Him to do that. But I don't want to give up control to Him. I just don't know what He would do with me. Think of Jesus. He was all into this business of doing His Father's will and look what happened to Him. I don't want that to happen to me. No thank you."

Joyce, who still didn't smile reassuringly, or pat Janet on the back comfortingly, said, "Then, Janet, I think you have some very serious decisions to make. The matter of who is in control of your life is crucial, not only for your progress in prayer, but also for the progress in your whole Christian life. But make no mistake about it. God wants to be on the throne of your life. Jesus wants to be King of your life. He is looking to you to make a commitment of yourself to Him. In fact, this becomes the great issue in every Christian's life, when our own self-will rises up and objects to yielding to the will of God. It is a matter that all of us who are making progress in our walk with God, and also developing in our prayer life, will have to face and deal with. You have arrived at that place. Will you yield your all to Him? Will you commit to doing His will? He asks us to yield. The prophet Isaiah deals with the issue beautifully when he likens God to the potter and likens us to the clay. But the prophet leaves no doubt that the clay has to yield to the power, authority, and skill of the potter. He says, 'Yet, O Lord, you are our Father. We are the clay, you are the potter; we are all the work of your hand' (Isa. 64:8). The clay does not say to the potter 'don't do this' or 'don't do that.' The clay does not say, 'I do not wish to be made into this or into that.' The clay simply places itself in the hands of the skilful and loving master potter and says, 'Here, make of me what you will. Mold me and shape me as you will.' The faith and trust of the clay is that the master potter has the skill, the wisdom, the love, and the care to make something beautiful out of the clay. Clay in the hands of the master potter can become something far more useful and beautiful than it could ever become by its own efforts or skill. The hymn writer expresses it well when he says,

> 'Have Thine own way, Lord! Have Thine own way!
> Thou art the potter, I am the clay.
> Mold me and make me, after Thy will,
> While I am waiting, yielded and still.'"[1]

"I am not at all sure that I can do that," said Janet unhappily.

"This is a crucial decision for you, Janet, and we will pray for you." With that we all bowed our heads, and Joyce prayed for Janet and Helen. After the prayer, Janet still did not seem to be at peace, but as there was nothing else we could do at the moment, Joyce called the class together to finish the teaching on the Lord's Prayer.

TOPICS FOR DISCUSSION—CHAPTER SIX

1. Discuss the whole matter of the effectiveness of prayer for others, given that God will respect their free will and their moral choices.
2. What does "daily bread" stand for?
3. What is meant by the statement "God will help by providing the processes by which the needs of daily bread are met?"
4. Consider the statement "When God answers this petition in our lives. There are three results or fruits that begin the blossom in our hearts."

    - What are these fruits?
    - Compare these fruits to the greedy hungers of the world.
    - What is Christian simplicity?

5. What do you perceive is the heart of Janet's problem?

    - How would you deal with it?
    - Was Joyce too hard on Janet?

CHAPTER SEVEN

THE LORD'S PRAYER—DELIVER US

Joyce began, "The next statement in the Lord's Prayer, in fact the next series of statements, introduces us to a new and very fundamental subject. They are prayers to help us deal victoriously with our greatest enemy. There is a dreadful disease that has afflicted the whole human race. This horrible affliction is the source of great suffering and misery to all of us. Unless we learn to understand this enemy and deal with it effectively, then it will, in some form or another, overwhelm us and destroy us. The next statements in the Lord's Prayer are designed to help us confront and overcome the deadly enemy of evil. Because we are so used to evil in our world and in our personal lives, we tend to want to minimize its importance and trivialize its influence. Some view it as nothing more than a necessary but inconvenient nuisance. Others think that since it is so universal, it has to be considered as a monstrous but inevitable problem which we can't really do much about, and so we need to accept it as part of human existence. They think that evil is God's problem, and He will have to deal with it somehow and in His own way. Since the problem is beyond us and there is little we can do about it, we do not need to get too upset over it. The concept that we must personally become involved in the battle against evil is not a prominent idea amongst many Christians today.

"The Bible, however, holds no such false illusions. Evil is not trivial. It is the source of unspeakable suffering in the human race. It is the root cause of much of our disease, wars, pain, and cruelty. And evil is more than a social or racial blight, it is also intensely personal. It takes hold of the individual human heart and expresses itself in our pride, greed, selfishness, and hatreds. Collectively it also spoils our social lives by creating jealousy, bitterness, and divisions between people. It destroys our fellowship with God and will ultimately damn our souls unless we learn how to deal with it. The fact that three out of the eight statements in the Lord's Prayer are devoted to the subject of evil is an indication that Jesus did not take this lightly. It is a major concern. Neglect and weakness here could destroy us. How to deal successfully with the evil in us and around us should form an important part of our prayer life. In the house of prayer, these three rooms are not the most comfortable, but their importance cannot be overstated.

> "The three statements that deal with our struggle with evil are:
> Forgive us our sins as we forgive those who are indebted to us.
> Lead us not into temptation.
> Deliver us from evil.

"Although we have distaste for this subject and we would rather not go here, an earnest intent in our prayer life indicates that we must give serious attention to evil. The encouraging factor is that this can be a victorious and conquering part of our prayer experience. It is neither inevitable nor acceptable that we are going to be defeated by evil. Indeed the very opposite, God has, through Jesus Christ, made possible a life of victory and triumph over sin and evil. The three statements each deal with a different aspect of how evil tries to infect and destroy our lives, our souls, our contact with other people and with God. They also indicate the provision that God has made to help us become conquerors in this battle. Let's look at these three important statements.

"The first one says, 'Forgive us our sins as we forgive everyone who is indebted to us.' In this prayer we pass through a doorway in the house of prayer that leads us into a room in which we deal victoriously with the conscious sins that we may commit. If we have knowingly done something wrong, this becomes a very important room in the house of prayer. The sins we commit can be placed in two categories. First, there is the sin that is defined as a 'willful transgression of the known law of God.' When we commit this type of sin, then two important ingredients are in it. The first ingredient is knowledge, we know it is wrong. The second ingredient is our own will or choice. We know it is wrong, but we decide to do it anyway. To know it is wrong but to decide to do it anyway is what some call 'sin, properly so called.' Knowledge and will are involved in this kind of sin. Actually, the reverse is also true, when you know you should do something and you decide not to do it, then that is still sin properly so called. James states this in his epistle. He says, 'Anyone, then, who knows the good he ought to do and doesn't do it, sins' (James 4:17). When you know you should have done something and you chose not to do it, or you know you should not have done something and you chose to do it, then you have consciously and willfully violated the will of God and you have sinned.

"This kind of sin, this willful violation of the known will of God has immediate and powerful repercussions in our lives. It is real sin. It brings immediate negative results. This type of sin makes you feel guilty. This sin immediately begins to disturb your relationship with God, and if it is not dealt with will disrupt and finally sever your fellowship with Him. You cannot continually and habitually keep on doing this kind of sin and expect to maintain an intimate and satisfying relationship with a Holy God. To continuously violate what you know is the will of God is contrary to the whole spirit of faith in Christ. It denies the purpose of redemption. John states it quite bluntly in his epistle, with this kind of sin in mind, he says, 'No one who continues to sin has either seen him or known him' (John 3:6). Or even more bluntly in 1 John 3:9, 'No one who is born of God will continue to sin.'

"The power of this kind of sin to destroy our spiritual life is clearly seen in the Bible. Go right back to the very first sin, with Adam and Eve. God made it abundantly clear that they could eat of any tree in the Garden of Eden, but must not eat of the fruit of the tree of the knowledge of good and evil. They knew and understood this was the command of God. But even when they knew it, they still went to look at the tree and by their own choice picked its fruit and ate it. They did not have to do this. They were not forced into it. But in full knowledge of the command of God and by their own moral choice, they ate the forbidden fruit. They had knowledge of God's will, and they choose to violate it. The results were immediate. They saw they were naked. They hid from God. They felt guilty and were alienated from God and His presence. The sin also had long-range consequences. They were banished from the garden and from God's presence. The natural world in which they had to live was now spoiled. Pain, suffering, and disease were introduced. Enmity and selfishness invaded their relationships. Sinfulness became the habit and the state of the human race. We must clearly understand that this kind of sin, this willful, conscious violation of the known will of God will have immediate effects in our life. If you participate in this kind of sin, you must understand that it is a fatal poison that must be dealt with. 'The wages of sin is death' (Rom. 6:23).

"The wonderful news is that God has provided an antidote for this poison. That is why we must enter this room in our prayer life and take time to wait on him and make sure that this poison is not active in our lives. This is the room of reconciliation. In here we drink in the antidote for the poison. When we sense that something is wrong in our relationship with Him. When our conscience is disturbed or we feel uncomfortable and out of peace in the presence of God, then we need to enter into the spirit of this prayer. Forgive us our sins. It is an open confession, 'I have consciously violated what I know is your will. I have disobeyed what I knew to be your command. I confess and repent and ask your forgiveness,' God will respond to this penitent prayer by offering His free forgiveness. The sin will be forgiven, we will be released from guilt, the peace of God will be restored in our hearts and the fellowship will be renewed. Wonderful. John describes this process for us in his epistle. He says, 'My dear children, I write this to you so that you will not sin, but if anyone sin, we have one who speaks to the Father in our defense—Jesus Christ the Righteous one' (1 John 2:1). The expectation is that we do not sin like this, but if we do, then immediate action must be taken, and if we are genuinely repentant, we will find a readiness and willingness on God's part to forgive, through Jesus Christ the Righteous. John makes the same promise earlier in his epistle when he says, 'If we confess our sins, he is faithful and just and will forgive us our sins and purify us from all unrighteousness' (1 John 1:9).

"You must not expect any meaningful fellowship or unity to happen between you and God until this matter is cleared up. When you know it is wrong and you choose to do it, you have driven a wedge into the relationship between you and a holy God. When you do this, then you need to enter this room and pray this prayer. Not flippantly, or carelessly, but remorsefully and repentantly. If you are truly repentant, then you can have faith that this is the kind of prayer for forgiveness that God will forgive. You need to acknowledge your sin, repent, and trust God for forgiveness.

"King David understood this when he grievously sinned in the Bathsheba incident. Eventually, with a disturbed soul he entered this room in the prayer house and cried from his heart, 'Create in me a pure heart, O God, and renew a steadfast spirit within me. Do not cast me from your presence or take your Holy Spirit from me. Restore to me the joy of your salvation and grant me a willing spirit to sustain me' (Ps. 51:10-12). Your loving heavenly Father, who wants clean and true fellowship with you, will forgive you for Christ's sake. Remember the true essence of prayer is **learning to receive what God wants to give.** You can be sure and confident that God wants to forgive and that He will forgive in response to repentance and faith on your part. To try to carry on with your Christian walk, while you are knowingly violating what is the will of God for you will cause you great grief, and if you persist in it, it will eventually lead to a separation between you and God. If you have sinned like this, then this prayer is vital for you. In some ways, this is the 'sick room' in the house of prayer. If you know there is something wrong in your relationship with God, this is the place to go. If you are aware of unhealthiness in your soul, it might be good to go to this room first. To try to pray in other aspects of prayer while you are consciously sick in your spirit, is not likely to be rewarding. First get right with God and restore a healthy relationship with Him.

"Remember, however, that you are dealing with a powerful and disastrous poison here. You cannot be flippant or neglectful or careless about this. You need to enter this room. Quieten your heart. Search your heart honestly and openly before God. Confess to Him what you find is wrong there and ask His forgiveness. You should not leave until the sense of God's peace and forgiveness has returned to you conscience again. This is an important aspect of prayer when you are feeling guilty and need to get things right between you and God or you and other people.

"But this prayer 'forgive us our sins' also deals with another aspect of sin that invades our lives. In this second aspect of sin, the two critical ingredients of knowledge and will are absent. This type of sin, which some do not even consider to be real sin at all, is when you do something that God would not approve of, but you are not aware that you have done it, or you did not know that God did not approve. Often we make mistakes. We foul up in what we were trying to do, even when we had the best of intentions. We meant something for the best, but somehow it was misunderstood and caused offence. Unwittingly we treat other people in ways that damage them, but we are blithely unaware that we have done it. Even while we are doing our best, sometimes mistakes and errors happen. We fall short of God's standard, even though we did not mean to or want to, and in our own hearts we thought we were doing our best. Sometimes poor attitudes creep into our heart, and we are, at first, unaware of them. This kind of sin is different to 'sin properly so called.' This is not a conscious violation of the known will of God. We do not know we are doing it, and if we were aware of it, we would choose not to do it. But nevertheless, whether we meant it or not, whether we knew it or not, we have still fallen short of God's standards and perhaps caused some damage to other people, to ourselves, and to the kingdom of God. That is why we need to pray 'forgive us our sins.' For we have sinned. In this respect we sin in word and thought and deed every day and need forgiveness.

"We all have things to learn. We all still have to grow in grace and in wisdom. The more we grow and the closer we get to Him, then the greater will be our understanding of how He wants us to live and the fewer errors and mistakes we will make. We will learn to treat people with greater respect and see better ways to love them more effectively. But no matter how far we advance in the Christian life we will never, in relationship to this sin, be perfect. There will always be room for improvement. Even the great people of God need to pray this prayer. We need to pray this prayer in order to keep our hearts and minds clear before God. We need to enter this room in our prayer life and pray that God will forgive us for our shortcomings and mistakes.

"To pray in this spirit helps us grow and develop in our Christian life. John tells us that 'if we walk in the light, as he is in the light, we have fellowship with one another, and the blood of Jesus, his Son, purifies us from all sin' (1 John 1:7). Often in this quiet, honest openheartedness before God, He will reveal things to us that we never understood or grasped before. If we listen to His voice and respond to His light, we will grow and develop in our walk with Him in exciting and fresh ways. It is this walking in the light that keeps our experience with Him fresh, new, and ever changing. We see new things, experience new truth, we face new challenges, we understand adjustments that need to be made, we grow in grace and get more like Him all the time.

"Sin in all its shapes and forms is the very thing that will separate us from God and disturb and destroy our fellowship with Him. If we do not humbly search our hearts and ask forgiveness, then things can creep into our lives that bring a cloud and shadow over our fellowship with God. So when we enter this room in our prayer life, we need to search ourselves. Open our hearts honestly before God and without excuse acknowledge our sins and failures. And seek forgiveness. Optometrists tell us that there are small particles of dust and dirt that land on our eyes all the time. To deal with this, there is a thin stream of fluid that flows over our eyes to keep them clean. When we blink, this is a cleansing operation that keeps the eye clean of any unwanted dirt. Without this constant attention to cleansing, the eyes would become dry, clogged, and eventually pain and blindness would set it. It is essential that constant attention be given to cleansing the eyes. So in this way, this prayer helps us to give constant attention to cleansing our consciences before God. We open ourselves to His spirit and respond to what He tells us and impresses upon us. The hymn writer expresses the attitude and approach to this part of the prayer life well when he says,

> Search me, O God and know my heart today.
> Try me, O Savior; know my thoughts, I pray.
> See if there be some wicked way in me,
> Cleanse me from ev'ry sin, and set me free.[1]

"If this seems like an odious and burdensome task to you, let me remind you that the outcome is wonderful. You know you are right with God. You are aware that there is no impediment between you and your Savior. When you leave this room in your prayer time, you have a wonderful sense of peace with God. Your heart is right. There is nothing between your soul and your Savior.

There is no barrier between you and other people. All is forgiven. All is right. There are no remnants of bitterness or resentment. This is peace indeed. This is the joy of being at one with God and your neighbor. This is what Jesus died for, to bring us back into fellowship with a holy God. Do not avoid this. Do not try to escape it. It is an exercise of the soul that brings instant and immediate results. With these prayers, you can have absolute confidence and faith that God will answer.

"The prayer goes on to say 'forgive us our sins as we forgive those who are indebted to us.' This portion of the Lord's Prayer is rather dangerous. We pray, 'Father, forgive us our sins in the same measure that we forgive those who sin against us.' The purpose of this kind of praying is to keep our relationships with other people as right as it is possible for them to be. We are asking for a spirit of forgiveness towards others, even to those who have sinned against us and have not treated us the way we think we should have been treated. If we are willing to forgive others, then we will not carry around in our hearts a spirit of resentment, or hostility. We cannot carry grudges or maintain a bitter attitude and at the same time exhibit a forgiving spirit. Inevitably, other people will behave badly towards us. Whether knowingly or unknowingly, they will not treat us in the way we feel we should be treated. We will be hurt and grieved by the behavior of others towards us or towards those we love, but rather than let their bad behavior sour us, and poison our spirit, we express an attitude of free forgiveness. We would willingly forgive them just as God would willingly forgive us.

"So much of the pain and suffering we experience in this life is because of broken, fractured relationships. We long for love and unity with others, but so often we encounter, bitterness, jealousy, and hostility. Personal relationships break down. Sometimes there is nothing we can do about it. We may not be at fault. The other person is creating problems by their actions or their attitudes. It hurts. It disappoints us. But in order to keep our own spirit free and unpoisoned by the bad atmosphere, we must maintain a loving spirit of generous, willing forgiveness. We cannot determine, nor are we responsible for, the attitude and spirit of others. Inevitably there will be those who sin against us in act or in attitude. How we respond to them is vital. If we respond with hostility and anger, if we harbor bitterness and spite, then we ourselves are poisoned in spirit. We allow them to harm us. Thus this prayer is very important. We keep our spirit free. We keep our attitudes clean. We are not being damaged and spoiled by a bad or hostile atmosphere. Our spirits are free. Our conscience is clear, and the way is open for good relationships to be restored and renewed if the other person is willing to cooperate.

"The prayer, does, however, give us a warning. If we will not forgive others their sins against us, then neither will God forgive us our sins. Jesus refers to this in the version of the Lord's Prayer that is given in the Sermon on the Mount in Matthew's Gospel. In the only commentary on the prayer that Jesus gives he adds at the end of it the comment, "For if you forgive men when they sin against you, your heavenly Father will also forgive you. But if you do not forgive men their sins, your Father will not forgive your sins' (Matt. 6:14-15). When you carry about in your heart an unforgiving spirit, it means that their sins are also damaging you and your spirit. You are the loser when you allow bitterness and hostility to linger in your heart. This is true even when you feel you are very justified in your attitude. The spirit of willingness to forgive frees your spirit, and you do not become hostage to the actions and attitudes of others. In the moment of His greatest suffering, a suffering imposed upon him by jealous and greedy men, Jesus cried out to the Father, 'Father, forgive them, for they know not what they do.' I ask you, who at that moment was free in spirit and at peace with himself? Who carried the burden of guilt and shame and the never to be satisfied greed for power and authority?

"If you maintain a bitter and resentful attitude to those who sin against you, then God will find it impossible to forgive you your sins as well. How can God forgive you when you insist on being unrepentant and unforgiving in your attitude to others? A generous and forgiving spirit towards others releases God to have the same spirit toward you."

This was heavy stuff for us to absorb, and there had not been much response or questions from the class. At this point, however, a hand went up. The question was asked. "A lot of people say you are supposed to 'forgive and forget.' I can understand how you can be willing to forgive, but how do you forget? If a man rapes your daughter and ruins her life, I can see that you could be willing to forgive, but how in all the world do you forget? You live with your spoiled and broken daughter every day of her life—you cannot forget."

"Thank you for that question," replied Joyce. "'Forgive and forget' is not a scriptural statement. It is a statement of folk theology and folk wisdom. God nowhere asks us to forgive and forget. So the statement does not carry the authority and truth of scripture. We cannot, of course, forget, in the sense that we have no memory of what happened or what was done to us. Sometimes the hurtful and harmful things will live with us for the rest of our lives. The parents of a girl who was raped and beaten will have to take care of her wounded soul and broken body for the rest of their lives. They live with it every day, they cannot forget. When people say 'forget,' I do not think they mean that you now have no memory of what was said or done, they mean that in your own heart and your own spirit you now have victory over the negative and harmful emotions that often accompany the memory. A willingness to forgive a wrong done to you will rob that wrong of its ability to harm you and cripple your own emotional and spiritual life. Many live soured and broken lives because they carry resentful, bitter, and revengeful desires in their heart. Although they did not do the wrong, although they were the wronged party, they are allowing the event to spoil and destroy their own life and happiness by letting these negative emotions sour and twist their own soul. Forgiveness of spirit frees you from this domination. So to forget does not mean you have no memory of the event, but it means that even when you think about it, it no longer has the power to arouse negative emotions in your heart. You are free from the emotional resentments and anger that cripple your own spiritual experience. To be willing to forgive means that the situation has lost its power to stir up within you hostile feelings. When you are openly willing to forgive, that generous and loving attitude then frees you to get on with your own life and your own spiritual development.

"The matter of forgiveness needs to be talked about too," continued Joyce. "Forgiveness is a mutual experience in which both the offender and the offended participate. Remember that even God does not forgive without repentance on the part of those seeking forgiveness. Those people who refuse to repent and insist on embracing their sinful way of life will not experience the forgiveness of God until such time as they repent. If they never repent, then they will experience the final separation from God and the pain that that will bring. Forgiveness is a mutual experience. The offended person must be willing to forgive. The offender must be willing to repent and show remorse and wish for forgiveness. When both of these conditions come together, then you have the experience of forgiveness. If, however, the offending party feels remorseful and repentant, but the one they have sinned against will not forgive, then the mutual experience of forgiveness does not happen. Or if the offended party shows a generous spirit and is willing to forgive, but the offender shows no remorse or repentance for what he has done, even though there is a willingness to forgive by the offended party, the actual experience of forgiveness does not happen.

"Even God does not forgive without repentance on our part. He loves us. He is willing to forgive. He works hard to bring forgiveness to us. But if we do not repent then actual forgiveness does not take place. It requires the cooperation of both parties. Jesus said, 'If your brother sins, rebuke him, and if he repents, forgive him. If he sins against you seven times in a day, and seven times comes back to you and says, "I repent," forgive him' (Luke 176:3). Forgiveness is a wonderful thing. It brings healing and reconciliation to many broken and ugly situations. But for forgiveness to be experienced, the two elements must be present—repentance on the part of the offender, and gracious forgiveness on the part of the offended. If we have offended someone, then our responsibility is to confess and ask forgiveness. If someone has sinned against us, then our responsibility is to graciously offer forgiveness. If they repent, then beautiful forgiveness and reconciliation takes place. If they refuse to repent, then, forgiveness does not happen. On your part, however, the situation is robbed of its emotional power over you, because of your willingness to forgive. What is called for is the willingness to forgive. Being willing to forgive keeps your own heart clean and free. To repent or not to repent is the responsibility of the other party.

"Take time in this room. Quietly go before God and open your heart to Him. Ask if there is anything between your soul and Him that should be revealed and spoken about. Make sure your heart is right with Him. Take time over this. Linger. Do not rush. It will bring you great joy and peace when you know that your heart is right with God, with your neighbor, and with yourself."

Joyce closed her notebook, and looked at the class. "This is a very serious moment for us in the class, just as it is a very important time for all of us in our prayer life. Before we continue, I would like us to sing quietly and thoughtfully a chorus that you may know:

> Let the beauty of Jesus be seen in me—
> All His wonderful passion and purity!
> O Thou Spirit divine, All my nature refine
> 'Till the beauty of Jesus is seen in me."[2]

Most in the class knew the chorus. With reverence we all bowed our heads and sang it together. After a few moments of silence, Joyce was ready to continue the instruction.

"Now, let's go on to the next of the petitions," said Joyce. "When you pray say, 'lead us not into temptation.' This part of the Lord's Prayer continues to help us deal with evil, the great enemy of our soul. Inevitably evil will tempt us to move away from God and participate in some sinful activity or attitude that will corrupt our soul. Temptation happens. Even Jesus was tempted. He was tempted by the devil in the wilderness at the beginning of His ministry. The writer to the Hebrews says of Jesus, 'For we do not have a high priest who is unable to sympathize with our weaknesses, but we have one who has been tempted in every way, just as we are—yet was without sin' (Heb. 4:15). If Jesus was tempted in the battle against evil, then we can have no other expectation than that we too will be tempted. Evil is in this world. Sin is rampant in our society. So we can only expect that there will be times when Satan will entice us to evil. He will make sin look easy and desirable. He will try to convince us that we are well within our rights and that it will be to our advantage to do, say, or act in the wrong way. He can make sin look very acceptable, unimportant, and desirable. We must be alert to this and expect temptation to happen in our lives. This statement in the Lord's Prayer is a request for God's help and guidance in the difficult and trying times of temptation. It is very important that we learn how to deal with temptation, for to yield and be drawn away by it will be destructive to our relationship with a holy God.

"As we enter this room in our prayers, there are three things we need to keep in mind that we want to explore with God. The first is the way the statement is made. It says, 'lead us not into temptation.' It would appear from the way it is stated as if God is the one who is doing the leading and He is deliberately placing us in temptations way. This is not at all what is meant. In fact James says, 'When tempted, no one should say "God is tempting me." For God cannot be tempted by evil, nor does he tempt anyone: but each one is tempted when, by his own evil desire, he is dragged away and enticed. Then, after desire has conceived, it gives birth to sin; and sin, when it is full-grown, gives birth to death' (James 1:13-15). Temptation will come, but it does not come from our heavenly Father, it comes from the enemy of our soul the devil and his spirit of evil.

"The second thing that we should notice is what we are actually asking for in this prayer. The prayer is that we will not be led into temptation. That suggests that there are lots of ways in which we ourselves can avoid being tempted. Often we can place ourselves in the path of temptation. The prayer should perhaps say 'make us wise enough to avoid temptation.' William Barkley the great Bible scholar has a section in his daily Bible readings under the heading 'We will be saved from temptation.' He says, 'If a man knows his own weakness, he will know the situations which he must avoid.

If a man has a weakness for too much liquor, he will be a very foolish man if he frequents inns and taverns.

If a man has a passion for gambling, he will be most ill-advised to frequent places and company where he will be tempted to gamble.

If a man knows that certain things make him lose his temper, he will do well to avoid them.

If we know our own weakness, and wisely remember it, half the battle with temptation will be won.'[3] This is good advice. So often we place ourselves in the position for being tempted.

"Eve in the Garden of Eden, let herself be led into temptation. She went and looked at the tree. And when she saw it, and feasted her eyes on it, she was in fact, allowing herself to be tempted, and the desire to indulge in the wrong thing was stimulated into a serious passion. 'When the woman saw that the fruit of the tree was good for food and pleasing to the eye, and also desirable for gaining wisdom she took some and ate it' (Gen. 3:6). If only Eve had not allowed herself to go and look and place herself in temptations way, the whole catastrophe might have been avoided. So we pray that we will not allow ourselves to be led into temptation. When we don't place ourselves in the position of being tempted then we have won half the battle. If you know that you have a weakness to feel sorry for yourself, then do not mull over the hurts and offenses. If you know that you can easily allow bitterness to take root in your heart, then do not 'nurse your wrath to keep it warm.'[4] If you know that you are prone to sexual temptations, do not look at that magazine or watch that movie. We must not trifle with sin. We must not play with it. It can suddenly turn on us and consume us.

"The third thing we need to understand about this petition is that it is an invitation to pray for strength when temptation does come. We can, by wisdom and discipline, avoid many temptations. There is moral and spiritual danger in deliberately placing ourselves in the way of temptation. But even when we are careful, there will still be times when temptation will seek us out. No one can live without temptation. Especially if you are seeking to live a holy and a godly life, you will be the special target of Satan. Temptation will come. But we are praying that when that time comes and the battle is on, that God will give us strength to be able to resist the temptation and not to yield. It is better to pray this prayer regularly each day even though you are not presently being tempted. You should not wait until the power and heat of the temptation is upon you before you start to pray for strength. But build yourself, reinforce yourself, so that you are in a position of strength when the temptation comes.

"Consider a man out on a mountain slope trying to learn how to ski. He is a novice and has not developed his skills. Suddenly he hears an avalanche rumbling down the mountain above him. He thinks, I will use my skiing skills to ski down the mountain and stay in front of the avalanche and so save myself. But he has not prepared for this. He has not developed the skills. His level of ability and strength are not meant for this kind of a test, and so, in spite of his best efforts, the avalanche overtakes him. The idea of skiing down the mountain with speed and skill might have saved him if he had been a professional skier and had spent time preparing himself and building his skill and expertise. But in his weakness he was not able to perform at the level that was needed to avoid the avalanche. When the power and fury of a temptation is upon you, it may be too late to pray for strength. Jesus realized this when he prayed for Peter. He said, 'Simon, Simon, Satan has desired to sift you as wheat. But I have prayed for you, Simon, that your faith may not fail. And when you have turned back, strengthen your brothers' (Luke 22:31).

"There is a further point to make here and that is that temptation also has a positive side. It is seen in the Bible as not just a seduction to evil but, when resisted, it is a positive strengthening point for the Christian. It is a test from which it is possible to emerge stronger and better. Its purpose, as far as the devil is concerned, is to make us sin and destroy our relationship with God. But God has the wisdom and ability to turn this solicitation to sin, which was meant for our bad, into something that is good. We can emerge from this time of testing with a deeper sense of loyalty, a firmer faith, and a developed self-confidence and trust in God. This way, temptation is not just a seduction to evil, it become a means for our growth and maturing in the Christian way. It can become a victory. It can produce fruits in our lives that nothing else could do. If you view your temptations as a test of your faith and loyalty, then you will come out of it a better, bigger, and more mature person. Victory over temptation has very positive results in our lives. Jesus came out of the temptation in the wilderness in the power of the Spirit and was ready to start His public ministry on a note of victory and power. Peter expresses it well when he says, 'Though now for a little while you may have had to suffer grief in all kinds of trials. These have come so that your faith—of greater worth than gold, which perishes even though refined by fire—may be proved genuine and may result in praise, glory and honor when Jesus Christ is revealed' (1 Pet. 1:6-7).

"So this is a prayer for wisdom and for strength. Wisdom, so that we are smart enough to avoid temptation when we can. Temptation is never nice and enjoyable, and we would be wise to not walk into its pathway if we can avoid it. And strength because we need to prepare ourselves for the battle. A soldier who has not prepared himself or his weapons for battle must not be surprised if he loses the conflict. But when the victory is won, then we rejoice in the fruits of victory.

"The last statement in the Lord's Prayer, continues to deal with evil. God clearly wants us to come out of this conflict with victory and blessing. The statement says, 'Deliver us from evil.' Perhaps better understood as 'deliver us from the evil one.' The evil spirit in the world is personified in the person of Satan. He is the true enemy of your soul. He has plans for your life and plans for your soul. His plans are bad, destructive, and harmful and painful. But God can deliver us from the evil plans of Satan. The destructive forces of evil must not be minimized or ignored. He is powerful, but not as powerful as God. He is wise, but not as wise as God. He works hard at our destruction and damnation, but not as hard as God works for our redemption and salvation. God is able and ready to keep us in victory over the plans of the evil one. You do need to notice that the prayer is for deliverance. You are not expecting that you will be exempt from the efforts of the evil one. Or that you will be sheltered from all of his schemes. You are promised, however, that even when the Satan does his worst, God is able to deliver you from evil and keep you in victory so that it does not harm your walk with Him or disturb the state of your spirit and soul.

"The power of evil has infected the world of nature, so that nature does not operate the way God originally planned. Nature can be furious. Tornados happen. Hurricanes take place. The prayer is not that God stop these things or that when they happen we will not be affected. We will be affected by the evil breakdown of nature just like everyone else. When a hurricane blows through town, it does not blow down all of the houses of the unrighteous but let all of the houses of the righteous stay standing. Even churches are not exempt and can be destroyed. But in the midst of these catastrophes our spirits are not defeated, and the devil's purposes to destroy and defeat us and cause us to doubt God and question His authority and power, need not be fulfilled. We can rise above the discouragements—God can deliver us from it. So when we pray 'deliver us from evil,' we are not asking that He will shelter us so that all of these evil things will not happen to us, but rather that He will deliver us in the sense that our spirit and faith will stay on top of the disastrous situation and we will be kept victorious. The evil in the world has brought sickness and decease. This is not the act of God, this is part of the action of Satan. So when God promises to deliver us, He is not saying that no sickness will happen to us or our loved ones. That is clearly not the case. But what is promised in this prayer is that in the midst of this evil and horrible thing that Satan has planned for us and brought on to us, God can keep us in victory so that our spirits rise above the pain and the weakness and maintain an attitude of victory.

"'Deliver us from evil' means something else. The evil in the world has affected the hearts of people. There are greedy, selfish, angry, and cruel people in this world. We are not to be sheltered from them. People will say things, do things, and act in ways that are hurtful, hostile, and sometimes cruel. Some people will, for their own selfish ends, seek to crush us and demean us. We cannot avoid this. So to pray 'deliver us from evil' does not mean that God will shelter us from the selfishness, greed, and cruelty of other people. God does not guarantee that we are only going to meet nice and pleasant and positive people all our lives and never encounter the other kind. But God can help us in the midst of a human society that can be godless, selfish, and cruel to live a victorious life and overcome the selfishness and hostility so prevalent in the environment around us. We can live 'self-controlled, upright and godly lives in this present age' (Titus 2:12). It is inevitable that we will all meet up with people who will not treat us the way we think we should be treated. They will be hostile, bitter, or jealous. But we are praying that our attitude to them will not be hostile, bitter, or jealous. Even when people, motivated by the evil in their own hearts seek to do us harm, we are praying that in return we will show a spirit of love and kindness. In interpersonal relationships our attitudes will be Christlike and pure. Because of the selfishness and greed that operate in peoples' hearts, it is inevitable that this will produce stresses in human relationships. We are not praying that none of this will happen to us. We must expect that we will on occasion be cheated, gossiped about, demeaned, bullied, and unjustly treated. What we are praying for is that when it does happen we will be able to keep our own spirits pure and free from sin. We praise God that He can deliver us from evil.

"But this prayer 'deliver us from evil' can become even more personal. The spirit of evil cannot only affect the hearts of other people, it can also affect our own hearts. Christians find that as they grow in grace and live closer to God, that there is an element of evil still residing in their own heart. This state of evil in the heart is different from sinning or willfully disobeying God. This evil is not so much something we do as something we are. Christians often find that there is a spirit in their hearts that is quite contrary and foreign to the Holy Spirit of Christ. They do not choose it to be there. They do not wish it to be there. They try to live so that this inward evil does not express itself or reveal itself in the attitudes that they have or in the way that they live. But in spite of their best efforts, it raises its ugly head now and then. This presence of sin in our heart mars the spirit of Christ in our lives. This condition of sinfulness residing deep within reveals itself in different ways in different people. In some it shows itself in an atmosphere of jealousy or spite. In others it can rise up as a spirit of hostile anger. Christians can find themselves bloated up with worldly pride. Others find it manifests itself in an inner rebellion against God and His will. When these spirits arise in our hearts, against our will and wishes, we are experiencing what the apostle Paul calls the 'works of the flesh' in our own hearts. He says, 'The acts of our sinful nature are obvious: sexual immorality, impurity and debauchery; idolatry and witchcraft; hatred, discord, jealousy, fits of rage, selfish ambition, dissensions, factions and envy; drunkenness, orgies, and the like. I warn you as I did before, that those who live like this will not inherit the kingdom of God' (Gal. 5:19-21).

"This aspect of sin in our hearts affects us so that we cannot love the way we want to love. We are envious when we do not want to be envious. Instead of peacefulness there is hostility. Pride mars our humility. Greed overcomes our simplicity. Even the apostle Paul himself struggled with this. He describes his inner struggle in Romans 7:15-20. 'I do not understand what I do. For what I want to do I do not do, but what I hate. And if I do what I do not want to do, I agree that the law is good. As it is, it is no longer I myself who do it, but it is sin living in me. I know that nothing good lives in me, that is, in my sinful nature. For I have the desire to do what is good, but I cannot carry it out. For what I do is not the good I want to do; no, the evil I do not want to do—this I keep on doing. Now if I do what I do not want to do, it is not longer I who do it, but it is sin living in me that does it' (Rom. 15:15-20). Paul is recognizing that there is a principle of sin in his heart which, in spite of his best efforts, he cannot fully control. It prevents him always exhibiting the Spirit of Christ. It causes him to adopt attitudes that are contrary to the love of God. It makes him, on occasions, rebel against the Spirit of God in his life. But Paul realizes he does not have to live with this sin in the heart. He cries out in frustration 'What a wretched man I am! Who will rescue me from this body of death?' He then goes on to cry in victory 'Thanks be to God—through Jesus Christ our Lord' (Rom. 7:24-25).

"Paul is describing an aspect of sin that lives in the heart of a person. This is not a sin that you do, so much as a sin of what you are—you are jealous, you are proud, you are hostile. It is not a choice or an action, it is a state of sin in the heart. You do not choose to be bitter, or envious, or selfish. Indeed you do not like these things and would rather do without them. To be sure, this sinful state in your heart sometimes causes you to act, speak, or think in ways that violate the Spirit of the Lord. But these outward actions are really only a response to what is in your heart.

"So when Jesus calls on us to pray 'deliver us from evil,' He is including in this prayer the spirit of evil that resides in our hearts. But to be delivered from this evil is not so much a matter of forgiveness and repentance, it is a matter of cleansing. God cleanses this from our hearts. The apostle John tells us that God has the ability to give us victory over this inner selfish sin that lives in our hearts when he says, 'If we walk in the light as He is in the light, we have fellowship with one another and the blood of Jesus Christ His Son, purifies us from all sin' (John 1:7). Especially note the words 'purifies from all sin.' There is no sin that can withstand His power or His grace. Jesus Himself urged this victory upon us when He said, 'Blessed are the pure in heart for they will see

God' (Matt. 5:7). When your heart contains jealous, hostile, or lustful spirits, it is not 'pure.'

"So this section of the prayer is recognizing that we are living in a world that is infected by evil. The evil expresses itself in many different ways. We must live in this world. We must seek to live for God in this world. So we pray that we will be delivered from the evil that is all around us and the evil that is in us. To deliver us from evil means He will give us the power to rise above it. To keep it from corrupting us. To help us fight off its effects, so that we are not defeated by it or overcome by it. But have the inner power, strength, and purity to live victoriously. This is the power and the help that God gives to those who ask for it in faith, 'deliver us from evil.'

"In the Gospel of Mathew's version of the Lord's Prayer, it ends with a benediction that is not included in the version in Luke's Gospel. The benediction in Mathew's Gospel once again turns our attention away from our own needs and directs it back again to God, 'For Thine is the Kingdom and the Power, and the glory.' This benediction at the end of the prayer helps us once again to focus on God. It reminds us who is supreme and who is on the throne. It reminds us that ultimately all glory and honor belong to him. I sometimes think I deserve a little of the glory. Or that some of the credit should come to me. I don't mind Him getting a lot of glory and a lot of power, but I sometimes wish I could keep some of it for myself. I want to keep some of the credit for me. But in God's scheme of things I must empty myself of all self-glory and all self-pride, and give Him all the glory. That is where it belongs. That is where it should be given. And that is where it should stay."

With that, Joyce closed her book of notes and said, "Amen, that is the Lord's Prayer. You can see that if you follow this outline, you will cover all the important subjects, and there will be no lack of things to say."

I looked around the class when Joyce stopped talking. All faces seemed absorbed, and everyone seemed in deep thought. She had certainly given us a lot to think about. One or two, however, seemed to be troubled and uncertain about what they had heard. Clearly the Lord's Prayer was not quite as pretty and inoffensive as they had imagined it to be. It was made for life in the raw. It was made for spiritual struggle and warfare, and not for a sheltered and easy existence. Some, I was to find out, found this hard to accept.

It had been a long, full day. Most of those in the class decided to remain in the School of Prayer for the night. Accommodations were available for us all.

I quickly retired to my room and took out my journal. What could I say after a day like this?

THE JOURNAL: What else can I do but bow my head and say:

My Father, who art in heaven,
Hallowed be your name.
Your Kingdom come
Your will be done on earth as it is in heaven.
Give me this day, my daily bread
And forgive my debts, as I forgive my debtors.
Lead me not into temptation,
But deliver me from evil,
For Yours is the Kingdom
And the power
And the glory
Forever. Amen.

TOPICS FOR DISCUSSION—CHAPTER SEVEN

1. One aspects of sin is "a willful transgression of the known law of God."

    - What are the basic ingredients in this aspect of sin?
    - How do we deal with it in our lives?

2. Discuss the importance of the statement, "Forgiveness is a mutual experience in which both the offender and the offended participate."
3. Discuss ways in which we can avoid being "led into temptation."
4. In what ways does God purpose to deliver us from evil?

CHAPTER EIGHT

THE DARK CANYON

At breakfast the next morning Alvin, John, and I sat at a table with some of the others who had taken the class from Joyce. We were soon discussing what we had heard about the Lord's Prayer.

"Well," said John, "I will never need to worry again about what to say to God when I pray."

"No," Alvin replied, "the question will not be 'What do I say?' but rather 'How do I get it all in?"

"The idea that each petition in the Lord's Prayer is only the name on the door of a room, and that you need to open the door and enter the room and explore and enjoy all that is in it certainly opens up all kinds of possibilities in prayer that I had never realized," I said.

Someone else who was in our small group said, "My prayers have been very much dominated by asking God to do things for me and for other people that I am concerned about. Especially my family. Now I realize that I need to move away from being obsessed with my own needs and wishes and begin to reflect what God's will and wishes are."

"Yes," someone else said, "I am beginning to understand that prayer is more than petitioning God to do what we want Him to do. I know that may be part of it, but in addition to that, I am realizing that it is also important to seek to be in fellowship with Him and enjoy His presence. It is communion with Him."

"I hadn't bothered much in my prayer life," someone else said, "about listening to God. But now this opens up all kinds of exciting things to me. I understand that I can quieten myself, and in the stillness and restfulness of being in His presence, I can begin to sense His direction and hear His voice. This idea of quietly listening to God and resting in His presence is new and exciting to me."

I responded to this by saying, "When you think about it, I expect God has a lot of important things He wants to say to us. There are many important things that He wants us to hear. But we get so wrapped up in our own agendas that we do not develop the skill of listening to Him. Really, is there anything more important to me than hearing what God wants to say to me?" And so the conversations went on.

After breakfast, John and I prepared to continue our journey to the City of Prayer. We were delighted when Alvin came to us and asked if he could accompany us. We welcomed him, knowing that on our travels we would be encouraged by his presence.

We thanked Joyce for her help and for her teaching, and as we prepared to move out on the pathway, she explained to us that the pathway would pass through a very difficult valley. "It is really more than a valley. It is a deep canyon. The floor of the canyon," she explained, "is usually quite wet and marshy. It makes it very difficult to maintain good progress. In addition to this, the canyon is very narrow and dark. The nature of the place is such that it is not possible to build any prayer huts in there, so you must be prepared before you enter this Dark Canyon. Once you are in this difficult place, there is nothing you can do but persevere until you get through it. Do not stop or turn back but keep on going until you finally emerge from the marshy, dark, confines of the canyon. Remember, there is an end to it. When you have passed through this Dark Canyon, at the other end, you will find the path goes up a little hill and from the top of this hill you will get a splendid view of the City of Prayer. It will be closer and clearer than you have ever seen it. When you see it, you will realize that you are making good progress. It will be a great encouragement to you, but you have to get through the Dark Canyon first."

With that advice, we stepped out on to the path again. Just as we were about the start our walk, both Janet and Helen also came out of the School of Prayer. We invited them to join us and accompany us on our journey to the City of Prayer. Janet, however, shook her head. She seemed very disturbed.

"No!" she said. "I have come as far along this pathway of prayer as I wish to go. It just isn't leading where I thought it would lead, and I don't wish to go where it seems to be going. I am not going any farther." Remembering that we had prayed for both of these ladies, I looked at Helen. She seemed to have made a different decision. With quiet confidence she said, "Yes, I would like to accompany you."

We set off on our journey once again. We reluctantly left Janet, who seemed to be a little confused. She did not want to go on, but she did not want to go back. I wondered what would happen to her and her experience of prayer. I immediately joined up with Helen as we walked up the pathway of prayer. "What will happen to Janet now?" I asked.

"We talked about this with Joyce when Janet decided not to go any farther. She is in a strange position. She is unwilling to go on, yet she does not want to go back. Janet is very earnest and sincere about her desire to pray and her walk with God. What should she do? When we talked to Joyce about it, Joyce said that it was unfortunate that Janet had made the decision to go no farther toward the City of Prayer, but she emphasized that certainly the experience and knowledge she had gained so far in the journey into prayer need not be wasted. She encouraged Janet by saying that in prayer what she had learned would stay with her and give her an enriched prayer life. Her level of praying has advanced from the Viewing Platform, and with some effort and discipline, she will be able to maintain this. She will, however, never get past her present level until she deals with the matter of her own self-will and gets beyond the notion that prayer is there to get God to help us achieve our own selfish desires and wishes in life. She made it clear that if you do not respond to the spiritual realities of prayer, then you will begin to become insensitive and resistant to them. In many ways the principle of the Christian life is also true of our prayer lives, that if you do not go forward, you may begin to slip backwards. 'Prayer,' Joyce said,' is a dynamic thing. It is bursting with spiritual energy and power. It cannot be static. You cannot stay in one place all the time, it is too alive for that.' She made it clear that real communion with God will bring new light and truth into our lives, and if we fail to accept and obey these truths, then stagnation to our spiritual growth and progress will set in. In Janet's case, unwillingness to submit to the will of God will hinder progress, not only in prayer, but in all aspects of the Christian life."

"Joyce is pretty tough," I said, "but she seems to be saying that it is better to keep on praying even if we encounter roadblocks like Janet's unwillingness to trust in God's will. This kind of prayer will not give her the rewards of personal power and intimacy with God that come as she gets closer to the City of Prayer, but it will still have some value for her. In fact even those who only pray in a superficial and fleeting way still obtain limited blessing from it."

"That is what I understand," said Helen. "Not everyone wants to devote the time, effort, and sacrifice involved in developing a dynamic life of prayer. This is unfortunate and perhaps the time will come when they will sense a desire and hunger to move up the pathway of prayer to a closer fellowship with God. In the meantime, however, it is better for them to continue to pray at whatever level they have reached, than for them not to pray at all. Prayer is for everybody, but it will become more and more valuable and effective, the farther along the pathway you go."

"So Joyce would encourage everybody to pray, no matter what level they are at. And it could be as they continue to pray that the circumstances of their life will change. Or there may develop in their heart a greater hunger for better prayer. Or as life goes on they may have more time, or find they are less involved in other matters, and they will be able to move farther up the pathway."

"Yes," said Helen. "Joyce encouraged Janet to keep on praying. Certainly it would help her, and who knows, but that the time will come in her life when she will be prepared to make the commitments and follow the faith that will enable her to move on farther than she has ever been towards the City of Prayer."

"Well, that is encouraging," I said.

"I guess," said Helen, "that prayer is like singing. Nearly everybody can sing. Some are better at it than others, but everybody likes to sing at some time or another. If, however, you want to become really good at it, then you must take time to practice and develop your voice. A few people will become singing stars or opera singers, but not everybody will attain that level, but everybody should sing."

"And," I said, "it is often true that the more you sing, the better you will be at it, and the more enjoyment you will receive from it."

"Let's get everybody singing," Helen enthused. "Not everybody will become a star, but everybody can get started and participate."

"Right," I cried, "you don't need to become an opera singer in order to sing. So you don't need to pray like a saint in order to pray. And as people participate in prayer, it may create in them a greater desire, they will then be ready to move on farther up the pathway of prayer toward the City of Prayer."

This conversation made me feel better. There is no real failure in prayer. Prayer has value at whatever level you are at. Everybody should be encouraged to pray, even if that prayer is at the fleeting, superficial level of the Viewing Platform. Even this shallow or formal experience of prayer can generate a desire for a closer walk with God and for a better and more effective life of prayer. It is this hunger that makes people undertake the journey up the pathway of prayer. Some, like Janet, may never reach the City of Prayer, but even the journey has value and will help them into a more intimate and satisfying relationship with God.

I had been so engrossed in my conversation with Helen that I had not realized there was a significant change taking place in the journey. The trail was leading into a deep and dark valley. The walls of the valley closed in on us and were perpendicular and threatening. There was no other way to go than through this inhospitable and dangerous place. To add to our discomfort, the floor of the valley was wet and soft. The walls crushed in upon us until we could almost reach from one side to the other. John and Alvin had been walking ahead of Helen and me. Now they were waiting for us to catch up.

"This is not going to be easy," said John, "but Joyce did warn us about it. There will be no prayer huts here and no place to sit. She said we just have to persevere and get through it. There will not be much to encourage us."

The canyon did indeed look a foreboding and unfriendly place. I moved on into it a little and felt my feet sink into the soft mud of the canyon floor. I realized that the bottom of the canyon was marshy and soggy, and that was going to make progress even slower and more difficult. I turned to the rest and said, "Well, there is nothing for it but to get started. At least we are not alone, we can support each other as we go through this place." I peered ahead into the canyon, but it was so dark and musky that I could see very little. I bravely pulled my shoulders back and started into the Dark Canyon. It was so narrow that we had to go single file. Helen was behind me, followed by Alvin, with John bringing up the rear.

I had not gone very far before I realized that this was going to be an even more difficult part of the journey than I had anticipated. It was gloomy and dark in here. The sun did not reach the floor of the canyon. It was cold and damp. Worst of all, the pathway was soggy. My feet sank into the mud. It made walking very difficult. Soon my feet were uncomfortably cold and wet. Every step was an effort. I had to lift my foot from the sucking, sticky bog and put it forward, only to have it sink in again to the clinging mud. There was no wind, no birds singing, no color but depressing grey. None of us spoke. Apart from the squelching of our feet, there was just a gloomy silence. *I wonder why the pathway of prayer leads through a place like this*, I thought. *Surely there could have been some other way that would have avoided this?* We labored on. The marshiness seemed to get even softer until every step sank us past our ankles in cold, wet mud. It was slow, exhausting work. At every bend in the canyon floor I thought I might catch a glimpse of the end of this place, but around every corner, it seemed there was nothing ahead but more gloom and darkness.

I was getting tired and discouraged. I turned around to see how the others were coping. They too seemed weary and discouraged. John especially was having a harder time than any of us. But there was nothing for it but to keep going on our dreary way.

Finally I had to stop and take a rest. Wearily I turned round to see how the others were faring in this dreadful place. Helen was still behind me. Alvin still looked fairly strong, but John was clearly exhausted. "I am not sure I can keep going on like this," John said. "My strength is almost gone."

"But there is no place to rest in here," I said. "There are not even any prayer huts that we can go into. There is nothing else to do but to keep persevering." With no other available option we gathered our strength and plodded on around the next bend in this never-ending marshy canyon.

We had not gone much farther when there was a cry from Alvin calling on us to halt. "John is falling behind," he cried. "We must wait for him." Sure enough, John was not keeping up. He seemed to be in the last stages of exhaustion. He hardly had strength left to pull one foot out of the sticky, gluey mud and take another step forward. We waited until he finally caught up with us.

"I do not think I can go on any farther," wheezed John.

"What can we do?" asked Helen. "We certainly cannot stay here."

"Go on without me," John said. "Perhaps I will catch up later on."

There was a strained silence. None of us wanted to do this. We could not simply move on and leave John to his own devices. But what else could be done? Then Alvin, who was the strongest of us all, reached out and took John by the hand. "Brother John. Do you remember back down the pathway at the Pinnacle, you were a great help to me? At that time the practice of my prayer life consisted of duty, perseverance, discipline, and burden. You were the one, John, who taught me about joy and praise and celebration in prayer. You were strong on these things, and I was weak and needed to be taught."

"Yes! I remember," said John, who looked like he couldn't argue even if he had wanted to.

"You were strong in these qualities, John. You introduced me into a whole new atmosphere in prayer of which I had been unaware. I was focused on being strong and faithful. I developed a sense of duty and perseverance. Now the pathway of prayer has changed. In this canyon, the qualities that are needed now are the very things that I had developed and strengthened in my life. In here, there is no joy. Happiness has left us. We do not feel like celebrating. All the things that were important to you, John, are absent here. There is no joy and rejoicing in this canyon. The qualities that are called for to get us through this miserable place are perseverance, faithfulness, discipline. I have had plenty opportunity to develop these. You helped me back there, John. Now let me return the favor. Let me help you. Lean on me. Hold on to me. Together we can get through this thing."

John was obviously moved by this offer of help. He humbly acknowledged that if he was going to get out of this marsh, then he would need help. So he reached out and held on to Alvin. Alvin grasped him around the shoulder, and together, in this fashion, we carried on with the journey. But the canyon still did not come to an end. *What can we do?* I thought. *Will we ever get out of here?* Just then, a thought came to me. I stopped and turned to the others. "Do you remember," I said, "when Paul and Silas were thrown into the prison at Philippi? It must have been a very depressing time for them. In a deep, damp, cold dungeon. Their feet and hands were in the stocks. They had been poorly and unjustly treated. But in this depressing and discouraging time, what did they do? They began, at midnight, to sing praises to God. And when they started to praise God, then wonderful things began to happen. I think we should praise God right now, and that may lift our spirits and give us new strength."

"But I don't feel like praising God," mumbled John. "It is the last thing I want to do right now."

"Perhaps that is all the more reason for us to do it," I replied.

"I agree," said Helen. "I remember David in the book of Psalms, when he was going through a very difficult time said, 'Why am I so sad? Why am I troubled? I will put my hope in God, and once again I will praise him, my Savior and my God' (Ps. 42:11). David did not feel like praising God. In fact God's presence and blessing seemed far away from him at that time, but he concluded that even in these very adverse circumstances he should hope in God and praise Him. So maybe we should do the same thing."

"Yes, let's all sing a hymn of praise," said Alvin. "It certainly could not do any harm."

So we sang a hymn of praise. At first we were rather shy and uncertain about it. But as we sang on, our voices got stronger and our spirits began to rise. There was no outward change in our circumstances. There was no evident sense of God down here. We could not feel His presence or His blessing, but in faith we sang His praise. That very act seemed to bring new life and grace to us. So we sang on and on with renewed courage. And when we turned yet another corner in the long marshy canyon, we caught a glimmer of light in the distance. It was the end. We would soon be out. We had come through a very difficult part of the journey. The grim walls of the Dark Canyon began to recede. The ground under our feet became firmer. Light reached us, and we once again saw the sun and felt its warmth. It was with great relief and a sense of accomplishment that we finally emerged from that dark and dismal place and into the brightness and warmth of the sunlight.

"Let's take a rest," I said and threw myself down at the edge of the pathway. With thankful groans, my companions all did likewise. When we had somewhat recovered, Alvin suggested, "Before we go on, let's take time to pray together and thank God for helping get us through that place." This seemed the appropriate thing to do, so we linked arms and thanked God and praised Him for His help during that dreadful struggle in the Dark Canyon.

At he end of our prayer time, John, whose spirit seemed to be reviving again, reminded us that Joyce had told us that after we came out of the canyon, the pathway would climb a hill, and from the top of the hill, we would get a clear and encouraging view of the City of Prayer. "Let's climb the hill, and then at the top where we can see the city we can sit down and have a rest and discuss what lessons we learned while coming though the Dark Canyon." This seemed the right thing to do, so we climbed the hill, away from the canyon and the long marsh, toward the City of Prayer.

The view from the top of the hill seemed to be everything that Joyce had promised it would be. From up here, the air was clear and cool. The city, while still some distance, was much nearer than we had ever seen it. In the bright, cool air, we could see it much more sharply. Its beauty and design were more clearly in evidence now. Looking at it from up here made us want, all the more, to be there and to enter it. What was even more evident from this viewpoint, that had not been so clear before, was the atmosphere that surrounded the city. It seemed to have an attractive glow that permeated the whole city. It had a strange and indefinable aura about it. There was a presence emanating from it that could only be the presence of God. We stood captivated, more by the atmosphere than anything else. This is where we wanted to go. This is where we wanted to live.

"Isn't it beautiful," said Helen.

"Such an atmosphere," said John.

"Seeing it now makes getting through the Dark Canyon worthwhile," said Alvin.

After the struggles we had had getting through the canyon, it was indeed refreshing and rewarding just to rest here and view the city. As I sat there with my friends enjoying the view, I could almost feel new strength and courage flow back into my soul. No one in the group said much. We simply rested and enjoyed the atmosphere of the city, and the sense of healing and energy that was restoring our spirits. In addition to the growing appeal of the city, I also became aware of a strengthening bond and fellowship among ourselves. We had successfully come through a very difficult part of the journey. We had helped each other and encouraged each other. Perhaps, if we had been alone, we would never have had the courage or strength to come through the canyon. Now we felt like brothers and sisters. We had a growing comradeship that united us together and gave us additional strength and determination.

After a while, I said, "Let's follow up on John's suggestion and talk about the lessons we learned from the Dark Canyon. Everyone agreed. We turned around and looked back over the way we had come. Right at the bottom of the hill we could see the exit from the canyon. It formed a narrow cleft or split in the sheer rock of the mountain. The mountain face, where the exit lay, was almost a sheer cliff. Impossible to climb or to descend. The only way we could have arrived at this spot was to have come through the canyon that split the mountain. I made the comment, "Now that you see it, there was no other way to get over that mountain and arrive here than by coming through that Dark Canyon."

Yes!" said John. "I wondered why we had to come through that place. I questioned why there could not have been a better and easier route. But now that you see it, there is no other way. Every traveler to the City of Prayer must go through this canyon. Any attempt to avoid it will bring you up short of the destination."

"I felt as if God had forgotten about us in there. I did not feel His presence. I did not sense His Spirit. It was a time of darkness and heaviness in my soul. Now that you look back at it, you realize God really was there. He had not forsaken us, but it certainly felt that way when we were going through it," said Helen.

"Right," said John. "That is what I found most difficult about the experience. It was a time when there was no joy, no encouragement, and no uplift. I am not used to that. I rely heavily on the feelings of joy and celebration that come to you in prayer. To have all of that stop. To be denied the positive and uplifting sense of God's presence. To wonder if He had left us, and forsaken us, almost destroyed my faith and robbed me of my courage. In fact, if it had not been for my good brother here, Alvin, who supported and encouraged me, I do not think I would have made it." He reached out and touched Alvin's arm. Alvin's face, which was usually rather stern and serious, broke into a warm and appealing smile. Alvin actually looked attractive when he smiled.

"So, what we are saying is that on the journey into prayer, we must expect that there will be times when praying and getting into the presence of God seems unrewarding. There are occasions when our prayers seem to be getting us nowhere. We lose the awareness of God's presence. It seems as if He has forsaken us. We question if it is worthwhile going on with this business of praying. We feel discouraged and are tempted to give up on our commitments."

"I remember," mused John, "that some people used to testify that there were times when their prayers seemed to get no higher than the ceiling and then bounce back at them. I didn't understand what they were saying, but I think I grasp it now. There are dark times. There are times when the juices of the soul cease to flow. We think then that God is hidden, far away, not interested in our prayers. During these times, we ourselves don't want to pray, the hunger and desire for communion with God dries up. Prayer seems to lose its power and meaning, and we are just going through the motions, but not really accomplishing anything. Only, when it is all over and you look back at it, you realize, that is not at all what was happening, it only felt that way. I guess the important lesson for me is not to rely so much on what I am feeling, but to rely more on the unchanging love and nature of God and place my trust in that."

At this point, Alvin seemed anxious to get into the discussion. He said, "We have often been told that we are to go by faith and not by feelings. But this is hard to do when all of the good feelings are absent and we are being bombarded by negative doubts. Doubt and fear and disappointment seem to rob us of the good feelings of joy and faith and trust. But nevertheless, we must understand that feelings whether good or bad are not necessarily a true and accurate guide to our spiritual state. There may be times, like going through the Dark Canyon, when we feel that God has left us and is no longer interested in us, and that we are not making any progress in our journey, but in actual fact, even though we felt that way, we were truly making good progress and learning things that we otherwise would never learn. The lesson I learned earlier on from my brother John, however, is that there is something wrong and unbalanced if you never have joy and never enjoy the glory of the presence of God or experience the uplift of victory in your heart. There are times of great joy and blessing, like on the Pinnacle. There are times of deep struggle, as in the Dark Canyon. This is healthy and normal and should be expected in any progressive journey in prayer. There is something unhealthy about wanting joy and blessing all of the time. The Arabs have a saying 'all sunshine makes a desert.' But it is equally unhealthy to think that the only thing that can be experienced in the spiritual life is duty, sacrifice, and perseverance. I was strong on all of these things, and they were the qualities that helped me get through the Dark Canyon. The sense of persevering and being disciplined and being faithful to your commitment are very important, especially when the good feelings are not there, but by themselves, they do not make up mature and growing experience of God's presence and communion with Him. There is a time for joy and celebrating. There is a time for faithful commitment in the absence of joy. But we need both, and both need to be balanced."

"What I wrestled with going through the Dark Canyon," said Helen, "was the feeling that I must have done something wrong because God had left me. When I go through a hard time like that, a time when God seems to be remote and unattainable, then I think this must be happening to me because I have done something wrong, and I am out of touch with God. God has left me because I have sinned in someway or another. I feel that if everything was right between me and God, then I should not have these times when He does not seem near."

I turned to Alvin and asked, "What do you think of that Alvin?'

Alvin's response came after a great deal of thought. "No!" he said, "we must not assume that a dark spell in the soul is a necessary indication that we are not right with God. It could be, but not necessarily so. After all, the greatest of God's servants seem to have experienced times of spiritual dryness and dark nights of the soul. Even Jesus gave that heart-wrenching but mysterious cry from the cross, 'My God, My God, why have you forsaken me?' (Mark 15:34). However you explain what Jesus meant when He made that desolate statement, it was certainly not because He had sinned or was not right with God. King David is described as a man after God's own heart, but he had times when he too asked the question 'To God, my defender, I say, "Why have you forgotten me? Why must I go on suffering from the cruelty of my enemies? I am crushed by their insults, as they keep on asking me, 'Where is your God?'" But David does not stay down there in the depth, he goes on to ask, "Why am I so sad? Why am I troubled? I will put my hope in God, and once again I will praise him, my Savior and my God." In spite of the serious questions of where God was and why he, David, was so depressed in spirit, he does come out in the end hoping in God and believing that he will praise Him again. He was low and dejected, not because he had sinned, but because of the actions of other people. But his faith prevailed, and he believed that the time would come when he would praise God again.

"So the times of darkness in our soul need not be because we are not right with God. That is why Jesus told us day by day to pray 'forgive us our sins as we forgive those who sin against us.' We take time each day to examine our hearts and be sure we are right with God. Not only that, but we also have the assurance that if there was anything wrong between us and God, then the Holy Spirit would communicate this to us. Our conscience would become aware that something was wrong. Then we would seek God for a remedy and immediately deal with the problem. So a time of darkness like going through the Dark Canyon does not necessarily mean that we have gotten out of touch with God. Having said that, however, it must also be understood that if there is something that we are aware of that is wrong between us and God, then that will inevitably affect our relationship with Him and cause us to drift away from His presence."

"This is good," I exclaimed. "The thought that came to me was when we started to sing praises to God, like Paul and Silas in the prison, it was at that time that new strength and courage seemed to flow into us. I think that learning to praise God, even in the midst of the cold, damp discouragement of the canyon, is an important lesson for us to learn."

"That's right," Helen replied. "It was when we started to praise God, even though we did not feel like it, that the spirit of weary discouragement began to lift and new hope and courage began to grow in us again."

"I remember that," said John emphatically. "As Alvin has told me, I tend to be guided by my emotions rather than my faith. So I certainly did not feel in the mood for praising God. In fact my feelings were telling me the very opposite, that God had forsaken us and left us to our own devices in that terrible place. I felt lonely and discouraged. But when we began to praise God, it reminded me that while I did not feel like praising Him because I could not sense His presence, my faith told me He was there and with us, even though it did not feel like it at that time. To make the deliberate choice to praise Him in spite of the circumstances and feelings undoubtedly gave faith and hope a chance to reassert themselves."

I picked up the thought from John and said, "Yes! And remember what the apostle Paul said, 'In everything give thanks, for this is the will of God concerning you' (1 Thess. 5:18). 'Everything' does not just mean only the good things that happen, but even in the midst of the difficult and troublesome times, we need to learn to give thanks. It is the act of giving thanks and praising God that refreshes our spirit and renews our confidence."

"I remember," said Alvin in his quiet, steady way, "the story of Nehemiah, when the people heard the words of the law read to them and they wanted to grieve and be sorry, he said to them, 'This day is sacred to our Lord God. Do not grieve, for the joy of the Lord is your strength' (Neh. 8:10). There is certainly a time for us to mourn and grieve over our sins and failures, but when we are being tested and tempted, there is a place for us to deliberately praise God. It calls on us to rise above our feelings and our circumstances and praise God anyway. This very act of faith and trust in His greatness and goodness brings new strength to our souls. 'The joy of the Lord is our strength.'"

I tried to sum up our discussions, "Going through the Dark Canyon was not an easy experience for any of us, but it did seem to do us good, and we learned some important lessons from it. We understand that these experiences can strengthen us and develop our faith and trust in God. We can see the pathway of prayer is not all lightness and joy. We learn that sometimes the sterner virtues of faithfulness, commitment, discipline, and perseverance are called for. We understand that while we should expect times like this, they are only for a season. The joy and blessing will return. If the joy and blessing leave us permanently, then something is wrong. We should persevere, so that even in these dark and dismal places of life, we practice praising God, for this is a positive expression of faith and trust in Him. The apostle Peter states it well, 'In this you greatly rejoice, though now for a little while you may have had to suffer grief in all kinds of trials. These have come so that your faith—of greater worth than gold, which perishes even though refined by fire—may be proved genuine and may result in praise, glory and honor when Jesus Christ is revealed'" (1 Pet. 1:6-7).

After these discussions we decided that since there were prayer huts available at this scenic point on the trail, and since the experience in the Dark Canyon had left us tired and weary, that we would go no farther that day but rest and recuperate by spending the remainder of the day and the coming night in the prayer huts. First we gathered together again and gave God thanks for His help in getting us through the Dark Canyon. Then we separated each to their own prayer hut for the night to rest and spend time alone with God and in fellowship with Him.

THE JOURNAL: The experiences of today have impressed some things upon me as we went through the Dark Canyon. Really three things were impressed on me after that difficult experience.

First, the importance of faith. In the canyon, about all I had left was faith. It was dark, and I could not see anything or see the way; I just had to believe in everything that had brought me to this place. All of the experiences, victories, and truths that had been built into my heart and my consciousness, although I could not see them, nor was I aware of them in the depth of the canyon, yet I had to believe in them and in their reality. Continuing to believe in them was like a solid anchor that held me steady when it would have been much easier to drift into doubt and uncertainty. My faith in God was essential. Faith in His goodwill, His love, His wisdom, even faith in His presence. There was no indication that God was there, nor was there any strong feeling of His presence or interest, yet I believed He was there and with me in spite of all indications to the contrary. Faith in the experience was essential.

Second, I was greatly encouraged by the way my sense of fellowship and brotherhood with my companions was strengthened. To pass through an experience like that with tried and true companions bound us together in a closer fellowship than we had known. Being with them helped me. I do not know if I would have made it without them and their presence and encouragement. The way that Alvin helped John was very moving.

Third, the power of praise. Yes! I need to learn to praise God even when I do not feel like it. Praise helps the spiritual juices to start flowing again and brings new courage to the soul.

TOPICS FOR DISCUSSION—CHAPTER EIGHT

1. Janet has decided not to go any farther into prayer. Joyce responded to this in part by saying, "Prayer cannot be static. You cannot stay in the one place all the time, it is too alive for that."

   - Discuss the implication of this statement.

2. The Dark Canyon represents those times when it is hard to pray:

   - Do you ever experience those times?
   - Describe what they are like for you?
   - What brings them on?
   - How do you deal with them?

3. In the Dark Canyon, they praised God, even though they did not feel like doing this.

   - Discuss the value of positive praise even when you are not in the mood.

4. What were the lessons they learned in the Dark Canyon?

CHAPTER NINE

THE STORM

The next morning, it was with strong and happy hearts that we set out again on our journey to the City of Prayer. The pathway here was easy. The sun was shining, and it was a pleasant and warm day. Around us, nature was beautiful. We could see the city quite clearly now. It was encouraging to know that our journey was nearing an end. I enjoyed the growing bond of camaraderie that continued to develop between myself and my companions. We were getting to know and understand one another better. We now had shared experiences that bound us together. The difficult passageway through the Dark Canyon had especially given us a feeling of mutual confidence and trust. I was well aware that even though we were quite different in personality and background, we were united together in a common purpose, goal, and faith. We relaxed in one another's company and gave to each other a sense of support and fellowship that enabled us to travel the journey with greater ease and confidence. We had this assurance that if any of us got into trouble, the others would come to their help. It was a good feeling of mutual care and goodwill, and it brought warmth and companionship to the journey.

The proximity to the City of Prayer and the realization that our travel was coming to an end made me start to evaluate the meaning and purpose of this journey. My thoughts were rather challenging. *Why am I doing this? Do I really want to live in the City of Prayer? Why did I want to do this in the first place? What motivated me to start on this journey?* The ever-increasing presence of the City of Prayer seemed to bring these thoughts to the foreground of my mind and added a sense of urgency to my considerations. *Did I really want to enter the city? Did I really want to live in the City of Prayer? Would it really be what I thought it was? Would I be disappointed?* My thoughts disturbed me, and so I decided I would share my concerns with my traveling companions.

First, I approached Helen, who's compassionate and understanding nature made it easy to confide in her.

"Tell me, Helen," I asked, "why did you come on this journey in the first place? Why do you want to reach the City of Prayer?"

"Philip," she said, a little reluctantly, "I hesitate to tell you why I got started on this journey, because as I remember it, I now realize my motivation was not very good. When I considered prayer, I was thinking mostly of all of the things that I wanted God to do for me. I had a long list of prayers that I wanted Him to answer, family matters, health concerns, financial and social status, internal personal tensions, and many other problems that I wanted His help with. So I thought, if I get better at praying, then God will answer more of my requests. It was really rather self-centered. I imagined that if I got good at prayer, then I could persuade God to be more active on my behalf. To be honest, when I started out, I did not see God as very active, and I secretly thought He ought to be doing better."

"But not all of your requests were bad or selfish," I defended.

"Oh no! Many of my requests were for other people and for God's blessing on them. I wasn't only asking God to provide for my personal needs such as give me more money, more health, and more success, although these things were part of it. But, Philip, as I have journeyed up the pathway to the City of Prayer, you know I have learned a lot and my motivation has changed somewhat. I now realize that prayer is not so much a matter of me getting God to do everything I want Him to do, as it is a matter of bringing me into touch with Him and enjoying His fellowship."

"Remember what the trail guide said, **prayer is learning to receive what God wants to give."**

"Yes, I remember," said Helen. "But the fact is that I was not thinking like that when I started. I was thinking more along the line that prayer was learning how to get God to give me what I asked for, and I felt, the better I was at prayer and the more faith I had, then the more likely He would be to answer prayer and respond to me favorably. As I think of it, it was not a very good motivation to get started on the journey into prayer. But you know, as I go on with this journey, my motives are being purified of their selfishness and my priorities are changing. Now, it is not so much what do I want God to do, as it is what does God want to give?"

"Ah yes!" I said. "It helps me a great deal to know that your priorities and motives for praying are changing. I am aware of changes taking place in my own heart. When I started out on this journey, I too was rather self-centered in what I wanted out of prayer, but as I have progressed up the pathway, I am realizing that there are many more vital priorities in prayer than just getting from God what I want."

"I guess," said Helen, "as we get closer to Him, and get to know His will and spirit better, we feel safer in believing and trusting that what He wants for us is really the best possible thing for us."

"Yes," I responded, "but that is not always easy to believe. We really are afflicted with the notion that what we want must be the best possible thing for us."

"Right! It is rather humbling to think that He knows better than we do about what it is we really need."

Next I went to my friend John. Since he and I had already talked about this, I framed my question a little differently. "Just as we were starting out on this journey, I asked you a question. Now that we are approaching the City of Prayer, I would like to know if you still feel the same way? John, why do you want to learn how to pray better?"

"I remember you asked me that question. It was a hard question to answer," replied John. "I think there were a number of reasons why I wanted to learn to pray better."

"Yes! But do you remember what the primary one was? More than any other reason, why did you want to learn to pray better?"

"I think," said John thoughtfully, "it was because I was hungry for the blessing of God. My soul was not satisfied with the experience of God that I had, and I wanted His blessings in a much more vivid way. I wanted to feel His joy, His love, His power, His victory to a much greater degree than I had experienced up until that time."

"So have things changed any? Is that still your primary purpose in wanting to pray better?"

"Oh!" exclaimed John. "I am learning a lot of things since I set off on this journey to the City of Prayer. The most important lesson that I am learning is that a major purpose of prayer is to help us get to know God better and fellowship with Him, to interact with Him, to be in His presence. Knowing Him is more important than receiving His blessings. The giver is becoming more important than the gifts. Prayer is becoming more relational and not so transactional. Now I am much more anxious to know Him, and to get close to Him, and to drink in His presence and spirit, than I am to receive His gifts. The greatest blessing is to enjoy His presence. The best gift that He gives is the gift of Himself."

John continued, "Then in addition to that, I think I am also learning that God's blessings are more than just the good feelings of joy and peace and warm fellowship. I am beginning to realize that great spiritual benefits can come out of times of pain and testing. Sometimes rich and full blessings can come after times of great difficulty—as in coming through the Dark Canyon. I am learning that blessings are not just good feelings, but the establishing of a relationship, and sometimes relationships can demand a lot of work and some pain. When you asked me, as we were first starting out on this journey, what I wanted in prayer, I believe I said I wanted to have God's blessings, His joy, His power, His excitement. I wanted to see Him do great and mighty things. And while that is still part of it, if you were to ask me now what I predominantly want to get out of praying, then I would quote to you the words of the apostle Paul, who stated what his great ambition was, 'I want to know Christ and the power of his resurrection and the fellowship of sharing in his sufferings, becoming like him in his death' (Phil. 3:10). I think the best way to get to know Him, sense His presence, hear His voice, and share my heart with Him is through prayer. I still want His blessings, and I still like to feel good and joyful, but these desires are no longer dominant. What I want more than anything else is Himself."

"That sounds wonderful, John. I am not sure I am at that stage yet, but I certainly want to be. Your experience of prayer thus far seems to be similar to what Helen and I are experiencing. When we started off, although our motivations and ideas were not the purest or the best, they did help us to get started on the journey, and as we progressed, we matured and became purer in our motivations."

When I approached Alvin, he too confessed that his understanding of prayer was changing. "I started on the journey of prayer," he said, "because I believed it was the thing to do. Good Christians prayed. So I thought I had a duty to do it. I wasn't particularly inspired or excited about it, I just understood that if I was to be a Christian and a follower of the Lord, then I must discipline myself to pray. It became a daily discipline, like cleaning my teeth or getting my physical exercise—you had to do it, if you wanted good teeth or a healthy body. So if I wanted a healthy spiritual experience, I had to pray. Since setting out on the journey, however, I have learned some things. I realize now that while prayer is a discipline and it is a duty that I should faithfully attend to, it is far more than that. I now find prayer can be a delightful and exciting thing. I often experience a joy in being in the presence of God. It is a delight to praise and worship Him. My soul rises on the wings of praise and adoration. It is rich to be in His presence and humbling to hear His voice speak to me. The sense of contact with Him and fellowship with Him is soul satisfying. So prayer is much more than a discipline. It is a delight. I look forward to it. I revel in His presence and delight to do His will. But sometimes, when all of these good feelings are not there, I still rely on the discipline that I have developed to continue with my habit of waiting on Him and praying to Him about the matters that are in my heart."

These conversations on prayer intrigued me. What stood out in my mind was that none of us had been exactly pure and unselfish in our motivations when we started. But as we practiced and progressed along the pathway of prayer, we began to change. We were becoming much more sensitive to the value and need of simply being with and resting in His presence. Our prayers were becoming more and more associated with an expression of His will, instead of getting Him to do what we want. There was a growing awareness that what was important was not what I wanted from God, so much as what God wanted for me. Not my will but His will. Prayer was becoming much more an exercise in which we contacted him and enjoyed His presence. It was becoming an instrument for us to better understand His will and wishes for our lives. All of my companions had verbalized the experience that as we matured in prayer so our motivations in prayer were being cleansed of their selfishness and worldliness.

In the light of these discussions, I thought, it must be important to get people to begin the practice of prayer. If we insist that they get all of the motivations and purposes right before they start, then they are not likely to ever get going. Elementary prayer is better than no prayer. People should be encouraged to pray even though the prayers are not of great quality. I remember the trail guide telling me that if you are going to learn to play the piano, you must start with the simple things. As you improve, you can move on to better things. So it is with prayer. People have some very simple, unrefined, and erroneous ideas about prayer. But the secret is to sincerely get started. You will learn. You will improve. And as your ability to sense God's presence increases, and your spiritual skill at interacting with Him develops, then the first part of the Lord's Prayer makes more and more sense and becomes more in harmony with the priorities of your spirit. "Our Father who art in heaven. Hallowed be Thy name. Thy kingdom come. Thy will be done on earth as it is in heaven." The essence of prayer stated by the trail guide at the beginning was starting to make sense, **prayer is learning to receive what God wants to give.**

I had been so engrossed in these conversations with my friends that I had not noticed a significant change in the weather taking place. But I now became aware that the sky had become overcast with dark and threatening clouds. A sudden flash of lightning, followed by the rumble of thunder made me realize that a storm was approaching. I did not, however, appreciate how severe the storm was going to be. We could not see the center of the storm, for it was hidden behind the mountains that surrounded us. But we could tell that it was coming. The wind picked up, bringing with it a sudden coolness. The sky became so black that, even though it was only early afternoon, it seemed daylight was finished and dark night was taking over. The ominous atmosphere deepened. The thunder and lightning were almost constant now, and then the rain started. It was gentle at first but quickly increased in volume until it was pouring down in great torrents. Water began to gush down the pathway. The wind became ferocious. The noise of the thunder was constant. The flashing of the lightning was fearsome. The pounding rain instantly soaked us to the skin. The cloudburst was so intense we could not distinguish the pathway ahead of us. The wild wind pelted the rain against our faces. We bowed our heads to protect our eyes from the stinging power of the almost horizontal rain. We had never been out in such a ferocious storm in our lives. The howling of the wind and the noise of the rain, together with the deafening vibrations of the thunder, made conversation impossible. John, however, grabbed hold of my arm, and I could see that he was pointing off to the side of the road. Through the rain I could just see some large rocks that might afford us some shelter. I nodded to him, and we hustled Alvin and Helen over to the side and with profound relief found shelter in the rocks.

The shelter proved much better than we anticipated, for nestled in these rocks was a cave, which gave us immediate cover from the wind and the rain. We were breathless and rather stunned at the power of the sudden storm, but extremely glad to have found some form of shelter, even if it was rather primitive. It was, therefore, a great surprise to us, when we got used to the darkness of the cave, to find that there were other travelers in there besides us. Because of the noise of the storm, conversation was not possible, but we signaled a welcome to each other. The group of about five people was, like us, cold and wet. They were looking out at the storm and seemed bedraggled, glum, and discouraged. Since conversation at the moment was impossible, there was nothing to do but to patiently wait for the storm to pass over. So we all sat absorbed in our own thoughts looking out at nature's madness and anger.

Eventually the storm began to abate. The rain eased and the noise of the thunder receded into the distance. When conversation became possible, I introduced our group to the others. The spokesperson for the other group seemed to be a lady, who called herself, June. But June did not seem very happy at all.

"That was quite a storm," I said, in an attempt to make conversation.

June responded rather grumpily, "It caught us by surprise, we were just not expecting something like this when we were so close to the City of Prayer."

I was rather surprised by the resentment that was in her voice. So I said as pleasantly as I could, "I am certainly glad that we found this cave to give us some shelter. It would have been terrible to be left outside in these conditions."

"What I can't understand," she said, "is why God sent the storm in the first place." She pointed to her group of followers and continued, "We were doing so well. We were making good progress. We were almost ready to arrive at the City of Prayer, when suddenly God sent this storm and we had to delay our journey. We were forced to sidetrack in here for shelter. But why would God do that to us when we were so close to the destination?"

I was rather taken aback at this and did not know how to respond. I looked at my three companions, but I could tell from their body language that they were quite happy to let me handle the situation. I was rather perplexed by the attitude. All I could think of saying was "What makes you think God sent the storm?"

"He's sovereign, isn't He? He is in charge of everything, isn't He? He is all-powerful, isn't He? If he didn't send it, then who did? Even if He did not send it, He could have stopped it if He had wished." She looked around our group and did not seem impressed. She continued, "You were caught in the storm too. You had your journey interrupted. You got wet and cold and had to take shelter. Who do you blame for sending the storm?"

I was unprepared for this and did not know what to say. "I hadn't really thought of blaming anyone. These things just happen."

"If God is in charge, then He sent the storm, and I really think it is unfair, just when we had almost reached the City of Prayer, and after having worked so hard to get this far, that we should be delayed and sidetracked by a storm that He could have prevented. If God doesn't prevent these things, why bother to pray?"

I was beginning to recover from my surprise and get my wits about me so I said, "I think you are blaming the wrong person."

June did not seem to hear me, she angrily carried on, "I just don't understand it. I cannot understand why God does some of the things He does." She pointed to one of the ladies in her group and said, "She had a lovely, promising young son, and he died of cancer? Why was it God's will that he die of cancer? I cannot understand that." She pointed to another gentleman in her group. "Jim there lost his job and is struggling to make ends meet and feed his family. Yet somebody else who worked for the same firm and lives a godless and profligate life didn't loose his job. Can you explain that? It seems so unjust. It is so hard to say that that is God's will. Why does God do these things or allow them to happen?"

I was beginning to understand that it was not just the storm that was upsetting June and her companions, but the storm was just another incident added to many others in which God did not do what they thought He should have done.

"What you are saying is that you do not think God is handling things right."

June hesitated. "Well," she said with some uncertainty, "I do not know if I would want to say it that bluntly. It's just that I know so many good people that have some terrible things happen to them, and I cannot understand why these things should happen if God is in control of the universe. I came on this journey of prayer to try to understand this better. I was having a terrible struggle to trust Him and have faith in Him when I looked around me and saw so much suffering and injustice happening in the world, and often, it seems, these awful things happen to the best and the most righteous of people. I have a hard time having faith in God when He lets all of these bad things happen to good people." June was sounding a little softer now. "I want to be able to pray. I want to be able to trust Him. I want to understand His will and wishes for my life. But I have a hard time accepting His will. When I hear good, righteous people say in the face of dreadful pain and loss, 'Well, I must accept it, it is the will of God.' Or, 'He must have a purpose in this when He made it happen.' I find it very hard to pray the Lord's Prayer as we were taught in the School of Prayer, 'Thy kingdom come, Thy will be done.' I am not at all sure that I want His will to be done if so much of it brings suffering and pain. When I look around and see so much senseless cruelty and destruction, how can I trust His will to be good for me? It makes praying in faith very hard."

I knew I had to respond to this with great care. I realized that June and her companions were earnestly seeking God and His will, but were confronted with these doubts and injustices. I said carefully, "June, I think you are blaming the wrong enemy for all of these things. There are many things happen in this world that are not the will of God. For example the Bible says that God is not 'wanting any to perish, but that all should come to repentance' (2 Pet. 3:9). God's will is that none should perish, but in spite of this being God's will, some do perish, so God's will is not done. God's will is that all should come to repentance. But not all choose to repent, so God's will is not done. And if they remain unrepentant, they will perish. God does not want that, but God's will is not done. There are many things happen in this world that are not the will of God. When a child is born deformed, that is not the will of God. When a young man dies in an accident, that is not the will of God. When a person dies in terrible pain and suffering, that is not the will of God. When a well-raised, much-prayed-for son goes astray and makes a shipwreck of his life, that is not the will of God. To try to explain all the evil and suffering in the world as the will of God is an incredibly frustrating and discouraging process. In fact it cannot be explained, and we should not even try. God is not the author or initiator of the world's evil and suffering, and to try and make it so is really to insult the name of a holy and loving God.

"Let's put the blame for all of this where it belongs. Not with God but with Satan and with evil. The world as it presently functions, with its sin, selfishness, hostility, and pain, was not the world that God created. But God's creation has been invaded by an alien force, and it is that evil alien force that produces the pain and suffering. The apostle Paul refers to the pain presently experienced in the created world in Romans 8:22 when he states, 'We know that the whole creation has been groaning as in the pains of child-birth right up to the present time.' It was the coming of sin into the world, through Adam and Eve that brought the selfishness, greed, and violent hostility into the world. God gave authority to humanity to oversee the running of the creation systems of earth. The Psalmist declared that "the highest heavens belong to the Lord, but the earth he has given to man" (Ps. 115:16). It was the coming of evil that brought with it the pain and suffering of disease and the cruel destructiveness of nature."

"But," objected June, "God could have stopped it. God could intervene and prevent a lot of these things from happening? Why doesn't He? God could have stopped the storm from coming, and we would have avoided all of this delay, trouble, and discouragement. He could have, but He didn't. Why not?"

"Yes! God could have prevented all of this. But in order to prevent it, He would have had to change the whole nature of things, especially the nature and fundamental characteristics of humanity. When God created us, and the angels for that matter, He created us as moral, spiritual, and ethical beings. In other words, he gave us the power and authority to make moral and spiritual choices, as he did the angels. When He created us, He said, "Let us make man in our image, in our likeness, and let them rule over the fish of the sea and the birds of the air, over the livestock, over all the earth, and over all the creatures that move along the ground" (Gen. 1:26). That means that in addition to being given authority over the affairs of the world, we have also been given a spiritual and ethical nature and a responsibility, which allows us to make ethical choices. God understood the risk. We could abuse our authority. We could make the wrong choices. And the wrong choices would have some devastating results, both for human behavior and for the unfolding of the natural world. In God's estimation, the risk was worth it. The alternative was to create us as moral robots, having no choice. But if He did that, then incredible riches and potential would be lost. We would then not be in His image. We would not be truly spiritual beings. We would not be able to consciously fellowship with Him. We would be far less than God planned and wanted. So He took the risk and made us as spiritual beings with the awesome power of choice. We made bad choices. Satan and the fallen angels made bad choices. Adam and Eve made bad choices. Evil was introduced into the world and into the human heart. It was the presence of evil in the system that made the natural world and the world of mankind function in ways far from the plan and will of God. The presence and influence of evil in the world has brought upon us all kinds of destruction and suffering. That is why Jesus calls Satan the 'Prince of this world' (John 16:11). Satan and sin have power and authority in this world because we, by our actions and choices, have given it to them. Evil operates in this world, so let's blame it for the pain and suffering that goes on. And also blame ourselves, for we have chosen to agree with evil in so many ways and give it authority. If God had had His way, it would never have happened."

"I can understand that," said June. "But still God could prevent a lot of things happening to righteous people."

"I think God could, and sometimes God does protect the righteous, but often He does not. Righteous people live in the world, and the sin and evil of the world spills over and affects them too. Indeed, since God's people are often considered the enemy of all unrighteousness and present a threat to the dominance of evil, they are often a target of Satan. Jesus never tried to avoid the issue, he said, 'Blessed are you when people insult you, persecute you and falsely say all kinds of evil against you because of me. Rejoice and be glad, because great is your reward in heaven, for in the same way they persecuted the prophets who were before you' (Matt. 5:11-12). The apostles were equally blunt in warning the early Christians. Paul said to Timothy, 'In fact, everyone who wants to live a godly life in Christ Jesus will be persecuted' (2 Tim. 3:12). The expectation of the Bible for righteous people seems to be that in a world dominated by sin and evil, they should expect to be a special target.

"So we should expect bad things to happen to us, just like they happen to everyone else in this world. When a storm comes, it does not avoid all the righteous people and blow only on the unrighteous. When a tornado rips through town, it does not just destroy the homes of the unrighteous but also the homes and churches of the righteous. When a pandemic hits the world, it not only brings disease and suffering to the unrighteous but also to the righteous. The Bible says, 'He causes his sun to rise on the evil and the good, and sends rain on the righteous and the unrighteous' (Matt. 5:45). Righteous people live in and share in the environment that sin has developed in this world. We will not escape it.

"But God does not leave us defenseless in the face of all of this pain and suffering. While we will have to be exposed to it, like everyone else, God will provide His grace, help, and strength so that it will not overpower us and destroy us. We have access to His grace and help so that in spite of suffering we can still rise above its depressing and discouraging influence and live in victory and in God's presence. God nowhere promises the absence of suffering in this world, but He does promise grace and help so that the suffering can be surmounted and not destroy our faith, spirit, or walk with Him. Indeed we can emerge from some of this suffering stronger and more mature in our faith and trust in him.

We are told by James, 'Consider it pure joy, my brothers, whenever you face trials of many kinds, because you know that the testing of your faith develops perseverance. Perseverance must finish its work so that you may be mature and complete, not lacking anything'" (James 1:2-4).

"So how about the storm?" asked June. "How can we emerge from that with stronger and better faith?'

"I think, instead of focusing on the storm and all of the rain and wind and cold that it brought, and the way it interfered with our pleasant journey, we should focus on the fact that God provided a place of shelter for us, and we did not have to face it without help. We should praise Him for His help. We should praise Him for the new friends and fellowship that we have found because of the storm. Without the storm we would never have met."

"True," said June, who now had a much lighter attitude. "And without the storm, we would have missed the teaching and encouragement that you have given us. I just never thought on things the way you have explained them. If the storm had not come, we would have missed that. So praise God for the storm."

With that I looked outside and saw that the storm had now passed over. "Well, things have cleared up outside. The storm has passed, so we can get on with our journey. But before we do, let's pray together and thank God for this time that we have had. It has enriched me, and I hope it has helped you." With murmurs of agreement, we all knelt together in our primitive cave and prayed together, especially giving thanks to God that he used the storm to bring us together and to help us on our journey of prayer.

With happier hearts we all left the cave and together as a group started up the pathway to the City of Prayer, which was now very close.

TOPICS FOR DISCUSSION—CHAPTER NINE

1. Philip discusses with his companions their motivations for wanting to become good at prayer. They all indicated that their motivations changed as they matured in prayer. This discussion led Philip to conclude: "It must be important to get people to begin the practice of prayer. If we insist that they get all of the motivations and purposes correct before they start, then they are not likely to ever get going. Elementary prayer is better than no prayer."

    - Discuss your opinions about this conclusion.

2. Did God send the storm?
3. Philip said, "There are many things happen in this world that are not the will of God."

    - Discuss this statement
    - Is everything that happens to you the will of God?
    - Has God planned everything, even evil, painful thing, as part of His design for your life?

The City of Prayer

CHAPTER TEN

SECOND SCHOOL OF PRAYER

We formed a fairly large group as we started on the last part of our journey to the City of Prayer. The "cave" group seemed a little happier and more encouraged now that we were on the move again. They were not overshadowed by questions and doubts about God's apparent absence and His lack of skill in handling things correctly. Now that the storm had passed, the sun came out again. The way was easy. We were full of anticipation and excitement as we looked forward to entering the City of Prayer. Even so, it was with some delightful surprise that we turned a corner in the pathway and discovered that the city now lay before us. We had in fact arrived. Our journey was complete. We could now enter the City of Prayer.

We had understood from our previous teacher that as soon as we reached the city, we should stop in at the Second School of Prayer. There we would get information and explanations that would prepare us as we moved into the city. The very first building we encountered, as we approached the city, advertised itself as the "Second School of Prayer." It was, therefore, without hesitation that we entered the building to receive our instructions.

Like the previous school of prayer, the building itself was fairly modest and quite devoid of any luxury or decoration. It was designed simply as a classroom that could hold a small number of students. Also there were dormitories attached to the building where we could stay overnight as we learned about the city. There was also a well-equipped kitchen that would provide good meals. Since our group was fairly large, we found, to our satisfaction, that a class could begin right way. We seated ourselves at the desks and with a sense of excited anticipation watched our teacher emerge from one of the doors at the front of the room. He welcomed us to the City of Prayer and introduced himself as George. George seemed a young, energetic man whose interest and enthusiasm for his subject immediately captured our attention.

George congratulated us in successfully completing the journey to the City of Prayer. He then continued, "This School of Prayer will be like a tourist information center, which you encounter when you are on vacation and visiting a strange city. Its purpose is to give you some basic information about the city and instruct you on some things you will need to know if you are to properly understand the nature and functions of the city. We will point out to you some of the highlights that you should visit and experience if you are going to adequately capture the flavor and the culture of the city. It is important that you get this basic information before you move into the city, or else a lot of needless time and effort can be wasted as you look for the places and the experiences that will be essential to you if you are to successfully live in the City of Prayer. The difference, however, between you and a tourist, who is on a casual visit, is that you will be deciding whether you want to live in this city or not. Not everybody who arrives here decides to stay. So it is important that you spend some time exploring the city. Find your way around. Capture the atmosphere. Enjoy the highlights. Experience the features. Then, once you have explored the city, you can make an informed decision as to whether you wish to actually live here or not."

I interrupted George at this point by saying, "This surprises me. I thought that everybody who made the effort of coming on the journey to get here would want to stay once they arrived?"

"Certainly," replied George, "we hope that everyone who arrives here will stay. But some, after they have explored the city and tasted its way of life and its culture, decide that it is not quite for them yet and so decide not to stay."

"But," said my friend John, who seemed as surprised as I was that not everybody would stay in the city, "what happens to those who decide not to stay?"

George, realizing that he had created a strong concern in the group, wanted to give a full answer to the question. He repeated himself, "It is important that you explore the city before you make up your mind. The city is rich and its way of life is very satisfying. If you stay, it will be a decision that you will never regret. The rewards and fulfillments of staying in the City of Prayer are spiritually abundant beyond anything else that you can experience on this earth. It provides you with an experience of God and a fellowship and communion with Him that will delight and satisfy your soul. The purposes and functions of the city will challenge and stretch you, but will also provide great spiritual enrichment and satisfaction. Make no mistake about it, there is no better place to live on this earth than the City of Prayer.

"But while life in the city is very rewarding and enriching, it is not always easy. The city does demand a high level of commitment and dedication from its citizens, and some decide they are not yet ready for this and so do not stay. I fully expect that some in this group, once you have become acquainted with the culture, values, and way of life prevalent in the city, will decide that you are not quite ready for this and will not stay."

John, feeling his question was not yet answered, persisted. "But what happens to those who decide not to stay?"

"If you decide not to stay," said George, who obviously did not want to get into the subject at this point, "then you must not consider it a failure. Nor must you think that the journey here has been a waste of time. The very fact that you have arrived here is an indication that you have already learned a lot about prayer. Your prayers have moved on from the primitive and immature style of praying with which you started out. You have overcome some of the elementary mistakes you made in prayer. On the journey you have learned many things and so have already made good progress. Your prayers are now more mature and your prayer life more satisfying. This progress in prayer will stand to you even if you decided not to stay in the City of Prayer. In addition to this, I will be encouraging you to spend some time exploring the city. There are still some essential lessons in prayer that you will learn as you become acquainted with the city. These too will be built into your prayer life and your experience with God. You will always benefit from them. You will never want to go back to the immaturities and uncertainties of prayer with which you started out. So even though you decide not to stay, you will have benefited greatly from the journey here and also from your exploration of the city. None of it will be wasted. The depth and influence of your prayer life will forever be enriched by these experiences."

John nodded and seemed to accept this explanation. But the fact that we would not all decide to stay here was still a surprise to us.

George, sensing that we were now ready to proceed with the lessons, said, "There are three things that I will talk to you about here in this class. First, I will describe the nature of the city to you. Second, I will point out some of the important highlights and centers of the city that I want you to explore and become familiar with. Third, I want to talk about the statement that you have all heard since you started out on the journey, that the essence of prayer is **learning to receive what God wants to give.** Understanding this statement is essential because it embodies the principles upon which the harmony and atmosphere of the city are based.

"First, let's talk abut the nature of the city. You will find, perhaps to your surprise, that this is just an ordinary city. The citizens are ordinary people who are living ordinary lives. They get up in the morning, and they make their way to a place of employment. They have to give the kids their breakfast and drive them to school. They live in homes and have gardens that require attention and maintenance. They eat meals, pay bills, see doctors, and drive cars. They have problems to deal with at work, at home, at church. The city carries on as any normal city. It has its commerce, its entertainments, its parks, and its roads. It is a successful, fully functioning, but ordinary city.

"The fact that this is a normal city comes as a surprise to many. It is commonly expected that the people here spend all of their time in prayer. Some have imagined that the people of the city would be so consumed by prayer that they would have no interest or time for the demands of everyday living and that all the people here are saints who spend all of their time in the activities of worship, prayer, and spirituality. You will find that this is not the case. This is an ordinary city populated by ordinary everyday people.

"The nature and atmosphere of the City of Prayer is not designed to get people to forsake the legitimate and necessary functions of life in order to pray, but rather to help them bring the spirit of prayer into the normal functions of life. Prayer does not so much demand that we leave the legitimate business of living, in order to pray, but rather that we carry the spirit and atmosphere of prayer into the everyday functions and purposes of life. In the City of Prayer, we do not stop practical living in order to pray, but seek to introduce the spirit of prayer into our practical living. It is another way of living normal life. It is a different approach to living. The spirit of prayer, the sense of fellowship and communion with God is something that we can experience and sense in the activities of our daily life.

"The Bible encourages us to develop the skill of carrying the spirit of prayer with us wherever we go. When the apostle Paul urges us to 'pray without ceasing' (1 Thess. 5:17 KJV), he is not suggesting that all other activities in life be stopped and we give ourselves unendingly to prayer. He is suggesting that the atmosphere of prayer be so real in our lives that we can, even in the midst of everyday business, be constantly referring things to God. Similarly, when Paul testifies to the Colossian Christians that 'we have not stopped praying for you and asking God to fill you with the knowledge of his will' (Col. 1:9). He was not suggesting that he had no other activity in life beyond that of praying for the Colossians. Rather, he is saying that his spirit was so sensitive to the atmosphere of prayer that even in the pressures and responsibilities of being an apostle for Jesus Christ, he often thought of them and prayed for them. The heart and spirit of the great apostle was never far away from his connection with God. He had learned to renew his interaction with his Heavenly Father regularly in the course of the day.

"Paul no doubt had his prayer times when he laid all other concerns aside and gave concentrated attention to the matter of prayer and fellowship with God. This is essential and must never be neglected. This regular time of concentrated prayer when we give full attention to God helps to keep open and ready the channels of connection between our soul and God. It clears the path. It is the foundation upon which we build into our lives the constant spirit of prayer. It is during those times of concentrated and intimate fellowship with God that the spirit becomes comfortable in His presence and learns to be more accessible to Him. When this habit of regular prayer is developed, it helps us to more easily keep the spirit of prayer alive and active during the day's activities. It helps us more naturally and normally keep in touch with God in the course of the day, even when other matters are pressing.

"Jesus was referring to the same continuing atmosphere of living in His presence, when, in John's Gospel chapter 16, He likened Himself to the vine and we, His followers, to the branches. The connection between the vine and the branches is a continuing experience. Branches do not stay connected to the vine for thirty minutes each day and then become disconnected for the rest of the time. Jesus calls it 'abiding in Him' or 'living in Him' or 'remaining in Him.' It means that we develop and mature our relationship with Him to such an extent that we seem to be in constant interaction with Him. Our spirit is naturally connected in fellowship with Him. Just as we breathe in air constantly without consciously thinking about it, so with the spirit of prayer we can develop a habitual, normal, well-travelled path into the presence of God. With discipline and practice, this pathway can become so well used that the soul often and comfortably refers matters to God and seeks out its natural home in the presence of God. It does this even as the duties and activities of normal daily life unfold. This practicing of the presence of God becomes the comfortable spiritual home of the soul. This is how we seek to live in the City of Prayer.

"Jesus links this 'abiding in Him' experience with the practice of our prayer life in John 16:7, when he says, 'If you remain in me, and my words remain in you, ask whatever you wish and it will be given you.' This is an astounding promise. It is not given flippantly or casually. The conditions that are laid down if this promise is to be fulfilled are 'if you remain in me and my words remain in you.' This implies a level of intimacy with God that has developed to such a state that the expressions of our heart also express the desires of God's heart. We have lived in His presence so often and so deeply and our hearts have soaked in His Spirit so completely that we begin to want what He wants and wish what He wishes. Our will and spirit reflects the will and spirit of God. It is to those who are living in this atmosphere of intimacy with the Spirit of God that God makes this promise. He can risk making this promise to those who remain in Him and His word remains in them, because He knows the promise will not be abused or used for selfish ends or worldly purposes. The richness of the promise is to be experienced only by those who have drank in the Spirit of God and lived so fully in His presence that their hearts reflect His will and wishes. The essence of prayer as **learning to receive what God wants to give** makes sense to these people. Such a person would agree that if God does not want to give it, it must be best for me not to receive it. If God does not want to give it, then I do not want to receive it. For if God does not want to give it, then it is not to my ultimate benefit for me to have it, and I must stop seeking it. If, on the other hand, God does want to give it, then I believe, in faith, that He can and will give it.

"So, if you are going to live in the City of Prayer, you will continue to pursue your normal life. You will still follow your career interests, take care of your family, live the lives of normal people, but the difference is that your daily life will be lived, in an easy atmosphere of prayer. You would practice the presence of God. You will not live in forgetfulness of God, or be disconnected from Him, for long stretches of time. But rather the activities of the day will be permeated with His presence. There will be constant readiness to stay in touch with Him. You will often refer matters to Him. Your spirit will often, in moments when the mind is free, find it the most natural thing to lift itself into His presence. Life never becomes so cluttered that neglect and carelessness develop about the presence of God or the will of God. The spirit of prayer is carried with you everywhere you go.

"The saints of all ages have understood that they must seek to develop this style of living in the presence of God. Thomas A. Kempis, in his devotional classic *The Imitation of Christ*, gives voice to the spirit like this, 'A man who is a lover of Jesus and of truth, a truly interior man who is free from uncontrolled affections, can turn to God at will and rise above himself to enjoy spiritual peace.'[1] Brother Lawrence in his little book *The Practice of the Presence of God* warns us 'we cannot escape the dangers which abound in life without the actual and continual help of God. Let us, then, pray to Him for it continually. How can we pray to Him without being with Him? How can we be with Him but in thinking of Him often? And how can we often think of Him, but by a holy habit which we should form of it.'[2] The same lifestyle of living in the presence of God is alluded to by Charles Swindoll. In his small book *Intimacy With the Almighty*, he says, 'Noise and words and frenzied, hectic schedules dull our senses, closing our ears to His still, small voice and making us numb to His touch.'[3]

"This level of interaction with God cannot be accomplished by casual acquaintance. This is something that is developed and cultivated until it becomes the habit of the soul and the home of the spirit. Those who live in the City of Prayer are learning that the real joy of life is unity with God. That true fulfillment and satisfaction are found in communion with Him. They understand that the reality of life is in fellowship with Him, and so this becomes the great object and aspirations of their soul—to be in touch with Him. Other matters of life still exist and need to be maintained. There are many things in life that should be enjoyed, and attention must be given to them, but the aspiration of the soul is increasingly absorbed in knowing God, resting in His Spirit and cultivating life with Him. And this can be experienced in the midst of the other aspects of living. The apostle Paul expressed this well in Philippians 3:7-8: 'But whatever things were gain to me, those things I have counted as loss for the sake of Christ. More than that, I count all things to be loss in view of the surpassing value of knowing Christ Jesus my Lord . . . and count them but rubbish in order that I may gain Christ' (Phil. 3:7-8).

"God expects us to live life in this world, and to enjoy it. He understands that we have obligations and interests that need our responsible attention. He created us so that we would be involved in the outcomes of life and in the running of the world. Even when he made Adam and Eve in the beginnings of things, he laid responsibilities and duties upon them. They were to rule over the world that he made and attend to it. They were to cultivate the garden and protect the animals. God made the world to be lived in, enjoyed, and maintained. Since He has given us life in the world, He expects and encourages us to live it to the full. Those in the City of Prayer understand this, but they also believe that there are spiritual values that are also important and that true life here can be lived only by participation in the spiritual values of life. They emphasize that they not only have a body with its fleshly and material concerns but they also have a soul and a spirit. They believe there is a God who is dominant in the universe. They are taught that Jesus constantly urges us to give precedence to the spiritual values of life. Material things are important but should never supersede the importance of the spiritual values. In the City of Prayer, the cultivation of unity and fellowship with God in the soul and spirit of the believer is considered the priority. And all of life flows out of that connection. The soul has found its natural home, and all of life is interpreted on that basis."

Someone raised their hand and asked, "This sounds wonderful, but what about the days when you do not feel in touch with God. I find that there are times that no matter how hard I try, His presence seems to have departed. My own spirit is sluggish, and my mind is distracted. Do people in the city not have days like this? Are they always in the spirit and always hungry for God and anxious for fellowship? Or are there times when all of this seems remote, when the pressures of life squeeze out spiritual awareness and they feel out of touch with God? Do they have experiences like this, and if they do, how do they deal with them, especially since everybody else around seems to be enjoying wonderful fellowship with God?"

"That is a good question," responded George, "and one that needs to be responded to. Remember that the city is just a normal city and the people who live there are just normal people. So they have their good days and their bad days. They have times when spirituality seems natural and easy, and they slip into fellowship with God with scarcely any effort. But there are other occasions when they have to work at it. Some days other concerns seem to invade them, and their mind is easily taken up with the affairs of life that have very little to do with spiritual values. So the answer to your question is yes! There will be days when it will be more difficult to fit into the spiritual atmosphere of the city than others. And there may even be times when we fail to do it. The important thing is to understand that the city is about cultivating this fellowship with God. It is about developing the ability to live in His presence more and more. Some in the city are more advanced at this than others. Some are better at it than others. Some have matured the system and have built it into their way of life. Others are still working at it. Everyone in the city, however, is cultivating and improving their practice of the presence of God."

"It sounds awfully hard," someone said, "and calls for lot of effort and discipline."

"True," said George, "it does call for effort and discipline. But remember that what we are seeking here is joy in His presence, enjoyment of His grace, praise for His greatness, peace in unity with Him. When your soul is rewarded with such realities, the appeal and hunger for this spiritual fruitfulness grows and increases so that there is a strong desire to pursue it. It becomes something you want to do. It is something that is remarkably rewarding. It is life at its best. When you experience the soul-satisfying fellowship with God, then living in the spirit of prayer is not so much an odious duty, but a rich and satisfying value that is worth any effort or discipline involved. Jesus once said that the 'the kingdom of heaven is like a treasure hidden in a field. When a man found it, he hid it again, and then in his joy went and sold all he had and bought that field' (Matt.13:44). Prayer is like the treasure hidden in the field. It is a treasure. For the soul and spirit of man, the spirit of prayer provides a rich, beautiful, and satisfying life. It may have cost them a great deal to obtain it. But once they possess it, they do not feel like they have been given a bad bargain. They do not feel like losers. Like the man in Jesus's story, they are filled with joy and rejoicing. Although it cost him a lot, he considered it well worth the cost. So the disciplines of prayer, which seem costly at times, can nevertheless develop into an ever-flowing relationship with God and become well worth the price. The rewards far outweigh the costs. As Jesus said, 'Come to me, all you who are weary and burdened, and I will give you rest. Take my yoke upon you and learn from me, for I am gentle and humble in heart, and you will find rest for your souls. For my yoke is easy and by burden is light' (Matt.11:28-30).

"It is clear that many of the people who are enjoying this kind of life have had to make sacrifices in order to attain it and maintain it, but do not feel sorry for them. They feel they have found life at its best. They are rich beyond measure. They experience joy, blessing, and love in great abundance. They are satisfied in soul and rejoice in the peace of God. Bernard of Clairvaux expresses it well when he wrote,

> We taste Thee, O Thou living Bread,
> And long to feast upon Thee still.
> We drink of Thee, the Fountain head,
> And thirst our souls from Thee to fill.[4]

Someone else in the class asked, "But what if we cannot achieve this kind of living and prayer spirit right away? Does that mean that we cannot live in the City of Prayer? I rejoice at the progress I am making in prayer. Since I set out on this journey, I have developed a much better and maturing prayer life, but I am not yet able to practice the presence of God in the way you describe it. Even though I want to, I am not sure that I am ready to enter into the spirit of the city?"

"No! Please feel relaxed. The spirit of the city is to be seeking after this life. To be pursuing it. Many in the city have not yet achieved this, the important factor is to want it and to desire it and to be seeking it and making progress toward it. In the city you will find that some are farther advanced in their prayer life than others. Not all are at the same level. Some have achieved this, some have not. What is common, however, is the strong desire to seek and pursue this way of life until they are experiencing it for themselves more and more. Be encouraged by what Jesus said when he stated, 'Blessed are those who hunger and thirst for righteousness, for they will be filled' (Matt. 5:6). In the City of Prayer, the direction is more important than the destination. Progress is just as important as achievement.

"I hope," said George, "that this gives you a good idea of the spirit and functioning of the City of Prayer. Now I would like to mention some of the special features of the city. As you explore the city for yourself, you will not want to miss these vitally important highlights. These dominant features of the city are not simply tourist attractions, they are functioning centers out of which the spirit and activities of the city flow. If you are going to understand the city and participate in its spirit and its life, you will need to understand the purposes and functions of these special features. Today I will mention five of them. Then when you go on to explore the city, these are the places you should seek out first. They express the values and the priorities of living in the City of Prayer. The five things are

1. The Central Cathedral, which also contains the Circle of God's Will
2. The Quiet Room
3. The Intercession Booth
4. The Celebration Center
5. The Palace, which also contains the Garden of Love and the Throne Room of the King

"I will give you just a brief overview of each of these features. When you visit them, you will find teachers who can answer questions and will give you a more detailed explanation as to why this particular feature is important to the proper functioning of the prayer life.

"The first feature that you should be well acquainted with is **the Central Cathedral.** As the name implies, this cathedral is at the very center of the city. On the main floor of the cathedral, exactly in the middle, you will find, inlaid on the floor, a circle of white marble. This is called the Circle of God's Will and is the symbol for the center of God's will. Everything in the City of Prayer is oriented around this circle, the Circle of God's Will. All distances are measured from here. All directions are given from here. The city is built around the Circle of God's Will. Everything radiates from this vital center. Until you become familiar with the city, you must begin your explorations at the Circle of God's Will. Some have neglected this. They felt that it was quite unnecessary to always take the time and effort to go the center of God's will and begin from there. They were quite sure that they could get to where they wanted to go without going to the bother of first standing in the Circle of God's Will. But if you attempt this, you will soon find that you will become confused, lost, and perplexed in the city. It is essential that you first go the circle, the center of God's will.

"The second feature is the **Quiet Room**. It is also located in the Central Cathedral, and you will want to visit it on a regular basis. In the Quiet Room, you will learn to soak yourself in contemplation. You quietly lay aside all distractions and center your mind and heart on the presence and nearness of God. In this feature of the prayer life, the focus is not on what you are asking for, or what you are requesting of God. It is allowing the soul to rest in the presence of God. It is a time when, in quietness, you focus your mind and spirit in connecting with His spirit. It is a season of being aware of His presence, of being in fellowship with Him, without request, or petition. It reduces life to just you and Him in quiet contact and fellowship. Those who enjoy the City of Prayer the most usually begin to spend more and more time in the Quiet Room. Their joy is to be in His presence. Their reward is to drink in His Spirit and feast upon His atmosphere. The purpose of the Quiet Room is to rest the soul in His presence. It is considered a successful time if you touch His presence. You may never make a request, or formulate a petition, but if you have sensed His presence and enjoyed it, then the main purpose has been fulfilled.

The third feature of the prayer life in the city is the **Intercession Booth.** The focus and purpose of the Intercession Booth is to pray for others. Here you will participate in prayer with the people of God around the world. Indeed, you will also join in the great prayers of the saints of the past ages as they pray for the souls and lives of others. The Intercession Booth is a plain and simple place. There are no decorations or unusual comforts. It seems more like a place of work. Prayers here are often very intense and burdened as people pray for loved ones, for friends, and for the lost souls of other men and women.

"The **Celebration Hall,** as you can imagine, is a place of rejoicing and singing and exuberant praise. It is often a busy place, for people enjoy getting together here and devoting themselves to the happy praise and worship of God. In the Celebration Hall, you let your soul soar into the realms of uninhibited praise and worship. It is a place of joy and thanksgiving. It is a time of release and refreshment. It is a feature of the City of Prayer, because being happy in the joy and wonder of God is part of the atmosphere of the city. I hope you will often visit the Celebration Hall. In this hall the people are experiencing what the apostle described when he said, 'You are filled with an inexpressible and glorious joy' (1 Pet. 1:8).

"The last feature I will mention is the **Palace.** This contains the **Garden of Love** and the **Throne Room of the King.** This is the center of power in the City of Prayer. It is the home of the King. When you visit the Palace, be sure and go to the Garden of Love. It is called the Garden of Love because it creates the atmosphere that dominates the rule and the kingdom of the King. It is a place of love. In the garden, you will sense and absorb the spirit of the King. In the Garden of Love, you eat the fruits of the Spirit that flourish there. Linger in the garden. Do not rush here. It is a beautiful place. Its fragrance and color will enrich your soul. In the garden, you are filled with His spirit. You receive into your own soul the spirit of the King. You will be filled with His love and his overflowing graciousness. As you open your spirit to this atmosphere and let the Spirit of Christ flow into you, you will experience what Paul speaks about in Romans 5:5, 'Because God has poured out his love into our hearts by the Holy Spirit whom he has given to us.' This atmosphere will enrich your own spirit.

"Also in the Palace is the **Throne Room**, here you will meet the King. He sits on the throne. From here radiates all of the power and authority of the Kingdom of God. Many wish to sit on this throne and display this power, but in the City of Prayer, there is only one who can sit on the throne—no usurpers or frauds—it is the King of Kings and Lord of Lords. In the Throne Room, you will humble yourself and accept His authority and power. You will submit to His will and wishes. He alone is on the throne. Here all thought of self-will and rebelliousness against the Lord is stripped from us. He alone is King. Here His power and authority are seen to be supreme. All self-will is dissolved in the mightiness of His presence. In the Throne Room, there is only one throne, and that belongs to Him. No smaller personal thrones exist. No minor powers compete for position. This submission to His power and authority is an essential part of living successfully in the City of Prayer. Those who do not accept this do not stay in the city very long."

With that George completed this part of his discourse to us. By way of conclusion he said, "I said at the beginning of our class that I have three things that I want to talk to you about—the nature of the City of Prayer, the special features of the city, and the essence of prayer. We have covered the first two subjects, but I suspect that you have heard enough for one day. You will all be tired from your journey. There are rooms available for you to stay in for tonight and during your days of exploration. I suggest you have a restful night, and then in the morning we will discuss the third item—the essence of prayer. Then, in the afternoon, you will be free to begin your exploration of the city. Before we retire for the night, are there any questions?"

I immediately put my hand up and asked, "When we are exploring the city, should we do it alone or should we do it as a group?"

"You will find it encouraging if you do it as a group. There are, however, parts of the city and some experiences in prayer that are best experienced alone. I would keep in touch with your friends and join them in some of the exploration, but in other parts, each of you will have to experience prayer alone. For example, when you go to the Quiet Room, it is important that you go alone. On the other hand, you will enjoy the Celebration Hall much more if you enjoy it with your friends. Since you will all be staying here in the rooms provided, you will have opportunity to make plans for each day and decide if you want to explore it together, or if you want to do it alone. Certainly at the end of each day, you should take time to share with each other your experiences and your questions. You will find your rooms if you go through that side door. Each person has a room to themselves. Each room has a prayer corner, which is set up to help you in your own private prayer time."

After the class dismissed, I gathered with John, Helen, and Alvin, and we each expressed a strong desire, when we were doing the explorations, to stay together as a group and when possible experience the city together.

"It would also be informative to gather each evening after the day's activities and have time together to share our experiences and to learn from each other," said Helen. To this we all agreed. We were all tired by now and retired to our rooms, with a sense of anticipation. The next day would be a very significant one when we would discuss the essence of prayer and start to explore the City of Prayer.

JOURNAL: It has been a long day, and I am very tired yet deeply satisfied. I have reached a significant milestone in my journey into prayer. I have completed the journey to the city but have yet to start my exploration. What have I learned so far in the journey? I can look back and see that I have made good progress in my prayer life. I can look forward with the understanding that there is still much more to learn. I can see that developing an effective prayer life is much more demanding than I imagined when I started out.

In some ways the journey is the wrong way around. I am realizing that the journey into prayer is a journey from complexity into simplicity, rather than the other way around. When I started out, I was a confusing jumble of mixed motives, uncertainties, doubts, and faulty thinking. I did not know how I was going to sort it all out. Now I am becoming much simpler. My motives are clearer and cleansed from a lot of ulterior self-centeredness and worldliness. I have learned a great deal so that many faulty ideas have been clarified. I am not wasting spiritual energy and resources by pursuing wrong concepts and unrealistic expectations. I have found there are so many false trails and dead-end streets in prayer that I could have easily been sidetracked. My doubts do not trouble and haunt me like they used to. I am not driven by guilt. I seem to be coming together. There is developing a simple unity between God and me—I have peace and security. There is a clarified motivation—I am not so divided in my purposes and desires. I am not mixed up in my objectives—I have a clearer understanding of what the objectives of prayer really are. All of this makes prayer simpler, not necessarily easier, but simpler; my journey so far has led me from complexity to simplicity. My heart is not divided. My eye is single. My desires are harmonizing better with God's desires. I look forward with great anticipation to exploring the City of Prayer and hearing what George has to say about the essence of prayer.

TOPICS FOR DISCUSSION—CHAPTER TEN

1. If you decide not to stay in the City of Prayer, was it worthwhile making the journey to get there?
2. Discuss the statement "The nature and atmosphere of the City of Prayer is not designed to get people to forsake the legitimate and necessary functions of life in order to pray, but rather to help them bring the spirit of prayer into the normal functions of life."

CHAPTER ELEVEN

THE ESSENCE OF PRAYER

When I awoke this morning, I realized that this was to be an important day. Today, in the School of Prayer, we would talk about the essence of prayer. I am looking forward to this since the principle has been emphasized to me from the very start of the journey, and I am not sure how well I have grasped its meaning. There are many questions I have, and I hope they will be answered as we talk to George. Also, today will be the day when I actually begin to explore the City of Prayer. I have anticipated this day for some time now. I came on this journey with this purpose in mind. I am filled with excitement and curiosity at the prospect. What will the city be like? Will I be pleasantly surprised, or will I be disappointed? All in all, this is going to be a pivotal day.

In my room in the School of Prayer, I took time to pray. The prayer corner in the room was quite simple. It had a plain wooden chair with a cushion. There was a small table with a Bible on it. On the wall behind the chair was a picture of Christ in prayer in the Garden of Gethsemane. Although unadorned, the corner seemed to be a sacred spot, and I found it easy to enter into the attitude and spirit of prayer. It was a blessed and worshipful time. It prepared me for the events of the coming day.

When the group had gathered in the classroom, George, after greeting us, expressed his hope that we all had had a good night of rest and were now ready to begin the study class. "Yesterday," he began, "I talked to you about the City of Prayer. I said it was an ordinary city with ordinary people. They go about the business of living just like everybody else. The difference is that while they do all of the ordinary things, they seek to surround these ordinary activities with the spirit of prayer. Then, secondly, we talked about some of the important features of the city that you need to become well acquainted with as you go about your exploration. I mentioned five of these important features. They were the

Central Cathedral, which contains the Circle of God's Will, the Quiet Room, the Intercession Booth, the Celebration Hall, and the Palace of the King.

"Today, before you begin your explorations, I want to talk to you about the essence of prayer so that you understand the guiding characteristic of true prayer. You have heard the statement given already by a number of your guides and teachers as you journeyed up the pathway to the City of Prayer. I think you will all be well acquainted with the statement by now. It says the essence of prayer is **learning to receive what God wants to give.** This is a simple statement but nevertheless captures the essentials of what mature and effective prayer is all about. This is the heart of the matter. There may be some aspects of prayer that are not covered by this statement. There are certainly common practices of prayer that are outside of this definition. Nevertheless, the heart and soul of what prayer is all about can be summed up in these simple words, **prayer is learning to receive what God wants to give.** Every word in this statement is important. Let's look at them.

"It is not a coincidence that the first word in the statement is the word *learning*. Prayer is something that is to be learned. When we start out on the journey of prayer, our prayers may be very elementary, fumbling, and rather self-centered. In fact this is how most of us probably took our first trembling steps into prayer. But we can learn. Our prayers can become more mature, wiser, more discerning, and effective. But we need to learn. I have a charming little daughter." Here the smile on his face and the twinkle in his eye announced to us all that this little girl had certainly captured George's heart. "When she was learning to walk, she did not wake up one morning and decide that she was going to walk. She did not jump up out of bed and run outside and sprint down the street for one hundred meters. That's not how she went about it. First she stood on her feet. She wobbled and fell. But she persevered, and soon she was able to stand with some confidence on her two feet. Then she took a step. Only one and then she fell again, but the first step had been taken. She became more confident. With her arms in the air, and excitement on her face, she would take a few steps and then fall into the arms of her encouraging and delighted mother. Soon she was able to walk from the chesterfield to the table—she never allowed herself to stray very far from something solid that she could hold on to, but she was making progress. It did not take long before she was running all over the house, getting into things that she should not get into, and in the process falling, bruising her knees and hurting her elbows, but learning to walk. She can't run one hundred meters yet, but she can go up some stairs. She's not ready for a marathon race, but she is gaining strength and skill. She is learning to walk, and she is getting better at it all the time.

"So we also learn to pray. At first we hardly know what to say or how to say it. We make mistakes and ask for the wrong things. We see others who can spend great amounts of time in prayer, while we seem to run out of things to say and do in a few minutes. We wonder if we are doing it correctly? Is God listening? How do we have faith? How do we sense God's presence? It is all very hesitant and uncertain. But we are starting to pray. We are making progress. Soon we experience times in prayer when we do indeed sense His presence. Sometimes we find that, yes indeed, there seems to have been an answer to some of our prayers, not all of them, but at least some of them, and this encourages us. Sometimes we wonder if we are asking for the right things. As time goes on, we learn to worship and praise in prayer. We become more alert to the presence of God. We begin to wonder whether what we are asking for is God's will or not? What is God's will? What does God want to give? So the progress continues. We learn more and more what is mature and reasonable in prayer. We begin to differentiate between realistic praying and childish dreams that are little more than wishing for magic. Prayer is a learning process. We find that we are becoming more and more interested and concerned about understanding what God's will is for us, than we are about getting God to respond to our will. It is becoming more and more important just to be in the presence of God than it is to be telling God all we want Him to do. We are growing and developing.

"We should not then be too upset if we discover that we have been doing some things wrong in prayer. Or that our prayers have been rather selfish and worldly. We are learning. We should rejoice when new elements come into our prayer life like joy, worship, praise. There may be occasions when we hear from God. We begin to learn to listen for His voice. We find we can comfortably take more time. Prayer becomes a more meaningful exercise. God's presence becomes more real. We improve at dealing with the problems of prayer, like distractions and sleepiness. We are improving. We are learning. The thing to be afraid of is not the realization that we have a lot to learn, but rather the bland assumption that we are already doing it right and have nothing much more to learn. As we improve, we grow in the ability to sense God's presence. We learn better to hear God and to understand His will. We learn to lay our own wishes and wants in the hands of God and seek in our hearts to reflect what He wants. We move away from the type of praying that concentrates on getting what we want from God, to praying about what God want to give us."

Someone interrupted with a question that I also had on my own mind. The person asked, "You keep on talking about selfish prayers. Are all prayers for ourselves selfish? Should we never pray about ourselves and our needs and desires?"

"That is a good question," replied George. "If I have given the impression that it is somehow wrong to pray for ourselves, then I must apologize, for that is not correct. There is a legitimate self-interest. In fact the Lord encouraged us to pray 'Give us this day our daily bread.' To have the needs of our daily life provided for is a legitimate and perfectly human desire. There are many desires that we have that are correct, human, and legitimate, and God really does want us to pray about them. What I am saying, however, is that as your prayer life matures, while these self-interest requests will still be part of your prayer life, they will become less and less dominant in the priority list of what we want from God. They will still be there and still should be there, but they will decline in importance. Other interests and values will grow in importance. We will always desire and wish for God's help in the legitimate affairs of our life, our health, and our family. As we develop in our prayers, however, we will more and more wish for His will, His presence, His worship. What seems to be important in prayer will change as your prayer life grows.

"Think about it like this," George continued. "Suppose there comes a day and you only have a short time to pray, you know you cannot cover everything in your prayer time. You have time only to cover quickly one or two priorities. When such a day comes and you find that you want to spend the precious moments in focusing on the presence of God, making contact with Him, sensing His nearness and Spirit, and letting His grace flow into your soul, then you will know that you are maturing in your prayers. When the hunger of your heart is to make sure you have this kind of contact, then good balance has come to your prayer life. When this is the major concern, rather than making sure that you press your own petitions and requests on Him, then the priorities of your prayers have advanced. His will, His presence, His worship, His grace, His assurance in your soul become the most important items. If we don't have time, then our requests can normally wait until tomorrow, but what is essential for today is to spend time enjoying His presence and making contact with Him, right now."

"Good," someone else said. "I can see what you are saying, but tell me, is there not a distinction to be made between legitimate self-interest prayers and selfish prayers?"

"Yes!" replied George promptly. "You have hit on a very important point. We must be careful that what we are calling legitimate self-interest prayers are not in reality sinful, selfish prayers. We have a great ability to clothe our sinful selfishness in very righteous garments. So we must be very diligent about this matter. Often, the real underlying reason we want God's help for things to happen in our lives or in the lives of our loved ones is quite selfish. God will not help us to feed our greed, if we are asking for far more than we need. God will not nourish our pride, when we really want things that will help us to glory in our success. God will not hear us when we pray so that we can triumph over those who are not being kind to us. There are a lot of prayers that can come from selfish and wrong motives. We need to examine our motives and ask ourselves, 'What do I really want this for?' 'What will this do to me if I get it?' 'In asking for this, am I really pressing my own will, or am I truly seeking His will?' It was probably this kind of prayer that James was speaking about when he said, 'When you do ask, you do not receive, because you ask with wrong motives, that you may spend what you get on your pleasures'" (James 4:3).

"But how do you differentiate between sinful, selfish motives and legitimate self-interest motives?" someone else asked.

George gave this some thought and then replied, "This is not always easy. And we do have a great capacity for deceiving ourselves. In this respect you may sometimes make mistakes and misinterpret your motives. Let me say two things that might help you here. First, remember, God is gracious. He knows that if you are sincerely seeking His will, and trying to be unselfish in your requests, even when you make a mistake, He understands and will be gracious to the sincere person. The second thing is that this is part of the wisdom that grows in you as you mature in your prayer life. You will get better at understanding your own heart and your own motives as you get closer to God. As you mature and grow in wisdom, the possibility of mistaking your motives becomes less likely. The main thing is to be aware of the problem and seek to be pure in your motives and to invite God's Spirit to lead and direct you. Remember, God is gracious and is much more anxious to help and guide you than He is to condemn you and punish you for being wrong. The prayer of the Psalmist is helpful here. In this prayer he expressed the correct attitude and the correct spirit, and if you are in doubt, you should pray in the same spirit as he prayed. He asked, 'Search me, O God, and know my heart; test me and know my anxious thoughts. See if there is any offensive way in me, and lead me in the way everlasting' (Ps.139:23-24). When this prayer is prayed sincerely, you can count on God's guidance and direction. And if you do make a sincere mistake, you can count on God's graciousness and help. Remember we are learning. One of the important features about learning is that we learn from our mistakes. Sincere mistakes can be used of God to help us in our learning process. The really big mistake is to think you are not making any. You should be far more afraid of ceasing to learn than you are afraid of making mistakes."

There was a period of quietness while we all digested this. When it was clear there were no more questions, George continued, "So learning, and the spirit of learning, is an essential part of the essence of prayer. How much you have learned and how far along the path you have gone is not really as important as the fact that you are making progress, moving farther along the path, and learning more and more all the time. Mature and effective praying comes from experience and maturity and wisdom.

"The second part of the statement about the essence of prayer says 'prayer is **learning to receive** what God wants to give.' In prayer we learn to receive. This places us in the right position. We are the receivers. God is the giver. We are in the position of need. God can supply that need. There is not much room for pride here or self-sufficiency. In prayer we take the humble stance of coming as a needy and hungry petitioner to a bountiful and gracious God. We are a needy people. God is a gracious God and will supply the needs. In prayer it is this humble and submissive spirit that is called for. David in his prayer of repentance expressed it well when he said, 'The sacrifices of God are a broken spirit: a broken and contrite heart, O God, you will not despise' (Ps. 51:17).

"You remember the story Jesus told about the two men who went up to the temple to pray, one man was a deeply religious, but self-righteous Pharisee, the other was a penitent sinner, a publican, one of the most despised men in that society. The Pharisee prayed in such a way as to tell God that He, God, should be grateful to the Pharisee for all of the good achievements that the Pharisee had accomplished. Jesus, with His tongue in His cheek, said, 'The Pharisee stood up and prayed about himself; "God, I thank you that I am not like other men—robbers, evildoers, adulterers—or even like this tax collector. I fast twice a week and give a tenth of all I get." Clearly, God was expected to be impressed and grateful for all that the Pharisee was bringing to Him. But Jesus goes on and says, 'But the tax collector stood at a distance. He would not even look up to heaven, but beat his chest and said, "God, have mercy on me, a sinner."' He had nothing to offer God. But he acknowledged that he did need God to help Him. Jesus concluded, 'I tell you that this man, rather than the other, went home justified before God. For everyone who exalts himself will be humbled, and he who humbles himself will be exalted' (Luke 18:11-14). The proper spirit and attitude that makes prayer effective and powerful is not the proud self-confidence of the Pharisee, but the broken neediness of the publican. Prayer is learning to receive.

"That is why many people prefer, when they pray, to kneel and pray on their knees before God. Kneeling is part of the body language that says, 'I am humbling myself before you.' 'I am acknowledging your greatness and my need.' And it is this sense of humble need that gets the spiritual juices flowing and causes the soul to make the right contact with God and open itself to receive the blessing that He has in mind. Jesus said, 'Blessed are those who hunger and thirst for righteousness, for they will be filled' (Matt. 5:6). The hungry need food. The thirsty need water. It is with this spirit of need that they approach God and He fills them. In fact if you go through all of the Beatitudes, which are the heart of the moral teachings of Jesus, you will find they are dominated, not by a spirit of pride and self-righteousness, but by a spirit of humble need and dependence. Jesus enumerates those who will be blessed by God, 'blessed are the poor in spirit. Blessed are those who mourn. Blessed are the meek. Blessed are those who hunger and thirst after righteousness. Blessed are the merciful. Blessed are the pure in heart. Blessed are the peacemakers. Blessed are those who are persecuted for righteousness sake' (Matt. 5:3-10). When it comes to a good relationship with God, there is absolutely no evidence of a proud, overbearing, self-reliant atmosphere.

"Learning to receive is an attitude which makes the power and grace of God flow to the individual," James says rather bluntly. "'God opposes the proud but gives grace to the humble. Submit yourselves, then to God' (James 4:6-7). God in a loving and generous way has so much that He wants to give. We, in our need and weakness, need so much of what He wants to give. It is in response to this recognition of need that God enjoys answering our prayers. He is not so anxious to respond to pride and a lack of need. So prayer is learning to receive.

"The next part of the essence of prayer is the key part. Prayer is learning to receive **what God wants to give.** First, we must not assume, with bland ignorance, that what we want to get is necessarily what God wants to give. Immature, thoughtless, careless, selfish, worldly, power-hungry desires can fill our minds and hearts. God is not interested in giving us all of that stuff, because it would harm us and others and because a lot of it is trivial. What I am saying is that if we are going to learn to receive what God wants to give, we need to give much thought and wisdom to determining that what we are asking for is, in fact, something God wants to give. Great discouragement and disillusionment occurs when we expect God to respond to every immature, thoughtless request that we come up with. I am urging you to give careful, wise, and prayerful thought into what you ask from God. Any expectation that God will always answer our prayers no matter how careless, shallow, or selfish they are is totally unfounded in scripture and is little more than delusions of grandeur on our part. Effort and thought must be put into our prayers. Does God want me to have this? Is this something that God wants to give? Why do I want to receive this? What would I do with it if I got it? Is this God's will for me? Have I really, carefully, and wisely considered this as God's will? The fact is that in our immaturity and often in our selfishness, we do not want to receive what God wants to give and sometimes we want to receive what God does not want to give.

"The second thing that needs to be said about this part of the essence of prayer is that this statement expresses the true nature of the promises given in the Bible regarding prayer. Many wild and thoughtless statements have been made about prayer by many good-meaning people. Prayer is nowhere promised to be a blank check and all we have to do is write in our own amount and expect God to come up with the necessary funds. Let's look carefully at the promises made about prayer by Jesus. A careful examination of these promises will reveal that what we are striving for in prayer is to achieve a harmony between God's will and what we are asking for. As we mature in prayer, there will be developing in our hearts a growing desire to receive what God wants to give. It is a uniting between the desires of our hearts and the desires of God's heart. When we want to receive what God wants to give, then our prayers are on safe ground and faith can flourish. When our hearts begin to long for the things that God wants to give, then we can have confidence in Him when we approach Him in prayer. Let's look at some of the promises.

"A promise about prayer that is commonly referred to is made by Jesus in John 14:13-14: 'And I will do whatever you ask in my name, so that the Son may bring glory to the Father. You may ask me for anything in my name, and I will do it.' This is an amazing statement. To state 'ask for anything in my name and I will do it' seems like Jesus is issuing blank checks. In fact I have heard the verse cut short and misquoted, so that people say, 'He has promised, that if you ask for anything He will do it.' He has, of course, promised no such thing. To say these things carelessly is to raise false hopes and expectations about prayer. It is important that in this promise, as in all of the promises of God, we take clear note of the conditions attached to the promise. When Jesus said, 'You may ask for anything in my name and I will do it,' He has attached a clear condition. The condition is that we ask 'in his name.' That means that when we make a petition to God in His name, He could sign His name to it. He endorses it. He agrees with the content of the petition. You are well aware of the importance of signing your name on a legal document. A document has no legal authority until you sign your name to it. Anyone could write up a document and say they are doing it in your name, but the document is worthless unless you sign your name to it and endorse it. When you sign it, then that means that you are aware of the contents of the document and you wish the contents to be implemented. The signing of your name is a very important procedure in the legal world. In fact the signing of your name often has to be witnessed by a notary to ensure its validity. The valid signature ensures that people cannot go around making up documents in your name and having their contents accepted as authoritative. For example, let us assume that you are very rich, and I am a good friend of yours. I might decide it would be good for you to make up a will so that your considerable estate will be properly shared when you die. So I proceed to make up a will in your name. I do, of course, generously include myself as a major beneficiary of the will. It might be a very nice document. It may express very well what I want it to say, but it is an empty and useless piece of paper. You have not read it. You are not aware of its contents. You were not consulted about it. You certainly have not endorsed it or signed your name to it. It is an expression of my will, not yours. Then the document is worthless. I may very much desire that you leave a lot of your money to me. I may even work hard at cultivating your friendship, so that you will give consideration to leaving me your money. But if you say, 'The document that you have produced is not what I want to do with my estate, that is not how I want it to be divided, that does not reflect my wishes or desires and I will not put my name to it or endorse it.' Then the document, regardless of my wishes and desires, will not become effective. So it is when we present a petition to God in the name of Jesus. Using the name of Jesus means that He is aware of the contents of the petition. He agrees with the petition. He wants to see its terms implemented. In other words, He endorses it and would sign His name to it. We are now asking 'in the name of Jesus.'

"Jesus is very careful about us using His name. He will not allow us to forge His signature. We will not deceive God into thinking Jesus endorses something when He does not. For us to be asking God for something that Jesus could not sign His name to is for us to be asking amiss, and we, therefore, have no promise that our requests will be answered. So you can see that for our prayers to be effective, we must take great care to make sure that we are asking 'in the name of Jesus.' This is His will. He wants this to happen. He approves of this request. We are asking for something that God wants to give. This is praying 'in the name of Jesus.' If you are not sure of His endorsement, if you are not sure He would agree to this and support it, then you cannot use His name.

"In the light of this, you can understand that the important matter in prayer is to bring our heart and spirit into harmony with Him, so that what we ask is what He wants to give. Our requests reflect His will. Prayer is powerful and wonderfully effective, when the desires of our heart reflect the desires of His heart, when our wills are united with His will, when our priorities are endorsed by His priorities. **Prayer is learning to receive what God wants to give.**

"Another great promise that Jesus gave regarding prayer is found in John 15:7. In this verse, Jesus promised, 'If you remain in me and my words remain in you, ask whatever you wish, and it will be given you.'

"Again, it is important that you do not misquote what Jesus said. He did not say 'ask whatsoever you wish, and it will be given you.' What He said was 'If you remain in me and my words remain in you, ask whatever you wish, and it will be given you.' The condition laid down for the promise being fulfilled is that we remain in Him and His words remain in us. If the condition is disregarded, then the promise is no longer valid. But if the conditions are met, then the promise is real, and a wonderful promise it is. In this passage, Jesus is describing a close relationship that should develop between Him and His disciples. He talks about this relationship as being like the interaction between a vine and its branches. The branches must stay connected to the vine. They cannot function effectively without this vital connection. They receive sustenance, support, food, and nourishment from the vine. Branches separated from the vine are going to wither and die. Well might Jesus say when He emphasized this relationship that 'apart from me you can do nothing.' (That, by the way is also a promise.) When a branch has this relationship with the vine, then it will become a fruitful branch. This relationship of fruitfulness is enhanced by the Father who will prune and shape the branches into even more fruitfulness. It is in the context of this close connection and interaction between the vine and the branches that Jesus makes the promise about prayer. He is saying, 'If you live in me and my words live in you, then you shall ask what you will and it shall be given unto you.' Living, remaining, abiding in Him and His words remaining, abiding, living in us. This reflects a close and continuing association between us. In this relationship, the branch is to receive a constant supply of the life, the spirit and the will that come from the vine. The responsibility of the vine is to provide for a continuous flow of spiritual sustenance which will make the branch fruitful and effective. In prayer it means that when we absorb His will, His life, when we receive in our hearts His spirit and His desires, when we are in harmony with His purposes and plans, then we can ask what we will, and it should be done. The promise is valid because what we are asking for reflects His desires, plans, and wishes for us. The desires of our heart are the desires of His heart. His will is our will. There is a unity here between what we want and what He wants. We are both striving for the same purposes and the same ends. There is no clash of wills, no contrary desires, no self-will trying to impose itself on God. Once again we can say it: **prayer is learning to receive what God wants to give.** The flow of grace, blessing, sustenance, and spirit that comes from the vine into the branches is exactly what the branches need and want for a fruitful and effective and fulfilling life. And prayer is a vital part of keeping that flow of nourishment open.

"A great deal is made of having faith in prayer. Another promise of Jesus that is often referred to is when He said, 'I tell you the truth, if you have faith and do not doubt, not only can you do what was done to the fig tree, but also you can say to this mountain, "Go, throw yourself into the sea," and it will be done. If you believe, you will receive whatever you ask for in prayer.'

"Clearly a key factor in the miracles that Jesus did while He was here on earth was that the people involved have faith. They were healed in response to faith. Demons were cast out in response to faith. In fact we are told that even Jesus could not do many great works in His hometown of Nazareth, because of their 'lack of faith.' So the matter of believing that God is going to answer our prayers is a vital factor in the effectiveness of prayer. But on what base can we have faith? The base upon which faith is built is the base that what we are asking for is something that God wants to give. True faith is built on the foundation of the will of God. If you know that something is the will of God and God wishes you to have it, then you have a base for faith and can ask believing. If what you ask is not in the will of God for you, then you have no base for having faith. Indeed you ought not to even to try and have faith. Our faith relies on the fact that God wants to give us what we are asking for. Our faith is built on the foundation that what we are asking for is just the very thing that God wants to give. If God does not want to give it, then there is no base for having faith. Jesus made a very wonderful promise in Luke 11:11-12. He said, 'Which of you fathers, if your son asks for a fish, will give him a snake instead? Or if he asks for an egg, will give him a scorpion? If you then, though you are evil, know how to give good gifts to your children, how much more will your Father in heaven give the Holy Spirit to those who ask him!' I have often wondered about the reverse of this promise. 'If the son asks for a snake—will he get it? If he asks for a scorpion will the Father oblige?' Our faith is based on us asking for the right things. A hymn writer expresses the faith well when he writes,

> Faith, mighty faith, the promise sees
> And looks to that alone;
> Laughs at impossibilities
> And cries: "It shall be done!"[1]

"Faith is believing that God has the power and ability and desire to bring about what is His will for you. To pray without knowing whether God wants you to have it or not is to pray on uncertain ground. And when there is uncertainty, then there is no strong faith. If you are not sure whether it is God's will or not, then you cannot have true faith until that matter is cleared up. You must be sure that what you ask for is something that God wants to give. If you are not sure, then you need to take time to seek His will and understand the mind of God on this matter. I am encouraging you to take much more time and give much more effort, at the beginning of your prayer, to determining what is God's will, rather than proceed to pray blindly, hoping it is God's will. This kind of careless praying, which says, 'I want it, so I will pray for it, and if it is God's will He will respond, and if it is not His will then He will say no' is sure to lead to many disappointments, and render us confused and uncertain about the assurances and promises of prayer.

"This matter of determining the will of God is also an essential matter in the growth and development of our prayer life. Growth in prayer and in our faith in prayer comes as we humbly seek to know God's will and wishes. As we get to know His will better, then our prayer life matures into a much more dynamic and dignified ministry. Power in prayer comes, not by spending more and more time in the confusion of not knowing whether something is God's will or not, but power comes when we are increasingly aware of the values and priorities and will of God and pray for these things. An unwillingness to seriously pursue the will of God in our prayers will cause stagnation and confusion in our prayer life."

At this point George stopped, for he sensed that we were having a difficult time accepting this. He sensed correctly, for we had questions on our minds. Immediately someone put her hand up and asked, "But if you do not know whether something is God's will or not, should you not then pray about it."

"There are three things I want to say in answer to that," responded George. "First, if you are not sure whether something is God's will or not, then the important thing for you to do is to find out. Until that is settled then your prayers are on uncertain and, therefore, on a doubtful base. Second, if you are not sure whether something is God's will or not, and you do not have time or opportunity to find out, then certainly you should pray about it. In the course of living, every day there are situations arise for which we have had no warning and have been given no opportunity for preparation. We do not have time to seek God's will, but we do want to pray about it. For most of us, it takes some time to determine the will of God. We are not very good at spontaneous and intuitive responses to surprise situations. So certainly in these times, we should pray and commit the matter to God and ask for His guidance, even though we are uncertain as to what His will is. This, however, will be more a prayer of commitment and resignation, rather than a prayer of faith. This kind of prayer is all right, but it is not the real home of what prayer is all about. In this circumstance you would pray something like this: "Father, I am not sure what your will is in this matter, and I have not had opportunity to find out, but I pray to you for your will to be done, and whatever your will is, I will accept it." There is a place for this kind of praying. The third thing I need to say about this is to remind you that real growth and development comes to us when we place ourselves and our hearts and spirit into the will of God. We are growing when, more and more, our requests and petitions reflect the will and wishes of God. Our constant effort should be to reflect the will of God in our prayers. For us to be content with 'not knowing,' or for us to fill our prayer lives with requests that we are uncertain about and then say whatever the results may be, then that is the will of God is to stifle the growth of our lives and let our prayers become bogged down in uncertainties. To be content with uncertainties is not good."

George could tell that we were having a hard time accepting this, so he said, "I think it would help us understand this better if we go on to the next stage of the essence of prayer. If prayer **is learning to receive what God wants to give,** then the most basic question for us is 'What does God want to give?' The answer to this question is actually a lot simpler than we often make it out to be. Basically what God wants to give to us, most of all, is Himself. He wants us to experience His life. He wants us to share in His Spirit. He wants us to participate in His joy. He wants us to be filled with His love. He wants to come and live in our hearts so that we taste His life and share His glory and drink in His power. The most wonderful thing that we could possibly receive from God is Himself. There is nothing that He could give us that would bring more life, reality, fulfillment, and joy than this simple thing. God, more than anything else, wants to give Himself. The main problem with prayer is that we do not always share in God's priority system. We do not mind Him giving some of Himself, but the fact of the matter is that our lives are full of other things and other priorities. We would certainly like God to give some of Himself, but we do not treat that gift with the priority status that God does. While in the background of our minds we may acknowledge our need of Him and His presence in our lives, nevertheless, we often are dominated by much more practical everyday concerns. I have a job, a family, money, status, health, career, to take care of, and I want God to help me take care of them successfully and to my own satisfaction. These things tend to be our priority, and the satisfying of their urgent needs tend to dominate. So while we don't mind receiving some of the things God wants to give, we are really much more interested in Him helping us with our life concerns."

Here George paused to let this sink into our minds. Then with great emphasis he said slowly but clearly, "And this is where we need to grow and develop and mature in our prayer lives and in our walk with God. We are growing and developing when our hearts desire more and more what God wants to give.

We are getting over our immaturities when we learn to seek what He wants to give. We are growing in grace when more and more our values change to loving and following Him. We are becoming strong in our Christian walk when we begin to make our priorities His priorities.

"We recognize and accept God's priorities in other parts of the Christian life. When Jesus said, 'So do not worry, saying, "What shall we eat" or "What shall we drink?" or "What shall we wear?" For the pagans run after all these things, and your heavenly Father knows that you need them. But seek first his kingdom and his righteousness, and all these things will be given to you as well' (Matt. 6:31-33). We accept this as a Jesus principle in our lives. But we should also accept it as a Jesus principle in our prayer lives. Seek first, make a priority out of the things of His kingdom, even in the things we pray about. Jesus stated His priorities when he was asked what He thought the greatest commandment was. He answered the most important commandment is: '"Love the Lord your God with all your heart and with all your soul and with your entire mind" This is the first and greatest commandment, and the second is like it: "Love your neighbor as yourself." All the Law and the Prophets hang on these two commandments' (Matt. 22:37-40). We understand and accept this as a basic Jesus principle for our Christian life. We also need to accept it as a basic principle in our prayer lives. Loving Him. Putting Him first. Seeking His kingdom and its values first should be reflected in the way we pray. Prayer then becomes more a matter of drinking in the Spirit of God, of loving fellowship with Him, of letting our spirit contact and communicate with His spirit. Prayer is getting into His presence, sensing His grace and goodness, loving and adoring Him, letting Him fill us with His love. Prayer becomes a joy in uniting with Him. It fills the soul with His grace. It helps us focus on the great factors of eternity and life. Prayer becomes the time when our soul and spirit are in touch with Him and receives from Him what He wants to give—His grace, His love, His power, His strength, His joy. When we learn this in prayer, then it becomes the most meaningful, satisfying, and exciting time of the day. This is when we experience life to the full. This is when our sprits soar and our hearts are lifted up into the heavenlies. This is life. This is joy. This is fullness, and this is satisfaction. This is the home of the soul. This is what we were born for. This is what we were created for—for unity and fellowship with him. This matters more than anything else. This should absorb our prayer time more than anything else.

"Let me share with you the testimony of Henri Nouwen, one of the great spiritual leaders of the twentieth century. He says 'Once, quite a few years ago, I had the opportunity of meeting Mother Teresa of Calcutta. I was struggling with many things at the time and decided to use the occasion to ask Mother

Teresa's advice. As soon as we sat down I started explaining all my problems and difficulties—trying to convince her of how complicated it all was! When after ten minutes of elaborate explanation, I finally became quiet, Mother Teresa looked at me and quietly said: "Well, when you spend one hour a day adoring your Lord and never do anything which you know is wrong . . . you will be fine! When she said this, I realized, suddenly, that she had punctured my big balloon of complex self-complaints and pointed me far beyond myself to the place of real healing."[2] Do you get the value system that Mother Teresa is referring to? "When you spend one hour a day adoring your Lord and never do anything which you know is wrong . . . . you will be fine."" In the light of that simple value system of prayer, all of Nouwen's complicated confusions melted away. To spend time each day with your soul focused on God and in fellowship with Him and do not consciously disobey Him is the base upon which you will experience real life.

"Understand," continued George, "that one of the things God wants to give is to give us a life here on earth that is full, satisfying, and good. He is not opposed to that. God is not against the good life. He wants that for us all. It is just that He realizes that if we are going to experience this abundant life, then we will find it in Him. Miss Him and you will miss life at its best. Find Him and you will find life at its best. It is not that these others things in our life are unimportant to Him. He cares about them. He will help us with them. It is just that He wants us to get things in their right place. 'Seek first the kingdom of God and these other things will be added to you.' Even if you get all of these other things and miss communion with Him, you will miss the real meaning of life. Jesus said it plainly, 'What good will it be for a man if he gains the whole world, yet forfeits his soul? Or what can a man give in exchange for his soul?' (Matt. 16:26.) Spiritual values outweigh temporal values. Kingdom values are more important than worldly values. Real life is found in spiritual experience rather than fleshly pleasures. So in our prayer life, the need for the soul to be in touch and fellowship with God predominates.

"**Prayer is learning to receive what God wants to give.** Mostly God wants to give Himself, for He knows that in fellowship with Him, we will experience life at its best. Jesus kept on saying this. He said, 'I have come that they may have life, and have it to the full' (John 10:10). He said, 'I am the bread of life' (John 6:48). Jesus said, 'He that drinks the water that I shall give him shall never thirst again. Indeed the water I give him will become in him a spring of water welling up to eternal life' (John 4:14). Jesus said, 'I am the light of the world.' Jesus said, 'I am the way the truth and the life.' Jesus was continually pointing to Himself as the way to real, full, and abundant life. God knows this, and so what He wants to give more than anything else is to give Himself, for in this we find true and full life.

"You can see that, this largely answers the question, "What is God's will?' We largely already know what God's will is. We are well aware of His priorities and values. And our prayer life should be a vital point at which these values and priorities are realized. We know God wants to give Himself. We know that God wants to share His love, strength, and power and joy with us. We know that in His presence, there is fullness of joy, and at His right hand, there are pleasures for evermore. So let's reflect this in our prayer life. Then most of the issues about which we should pray and what is God's will will be resolved. The fact is that we are already aware of what God wants and what He will give. The rest will fade in importance, and we will be much more balanced in how we seek them. In the matters that we still do not know what God's will is, we will be much more receptive to His guidance and direction. We will be much more sensitive to the voice of His inner spirit, because we are in contact with Him and are learning to listen to His voice. **Prayer is learning to receive what God wants to give."**

With that statement, George finished his dissertation on the essence of prayer. "Are there any questions?" he asked.

"Yes!" I said. "It seems to me that you are saying that it is immature for us to be blindly praying about everything, in ignorant disregard as to whether it is God's will for us or not. We are to become much more sensitive about the things we pray for and put effort into trying to determine if we are praying in the will of God."

"That is correct," said George.

"And," I continued, "as we mature and learn the joy and power of getting close to Him in fellowship, more and more of our time will be spent simply enjoying His presence and sensing the peace of His presence in our soul."

"Yes!" said George.

"And since what He wants to give more than anything else is Himself and His graces, do you ever then get to the place where all you do in prayer is flow into His presence and enjoy His fellowship and you never ask anything about your personal life, or the needs of living in this world?"

"No!" said George emphatically. "What I am urging upon you is a balance. As you mature in prayer, it is my hope that you will so enjoy your fellowship with God and your communion with Him that you will find it easy and more profitable to spend more of your prayer time engrossed in talking to Him and listening to Him talk to you. I want you to taste the beauty of communion with Him and delight your soul in His presence. This experience will make prayer rich and refreshing to your whole being. But that is not all of prayer. He indeed urges us to bring our needs and petitions to Him. So prayer should always have a part when we humbly present our petitions to Him and talk to Him about the concerns of our life. But if all we do in prayer is present our petitions and needs to Him, it is unbalanced. But equally, it is unbalanced if we fellowship with Him and enjoy His presence but never request anything of Him. You must not imagine that it is ultraspiritual to not ask for anything. You remember the talk you had on the Lord's Prayer at the First School of Prayer? That instruction told us what we should spend our time at in prayer and what the themes of our prayer life should be like. An important part of that prayer is about our relationship with God and our involvement in His Kingdom and His glory. But equally, on balance, we are told to make personal petitions about daily bread and not being tempted and so on. The secret is balance."

"So," I said, "you should keep a balance in prayer. Fifty percent in worship, fellowship, and enjoying His presence, and 50 percent in presenting our petitions?"

"No!" replied George. "Please do not make any such legal or formal division of time. Your own soul and spirit will guide you here on what you should spend your time at. Day by day and week by week, as the circumstances of life change, and the state of your heart changes, you will want to respond to the inner needs of your heart. Some days you will have pressing problems and needs that you want to talk to Him about. On these days you may spend a good deal of your prayer time, asking about these things that are urgent and necessary for you. On other days, you will be so hungry for communion with Him that you will spend much of your time glorying in His presence and enjoying His fellowship. There should not be a legal breakdown of time spent on the various aspects of prayer. Be led by your heart. Respond to the needs of your soul for that day. But whatever you do, keep the balance.

"Jesus urged us to ask God for things and to make our petitions known to God. Did He not say 'Ask and it will be given you; seek and you will find; knock and the door will be opened to you. For everyone who asks receives; he who seeks finds; and to him who knocks, the door will be opened' (Matt. 7:7-8). Jesus Himself prayed for the disciples. He prayed for Jerusalem. He prayed for the church. So He Himself had His petitions to set before God. But along with that, He had wonderful times of fellowship and communion with His heavenly Father. He found the balance. While I do not give out any homework for this class, I would urge you, when you have time after class to examine Jesus's prayer that is recorded in John, 17. Take note as you read the prayer how much of the prayer is an expression and affirmation of the relationship between Jesus and the Father. Even all of the petitions flow out of that relationship. The fundamental factor in the prayer is the ongoing unity between Jesus and the Father. When you explore the City of Prayer, one of the places I am urging you to visit is the Intercession Booth. There you will find that an important function of prayer is the prayer for others. We should certainly be holding other people up in prayer and praying about their spiritual needs and the state of their soul. People with a real burden for intercession will spend a great deal of time burdened and praying for others. So the need for balance is there in our prayer lives.

"What I have been trying to impress upon you, however, is that as you mature and as your heart gets closer to the heart of God and your spirit begins to reflect His Spirit more and more, you will find that what you consider your urgent and immediate needs will begin to change. You will have a greater desire for Him. You will long more for His closeness. You will need the refreshing of His presence in your soul every day. And this will go on increasing and building as your spiritual life develops. And this is moving in the direction He wants you to go. You are learning more and more to receive what He wants to give. The apostle Paul states this in his own vivid way when he says in Philippians 3:7-8, 'But whatever was to my profit I now consider loss for the sake of Christ. What is more, I consider everything a loss compared to the surpassing greatness of knowing Christ Jesus my Lord, for whose sake I have lost all things. I consider them rubbish, that I may gain Christ.'"

With that, George was ready to dismiss the class. He said, "This afternoon you will have your first taste of the City of Prayer. I remind you that the first place to visit is the Central Cathedral. You will find maps and directions on the table at the back of the classroom. Take your time. Absorb the meaning and atmosphere of the city, and examine the Central Cathedral very closely. And remember, I will be here if you have any questions or concerns that you wish to talk about. God bless you as you enter the City of Prayer."

TOPICS FOR DISCUSSION—CHAPTER ELEVEN

1. George compares learning to pray to his little daughter learning to walk:

    - What are some of the qualities needed?
    - What are some of the discouragements?
    - How long does it take?

2. Discuss the qualities that help us to receive from God what He wants to give?
3. Are what we want to receive and what God wants to give always in harmony?
4. What is the solid base upon which we build our faith that God will answer prayer?
5. What does God want to give most of all? Is this what we want to receive?

CHAPTER TWELVE

THE CENTRAL CATHEDRAL

Helen, Alvin, John, and I decided to make the journey to the Central Cathedral together. It was with great interest and excitement that we set out and for the first time walked the streets of the City of Prayer. At first, as George had told us, the city seemed like any other city. There were houses, businesses, parks, and people. The streets were crowded with cars. Everybody seemed to be going or coming. Our first impression was that this was just a normal busy city. But soon I began to sense an unseen but different spirit. Outwardly, the city seemed to function like any other city, but I was becoming aware of a different atmosphere here. All of the normal signs of city life were there, but underlying the activity there was a culture of peace and contentment. Indeed being here seemed to have a quieting effect on my own spirit. I wanted to enter into the atmosphere of the city. I was anxious not to exhibit any impatient or hostile attitude that would contradict the overall peace that surrounded me. I had the uncomfortable feeling that if I was to act in any stressful or irritable manner, I would be out of step with the general demeanor around me. I did not want to behave in any way that would be interpreted as stressful or anxious.

I wondered how my companions were reacting to the city. I looked at Helen and could tell that she was really enjoying herself. "You know," she said, "I feel safe. There is no sense of lurking danger here. I could walk these streets in open freedom at any time."

"I feel completely relaxed," said John. "There seems to be an absence of competition and a presence of courtesy and thoughtfulness."

Alvin reacted a little differently. He said, "I am comfortably at home here. Everyone keeps the rules. They appear to have made an agreement that they will respond to one another with kindness and treat one another with honesty and integrity."

"These are normal people living normal lives," I commented, "but they seem to be able to carry the spirit and atmosphere of prayer with them into their everyday lives. They do all of the things everybody else has to do to earn a living, but they appear to have an awareness of God about them and conduct their affairs from a deep sense of integrity and respect for others."

"I am sure that they have problems and stresses like all of us have," replied John, "but they are able to handle these stresses with confidence and strength."

"I believe that the peace and joy of their fellowship with God spills over and fills their every day life with a sense of His presence and Spirit," said Helen.

Farther on up the street, there had been a car accident in which someone had been hurt. As we gathered in to watch this scene, I noticed that amongst those involved in the mishap, no one was angry, or protesting innocence, or placing blame. I also noticed that nobody passed by in indifference. Nor was there a reluctance to get involved in the situation. Everybody wanted to be helpful. There is no doubt, I thought, these people are reacting to life and to one another quite differently. I remembered what George, our teacher, had said about the city, that it was a normal city and the people carried on normal lives, but what made it different was that they tried to carry the spirit of prayer with them into their everyday living. I thought, *Yes, they are learning what it means to handle the demands of life while maintaining the presence of God in their hearts.*

As we continued to walk the streets toward the cathedral, one or two other minor incidents illustrated for me the general spirit that seemed to pervade life in the City of Prayer. It was a hot day, and the walk was making us warm. We decided to stop and buy some ice cream. We inadvertently paid the girl too much for our ice cream. As soon as she realized this the girl brought to matter to our attention and quickly straightened the transaction out. A little farther on we noticed an elderly lady having difficulty crossing the busy street. Two young men quickly came to her rescue and assisted her across the road. At one point we were a little confused as to the best way to get to the cathedral. When we stopped a man to ask directions, we were surprised at his courtesy and pleasantness. These were incidental happenings, but they all added up to an atmosphere that made the city easy and comfortable. We felt accepted.

We were making good progress toward the Central Cathedral. As we approached it, we could see that it was a dominant building in the city. It was a large, solid, grey stone building, well constructed in cathedral style. Its main feature was a great spire that towered over the other buildings around it. This tower, with a cross on the top, could be seen from almost anywhere in the city. It was a landmark that gave people a direction and reference point from anywhere in town. We climbed the imposing stone steps to the massive front doors of the cathedral. The thick wooden doors swung open with surprising ease when we pushed them, and we entered the cathedral. After the noise and bustle of the city streets outside, it was cool and quiet in here. Our footsteps echoed as we walked over the stone floor.

The central auditorium of the cathedral was awesome and imposing. The vaulted ceiling towered above us. Large, thick, decorated pillars ranged around the outskirts of the large worship auditorium. The front section of the auditorium was dominated by a broad, expensive, but tastefully decorated altar. Over the altar hung a very large crucifix, carved beautifully in a dark hardwood. The whole auditorium was designed to direct attention to this great figure of the crucified Savior.

There were a number of people in the cathedral. Most of them were quietly meditating or praying. We were not sure where to go, but a man in a brown ankle-length, monklike gown approached us and asked if he could help. We explained that we were new to the city and that we had been encouraged by the teacher to come here and visit the cathedral.

"Aah, yes!" nodded the attendant, "it is very important that you start your exploration of the city by coming here. This Central Cathedral is at the center of the city. You noticed the high spire that reaches up from the roof of the cathedral?" We nodded. "That high spire can be seen from all over the city. People use it as a reference point and a guide to find their way around. The cathedral is the focal point of the city. The spire rises from the center of the cathedral. On the floor directly underneath the spire is a circle that marks the center of the cathedral. We call this circle simply the Circle of God's Will. I want you to understand two things about the Circle of God's Will. First, I will ask each of you to stand in the middle of the circle. For us, the Circle of God's Will is an important symbol and represents being in the center of God's will. If you stand in the middle of the circle you will experience in a vivid way what it is like to be in the center of God's will. Second, the circle is the reference point from which all directions and journeys start. It represents for us the fact that all effective prayers and explorations in the prayer life must start from, and be done in, the will of God.

"I would like to show you where the Circle of God's Will is. I would encourage each of you to stand in the center of the circle. Once you have done that I would like to explain its significance. After you have experienced the Circle of God's Will, why don't we meet at the back of the cathedral and talk there?"

We were quiet and hushed as we followed our guide to the central part of the cathedral. There on the floor was a beautifully inlaid white and black marble circle. The central piece was made of a very white marble. The margins were black marble. This circle, we understood, was a symbol representing the center of God's will.

"I do not wish you to rush this experience," said our guide. "Each one should stand at the center of the circle by themselves. The rest of you must wait and pray. Take as long as you like in the circle. It is meant to give you an idea of what it is like for you to live in the center of God's will. Living in the center of God's will is vital to living for God and for the effectiveness of our prayer life. This will give you a clear and condensed understanding of what it is like to be right in the center of God's will. The whole City of Prayer revolved around the Circle of God's Will. I expect you will, each one, find it a very vivid and impressive experience. I do not want you to talk to each other. Even after you have been in the Circle of God's Will, I do not want you to share your feelings or responses with each other. But after all of you have stood in the circle, then I would like you to meet me at the back of the cathedral and we will talk about it, and you can share in each others experience at that time."

With that, our guide quietly walked away, leaving us staring at the circle on the floor. Nobody moved. The stateliness of the vast building seemed to fill us with a quiet awesomeness. We sensed that we were confronted with a life-changing moment. No one wanted to break the solemnity of the atmosphere. We stood quietly and absorbed the spirit of the place. The importance of stepping into the center of the circle seemed to hush our sprits.

After a while I looked at my companions and said, "Who goes first?" The unspoken expectation seemed to be that I would go first. Feeling a bit like Columbus must have felt when he first stepped on to the soil of the new world, I stepped into the center of the circle. Our guide had said it would probably be a very vivid experience. He did not exaggerate. As I stood there, I was gradually possessed by the conscious reality of being in the very center of God's will. I was exactly where God wanted me to be. I was overcome by a deep feeling of well-being. Assurance flooded my heart, "this is what I was born for. This is exactly where I should be. This is the most fulfilling moment of my life." The center of His will. I lifted my eyes up and looked into the great vaulted ceiling. Almost unconsciously I lifted my arms up, and I stood with hands raised, looking up toward heaven. Who can describe it? Joy filled my heart. Sublime satisfaction flowed over my soul. The center of God's will was my home. I felt I did not need to seek or to wander any more. Such joy, peace, and well-being poured into me that I could scarcely contain it. It was overwhelming.

I do not know how long I stood there gazing upward with hands raised. I was "lost in wonder, love and praise." But gradually the waves of joy began to subside, and I became more aware of my surroundings. I realized that my companions were still there and were waiting for their chance to step into the Circle of God's Will. With my soul still overflowing, I stepped aside to let one of my friends take their place in the circle.

John was the next one to step into the circle. I could tell right away that John was also caught up in some kind of ecstasy. But I was surprised because he seemed to be experiencing something quite different to what I experienced. We never talked, but I watched his body language. This body language expressed a different kind of emotion than the ones that I had felt. John stood with his face looking upward. He also had lost awareness of where he was or that he had an audience. His whole body appeared to be filled with a pent up, dynamic energy. His fists were clenched. He swung his clenched fists over his chest continually and shouted, "Yes! Yes! Yes!" He seemed to be filled with a power and energy that was superhuman.

If I was surprised by John's reaction to the Circle of God's Will, I was even more surprised by Helen's. When she stepped into the circle, she bowed her head and soon began to sob. Her shoulders heaved. Her hands covered her face. Tears ran down her cheeks and dripped off her chin. She sobbed and sobbed. It was not, however, a sobbing of grief. She was not in pain or being burdened by some great weight. Her sobs were sobs of another kind. I could not quite describe what I was seeing, except that it was good. She was in the throes of a wonderful experience whatever it was.

Then it was Alvin's turn. He too was quite different. Alvin fell on his knees and lowered his head until his forehead touched the ground. He never moved from this position. He seemed absolutely quiet and still. After a while, still on his knees, he lifted his body straight. Raised his face and hands to heaven in an attitude of worship. His lips moved, but no words came out. Ecstasy shone from his face. He was lost. Then he began to whisper the words of a song. It was a well-known hymn of worship:

> Praise God, from whom all blessings flow.
> Praise Him all creatures here below.
> Praise Him above, ye heav'nly host.
> Praise Father, Son, and Holy Ghost.[1]

We respected the guide's request that we not talk to each other about our experiences until we met with him at the back of the cathedral. All we knew was that, within the Circle of God's Will, we had experienced a great experience. The center of God's will was a vivid and powerful place. We had been so engrossed in our experiences that we had hardly been aware of the passage of time. We were surprised, however, to discover that a great deal of time had passed, so we moved quickly toward the back of the cathedral for our meeting with the guide.

When we gathered around the guide, he smiled at us and said, "I have a small private room over here. Let's go in there and talk." We followed him into the room, and each took a seat. When we were all comfortable he said, "First, let's each one tell what he or she experienced in the Circle of God's Will. He turned to me first, and I tried to explain the experience of sheer unalloyed joy that had possessed me. Then John described his experience. He said he was fired with a tremendous feeling of power and energy. He was inspired by visions of what God wanted him to do for the Kingdom. "Nothing seemed impossible," he said. "I just kept on saying 'Yes! Yes! Yes! I want to serve You.'"

Helen reported, "With me, it seemed as if I was filled with great waves of love. They seemed to role over my soul until I felt that my heart would melt for love. I loved God. I loved people. I loved creation. I was overwhelmed by a great stream of liquid love flowing through me."

"What I experienced," said Alvin, "was an inexpressible sense of worship and praise. I felt my heart bursting with adoration and wonder at God's greatness. I felt I was rising on wings into heaven and worshiping Him there. I wanted to join with the great chorus of heaven and worship Him. Worship Him! Worship Him!"

While all of us seemed at a loss to describe our experiences at the Circle of God's Will, and were vainly grasping for words to describe it, the guide seemed to be satisfied with what we had experienced. "I am glad you have each had such a wonderful experience in the center of God's will. It is designed to let you know what a wonderful thing it is to be in the center of God's will. Today was just a visit. It gave you a taste. But you can live in the center of God's will as a lifestyle. Of course, the intensity you felt today would not continue. But it gave you an experience, so that you might know that to live consciously in the center of God's will is probably the most soul-satisfying, and reality-producing, experience we can have here on earth.

"While all of you were in the Circle of God's Will, all of you responded differently. Each reacted to the center in his or her own way. One was overwhelmed by joy, one was filled with love, one was inspired to serve, one was lost in worship. The Circle of God's Will is wonderful for all, but each experiences it differently. Each personality is treated as a unique individual by God. God reacts to meet the needs of each unique person, so He responds differently to all. But since He knows us all fully and completely, His will for each one is communicated in a way that fits that personality. To stand in the middle of the circle represents being at the center of God's will. So let me tell you some things about the center of God's will that will be important for you to know in your prayer experience and indeed for your whole walk with God.

"First, as you have already experienced, the center of God's will is a wonderful place to be. It is exciting, fulfilling, and satisfying. There is no experience more fulfilling to the human heart than to consciously be in the center of God's will. Once you have experienced this, all else will fade in importance and significance to you. The pleasures and values of earth will recede. Your joy and delight will be to do the will of God. You will join the psalmist who testified, 'I delight to do thy will, O my God' (Ps. 40:8 KGV.) Jesus expressed the same thing often. He said to the disciples, 'My food is to do the will of Him that sent me and to finish His work' (John 4:34.) This is food for the soul. Delight for the heart. This is what we were created for, and we will never find a more abundant life that being in the center of God's will."

"But if it is so great, why do we find it so hard?" asked Helen. I was not only surprised by Helen's question but also by the aggressive tone in her voice. Her question seemed to be out of keeping with the spirit that the rest of us was feeling.

"There are two main reasons why some people perceive God's will to be very difficult. The two reasons are lack of commitment and lack of faith. The first is a lack of commitment, or an unwillingness to yield to the will of God. The real pain and struggle that some people experience is not the pain of being in the center of God's will, but rather the pain of having to yield up their own will in order to get into the center of God's will. This yielding up of self-will can be an excruciating battle for some. In fact the apostle Paul describes it as dying a very painful death. It is like a crucifixion—one of the most painful forms of death. He says, 'I [the old selfish me] have been crucified with Christ and I [my old selfish me] no longer live, but Christ lives in me. The life I live in the body, I live by faith in the Son of God, who loved me and gave himself for me' (Gal. 2:20) (brackets my own). The same language of pain and death is used by Paul in Romans 6:6, where he says, 'For we know that our old self was crucified with him so that the body of sin might be done away with, that we should no longer be slaves to sin—because anyone who has died has been freed from sin' (Rom. 6:6-7). So the pain that some experience is not the pain of being in the center of God's will—that is rich and beautiful—but the pain of dying out to our own selfish will. To experience the center of God's will, you first must die out to your own selfish will. That means yielding all to Him. That means surrendering your will and desires to His will and desires. This call to surrender is not easy since we have developed the habit of doing our own will and giving our own desires' precedence, but it is necessary, if we are to experience the blessing of being in the center of God's will as a way of life. Jesus expressed the principle clearly when he said, 'If anyone would come after me, he must deny himself and take up his cross and follow me. For whoever wants to save his life will lose it, but whoever loses his life for me will find it' (Matt. 16:24-25).

"The second reason we may think God's will is painful is lack of faith. We don't believe that God's will is the best thing for us. We still think our own will and our own desires must be better for us than God's will and desires. There is a fear that if we give up our own will, we are giving up the greatest things in life. We are risking all that matters to us on the faith that God's way will be better for us than our own way. This feeling of fear comes basically from a lack of faith. To have faith in the character and generosity of God is to simply believe that God is love. If you cast your mind back, Helen, to the First School of Prayer when you were discussing the petition 'Your will be done on earth as it is in heaven' I think the teacher there told you that God, in His love, wants to give us what is the very best for us. God is rich and bountiful. He wants to bestow great blessings and grace upon us. He does not want to hold back anything that is best for us. God is powerful. He has the wisdom and the power to bring about His will in our lives. Do you remember that teaching, Helen?"

Helen nodded but made no comment.

"So," continued the attendant, "when we insist in pursuing our own way and our own desires, we are forfeiting all of the love and grace and blessings that God has planned for us. The richest and most blessed life is the life that is lived in the center of God's will. If you believe firmly in the love and generosity of God and in His undying goodwill, then to yield to His will is not so difficult. Faith in the loving kindness of our Heavenly Father would express itself in the simple trust that the path He wishes for us is the best possible path for us to take. We might think we know better, but faith tells us that our ability to understand and to see into the future is very flawed. His ability to choose the right direction for us is not in question. The Psalmist expresses this faith when he says, 'You have made known to me the path of life, you will fill me with joy in your presence, with eternal pleasures at your right hand' (Ps. 16:11)."

Helen thought about this for a while and then stated, "But if I yield to His will, He may ask me to do all sorts of things that I don't want to do?"

I was mystified by Helen's attitude. I thought she had come to terms with all of this already, but obviously she was still troubled about it in her own spirit. I scolded her by saying, "But, Helen, you are talking just like Janet talked at the First School of Prayer. She let her fears of what God might ask her to do if she yielded to His will overcome her faith, and she lost the ability to make any more progress. Can't you believe that God is your friend and not your enemy?"

Helen was not pleased with my comment. She said, "I know God is not my enemy, but I still find it rather scary to give up control of my life to Him."

"What you can be confident of," said the attendant, "is that God will not ask you to do anything that in the long run will harm your soul or your experience with Him. He loves you and understands you better than you love and understand yourself. His purpose is to give you the best and most effective and most satisfying life possible and in the end to save your soul for all eternity. If you think you can do better than that then go ahead, but if you believe in His wisdom and goodness, then the best thing you can do is to yield to Him and believe in His will. When all is said and done, Helen, the very best place for you is in the center of God's will."

This challenge seemed to quieten Helen. For the moment she had no more questions.

"The second purpose of the Central Cathedral," continued the guide, "is to give you a starting place for your exploration of the City of Prayer. It is important when you move out to explore different features in the city that you begin at the Circle of God's Will. In the City of Prayer, all direction and reference points start here. I warn you, that if you begin to explore the features of the city without first coming to the Circle of His Will, then you are likely to get confused and lost. All good directions start in the center of the will of God. It is important that whatever you pray about or seek in prayer that you begin the journey and the exploration by coming here and starting at the Circle of God's Will.

This experience in learning your way about the City of Prayer reflects the reality in your prayer life. If you start any enterprise in prayer and neglect the center of God's will, it is likely that you will not accomplish what you want to accomplish or get to the destination that you wish to reach. In prayer, everything reaches out from the center of God's will. Your faith is based on the center of God's will. The appropriateness of your petitions is based on the center of God's will. The prayer promises are built on the center of God's will. The priorities in prayer come from the center of God's will. If you neglect God's will in prayer, then you will likely end up being confused and disappointed. These points, you may remember, were emphasized by George at the School of Prayer.

"So," said the guide, "I am strongly advising you not to neglect the matter of the center of God's will. In exploring the City of Prayer, I urge you to begin each exploration by coming to the Circle of God's Will and start there. To many it seems difficult and unnecessary to go to the bother of coming here and starting here in their prayer explorations. They want to just move ahead on the basis of their own desires and their own ideas. They think they know the way. Only they find that it is too easy to get lost. They miss many of the places of blessing and power and reality, because they jumped ahead and did not take the time and effort to begin at the center of God's will."

Helen, who was obviously having difficulty with this whole matter, interrupted again and asked, "Does that mean that if you are not sure whether something is God's will or not, that you should not pray about it?"

The guide was clearly not going to make it easy for Helen. I think he understood that Helen's questions were not asked in order to seek new information but were coming from her own inner agitation over not being willing to accept what she already knew.

The guide said slowly but with great emphasis, "Helen, I think you already know, and you have certainly already been told, that if you want to make significant progress in your prayer life, if you want to develop a close relationship with God in prayer, if you want to have a powerful prayer life that achieves things for God and for others, if you want to experience definite responses from God to your prayers, if you want to be a person of faith and trust, then what I am saying to you is that you must give serious attention to praying from the center of God's will. To blindly push ahead in your prayers without first seeking His will is immature, impatient, and can be selfish.

"I have to tell you that many have come here to the City of Prayer earnestly seeking a real and effective prayer life, but have neglected this matter of the will of God and have spent a great deal of time aimlessly wandering about the City of Prayer. Sometimes they happen to strike the right place and enjoy some blessing of the city, but more often they simply grope about, hoping for the best, wishing for all kinds of things in prayer that they never receive, blindly seeking out realities that they never quite find, looking for power and grace from prayer that never quite comes. They never realize the power and the promise of prayer, and this is largely because they neglect to seek out the will of God. They pray like someone walking around in a fog. They know they want to get somewhere, but in the fog they cannot see their way clearly and keep on bumping into obstacles. They find they are not getting where they want to go, and they spend enormous amounts of time and energy just going around in perplexing circles. This blind hope that what we are asking for is God's will but, never really knowing, is not designed for us to make progress in our prayer life, but will condemn us to a shallow and inconsequential prayer life that hopes for the best but is often disappointed. In the end, these people usually have to decide that either the City of Prayer is not for them, or else they must make the commitment to yield themselves to the will of God and finally find the refreshing power of a real prayer life."

Helen was becoming increasingly frustrated. "Well! I think a lot of my prayers are prayed like that. I just do not know if what I am asking for is the will of God or not. In fact I think a lot of the people that I hear praying are praying in the same way, for they always end up their prayers by saying 'If it be Thy will.' It seems to me that they are saying, 'I don't know whether this is Your will or not, so answer it if it be Thy will.' So," continued Helen, "you have not answered my question yet. If you do not know whether it is God's will or not, should you pray about it?"

"OK, Helen," said the guide patiently. "What you are asking is a very important question, and many people ask it. I am not sure I will be able to answer it to your satisfaction, but let me try. I will say four things about it, for this is not nearly so difficult and complicated as people make it out to be. The first two things I will say about it you have already heard, so I will only touch on them briefly. The other two may be new to you.

"First, it is probable, Helen, that you know a whole lot more about the will of God than you think. Let me ask you to go back and remember what you learned in the School of Prayer from your teacher George. He talked about prayer as **learning to receive what God wants to give.** So the important essence in prayer is to know what God wants to give, or, what is the will of God? Do you remember Helen how he answered the question, 'What does God want to give?'

"Yes," said Helen. "He said that most of all God wants to give Himself. He wants to share His love, joy, peace, power, and holiness with us, so that we experience and receive what He is."

"Exactly," said the guide. "So a whole lot of what God wants to give is centered in that. He wants to flow into our life with His presence, His power, His love, and His Spirit. That is His priority, because He knows that this is what we need more than anything else. A great deal of what He wants us to experience is summed up in this concept of general revelation. So in actual fact, Helen, we already know what most of his will is."

Here the guide paused and gently looked at Helen and continued, "If, however, we do not share in God's priority system, if we do not primarily seek His Kingdom first, if we neglect these great spiritual values, in order to get going with our own lives and agendas, then we will begin to deemphasize God's values and desires in order to give front stage to our own. When this happens, then our prayers will begin to neglect God's obvious priorities and largely focus on the bits of God's will that we don't know. This is an unbalanced and unenlightened way to pray. In may in fact be our own selfishness asserting itself by trying to make prayer into a tool for getting God to do what we want, rather than getting us to enter into what God wants us to experience. The essence of prayer is **learning to receive what God wants to give.** So that is first Helen, most of us already really know a whole lot of what God's will and wishes are. If we are not interested in pursuing these values with God, then that is a reflection of our own faulty value system, and the remedy is to move our values into harmony with His values. If we do not center our prayer lives in prioritizing His values, then we will miss the essential point of prayer

The second thing that has already been impressed upon you on your journey into prayer is that it is our responsibility to make conscious efforts to understand what the will of God is. We are not encouraged to jump into prayer being uninformed and ignorant about the will of God. A responsibility is laid on us to seek, know, and understand what the will of God is and pray accordingly. I would make a comparison between praying in the will of God and praying rather blindly by presenting our requests without knowing whether it is God's will or not, to gambling with your money and investing your money. Prayer is not a gamble, it is an investment. In a gamble you sacrifice your money on a chance. You hope you will win, but you have no idea whether you will or not. It is like throwing the dice on to the table and hoping the right numbers come up. When you pray as a gamble, you say, 'If it is the will of God, He will answer. If it is not the will of God, He won't. I have no idea, but I'll take the chance.' It is a chance. It is a gamble. It is a random guess, and you wish by good fortune, not by faith, that things will turn out wonderfully well. And like all gambles, we find that occasionally they do, but most often we are disappointed and unhappy with the results. Prayer is not a gamble where you throw something on the table hoping it is God's will, and if the right numbers happen to turn up, you can claim it was God's will, and He answered prayer, but if the right numbers don't turn up, you can pacify yourself by saying, 'I guess it wasn't God's will, but I will try again.' When we gamble, we can risk a lot and not know what the outcome is going to be. Prayer is not meant to be a gamble. It is not throwing the dice and saying 'If it is God's will, it will happen, and we will all be happy, and if it is not God's will, then we will just have to be humble and accept it.'

Prayer is better compared to an investment. In an investment, after thoughtful consideration, you give something of value in the faith that in the process of time it will increase in value and stature. Investments usually increase more slowly, but they do increase. After a lifetime of gambling you are likely to end up poor and diminished. After a lifetime of wise investment, you are likely to end up richer and secure. Prayer is an investment. You invest in the Kingdom of God, and the values and treasures of that Kingdom grow and develop. With an investment you do not suddenly become rich overnight without effort or sacrifice, but your investment in the values and priorities of the Kingdom of God increases, and your treasure grows as your experience with God matures. So, Helen, invest in prayer, by developing what you know to be the will of God. Do not gamble in prayer by asking for things you have no idea whether God wants to give or not. It is wise, Helen, to invest in the values and riches of the Kingdom of God that you know about and not waste your prayer resources on blind chance. You will find they grow and increase. To blindly gamble in prayer, may on occasion bring results, but over the long run, will impoverish you and weaken your faith.

"Now, let's go on and look at the parts of life in which we do not know the will of God. We have already indicated that we already know the great values of the Kingdom of God in general revelation and should be pursuing them primarily in our prayer life. There are, however, issues that come up from day to day that are particular and personal to us, that are not covered in the general instructions regarding God's will. We would like God's guidance and perhaps need God's help for these special situations. We have problems that need to be dealt with. We have needs that need to be met. We have people that we love who seem to be going astray, and we want God to do something about it. We want God to be part of our lives and help us to live successfully."

"Yes," cried Helen rather angrily, "what about all of that? There is more to life than being spiritual and seeking God's interests. What about my interests? Doesn't God care about them?"

I was surprised at Helen's continued agitation. At this point I began to realize that Helen had arrived at a critical moment in her journey into prayer. Her problem was not lack of knowledge but an unwillingness to accept where that knowledge was leading. She was at the point of a spiritual crisis. A crisis of commitment and faith.

The attendant, I think, realized the real motivation behind Helen's resistance for he exhibited great patience and understanding. "Of course God is interested, and certainly He cares. But let me repeat it again, Helen, He realizes that it is in your best interests and also necessary, if you are to build a satisfying and fulfilling life, that you enjoy and experience real fellowship with Him. If you fail in that, then no matter what you accomplish in other aspects of life, you will end up missing the 'abundant life' that He promises. So let's look at the areas in our lives where we may not know what God's will is. There are a great number of issues large and small that come up each day for which there is no implicit instructions or guidance given in the Bible or in any word from God. What are we to do with all of these things?"

"Now you are getting to where I want to go," said Helen.

Our guide smiled and shook his head. "Listen carefully Helen, for at first you may not think I am going where you want to go. Some of the things we have said about praying in the will of God you have already heard from previous teachers. I think, however, you may not have heard this third thing I want to say about it. Do you know, Helen, one of the prayers that God has promised to answer? He will always answer this prayer?" It was a rhetorical question. The guide was not looking for an answer. He continued, "You find in the Bible in the book of James a rather remarkable promise that does not have attached to it too many conditions. James says, 'If any of you lacks wisdom, he should ask God, who gives generously to all without finding fault, and it will be given to him. But when he asks, he must believe and not doubt, because he who doubts is like a wave of the sea, blown and tossed by the wind. That man should not think he will receive anything from the Lord; this is a double-minded man, unstable in all he does' (James 1:5-8). God is promising to give us wisdom. Why, Helen, do you think God wants to give us wisdom?"

"Because he wants us to make wise and mature choices in life by understanding what is really important."

"That is a really good answer. God has promised to give us wisdom, because He wants us to make wise choices in life, and be wise enough to follow the correct priorities. So God is making wisdom available to us, because He respects our ability to make choices and decisions for ourselves. In other words God is not going to make every decision for us, while we simply respond like puppets on a string. He expects us to develop the responsibility and the maturity of making many wise and correct choices for ourselves. In fact this is part of growing up in spiritual things and maturing in our spiritual abilities.

"When we were young children, our parents made many of the decisions for us—what we should wear, what we should eat, where we should go, etc. But as we grew up and became more responsible, we began to make many of these decisions for ourselves, until we reached maturity, and then our parents made very few decisions for us, they expected us, as adults to make these decisions for ourselves. It is all part of growing up.

"Hopefully, our parents instilled into us the correct guidance systems so that we largely made the correct decisions and embraced the best values in life. But right or wrong, we became responsible adults and made our own decisions. So God wants us to grow up. He wants to see us develop as mature, responsible and reliable Christians, and so He does not plan to make every decision for us, but He will provide us with wisdom, if we ask, so that we will largely make wise and correct choices in life. This is part of developing a mature and sound experience. For our part as adults, we do not expect our parents to micromanage every detail of our lives. I do not ask my father what I should wear, or what I should eat, or where I should go. He expects me to make these and many other decisions for myself. It would, however, be proper for me to seek my father's advice and guidance in some of the major and difficult issues of life. What I really needed my father to do was to give me the training and discipline so that I could make many of these decisions with strength and wisdom. My ability to make mature decisions is a sign of grown-up responsibility. Any adult who keeps on running to his father and mother every time there is a difficult issue in his or her life is not really accepting proper responsibility and needs to learn to grow up. So God expects that as we advance in our Christian experience, we will make many choices for ourselves, based on the priority system and value system that He has outlined for us in the Christian way. God will not guide us in every detail of our lives. He will, however, provide wisdom and guidance systems to help us make the right choices. But He expects us to be grown up enough to make decisions on our own. The secret for a lot of Divine guidance is not hearing voices from God telling us what to do but an instilled wisdom and value system that helps us to make wise choices.

"In fact, if you check it out, you will find that wisdom was one of the things the apostles prayed for when they prayed for the Christians in the early church. Paul prayed for the Ephesian Christians, 'I keep asking that the God of our Lord Jesus Christ the glorious Father, may give you the spirit of wisdom and revelation, so that you may know him better' (Eph. 1:17). The prayer is that the Christian may be given wisdom so that they understand God and His ways better. Understanding God and His ways would help us make better and wiser choices in our lives. A similar prayer is offered for the Philippians, 'And this is my prayer: that your love may abound more and more in knowledge and depth of insight (*wisdom*) so that you may be able to discern what is best and may be pure and blameless until the day of Christ, filled with the fruit of righteousness that comes through Jesus Christ—to the glory and praise of God' (Phil. 1:9-11). According to this prayer, discerning what is the right and correct way to go is largely the function of wisdom and knowledge in understanding God and His ways.

"The importance of wisdom is constantly revealed in a number of stories in the Bible. King Solomon in the Old Testament is often praised for his wisdom and understanding. The story is told of Solomon in 1 Kings, chapter 3. Early in his reign, God appeared to Solomon in a dream and said, 'Ask for whatever you want me to give you.' Solomon, in response to this remarkably generous offer, did not ask for long life, or for riches or for success and power, he asked God for wisdom to wisely rule his people. God was very pleased with this choice and said, 'Since you have asked for this and not for long life or wealth for yourself, nor have asked for the death of your enemies but for discernment in administering justice, I will do what you have asked. I will give you a wise and discerning heart, so that there will never have been anyone like you, nor will there ever be. Moreover, I will give you what you have not asked for—both riches and honor, so that in your life time you will have no equal among kings' (1 Kings 3:11-13). Clearly in God's value system, wisdom tops wealth, power, success, and good health. The understanding was that God did not tell Solomon what to do in every situation but gave him wisdom to make correct decisions on his own.

"In the life and development of Jesus, the importance of wisdom is also underlined. There is a lot of speculation about what Jesus was like when He was a boy growing up in Nazareth. Did He perform miracles as a boy? Did He show his power and majesty by being better at everything than everybody else? Was He ultraspiritual? The Bible is silent about all of these issues, its only description of the developing years of Jesus's life is given in Luke's Gospel, where the important evaluation of the boy was made by saying, 'And Jesus grew in wisdom and stature, and in favor with God and men' (Luke 2:52). Clearly the important factor in Jesus life at this time was not the demonstration of miraculous powers or his superiority over everyone else, or in his undiluted success in everything he did, but in the development of wisdom. Wisdom is clearly important in the maturing and direction of the human life.

"It is interesting to note too that Jesus, at the end of the Sermon on the Mount, where he describes and outlines for us the way of life and the value system of the Kingdom of God, concludes this great dissertation with an appeal for wisdom. He said, 'A wise man built his house upon a rock. A foolish man built his house upon the sand. When the storms and floods came, the house of the wise man was able to withstand the storm but the house of the foolish man was swept away.' It is probable that the foolish man, in the midst of the storm, when he saw the catastrophe that was about to overtake him and his family, prayed to God for help and protection. His prayer was unavailing. His need was for wisdom, not a miracle. We really do need to live with the consequences of our decisions—wise or foolish. So Jesus calls for wisdom. And wisdom, He says, is found in those who 'hear those words of mine and do them.' In other words there is enough information and guidance available for us to be making the right choices in life. It is our responsibility to develop a wise attitude and wise approach. To many of the situations we encounter when we listen to His words and we are guided by them, then we will not make many mistakes in life.

"So there you are, Helen," continued the guide. "Most of your question is answered, *I* think. We already know much of what God's will is for our lives. We may not want to accept it. Or we may insist on another set of values and priorities, but that does not change the fact that God has already given us good direction. If we choose not to follow, then that is our choice and responsibility and not God's. In addition, God is prepared to give us wisdom, so that we can wisely discern what are the correct and wise choices to make in life. He does not propose to make every single decision for us, but expects us to develop maturity and responsibility in making choices that reflect His value system and priorities. So when you put together what God has already revealed to us and add to it the number of things he daily expects us to wisely choose for ourselves, then the vast majority of life's situations are already taken care of as far as knowing what is the will of God. On the basis of what is already revealed and living wisely in the light of God's principles, we are largely guided in most of life's situations.

"There are, however, times when wisdom and general revelation are not enough to give us the guidance that we need. There are occasional situations in life when we need some special guidance from God to understand what His will is. It is possible that in these unusual situations, God may communicate with us in order to give us the special direction that is necessary. We would never have arrived at this understanding of God's will by way of the ordinary channels of general revelation and wisdom. No matter how wise Moses might have been, he would never have dreamed up the ten plagues or the dividing of the Red Sea or the manna from heaven. This needed a special word from God.

"When the angel appeared to Gideon and told him that he was God's choice to lead Israel in the battle against the Midianites. Gideon immediately questioned the wisdom of the choice. He objected on the basis of wisdom, he said 'But Lord, how can I save Israel? My clan is the weakest in Manasseh, and I am the least in my family' (Judg. 6:15). When the best wisdom available was applied to the situation, Gideon was about the worst person to choose for a military leader. So special guidance was necessary. Also, when it came to the battle with the Midianites, who had a vast, well-equipped, and experienced army, then all of the military training in the world, and all of the current military wisdom available at that time, would never have told Gideon to approach this vast Midianite army, with only three hundred men, and a strategy that involved broken pitchers and flaming torches and loud shouting in the middle of the night. This ridiculous strategy needed special guidance from God and, I think, remarkable faith on the part of Gideon. It worked very well, but Gideon would never have arrived at that by himself, he needed special guidance.

"The evangelist Philip in the New Testament was experiencing a remarkable revival in Samaria. God was blessing mightily. So all available wisdom would have told him to stay there and reap this wonderful harvest of souls. No amount of personal wisdom would have inspired Philip to leave all of this and go down to the desert and encounter a single man, the Ethiopian eunuch. So God gave special guidance on this matter.

"When the apostle Paul, on the basis of his own wisdom and choice, was going to move into Asia Minor with the Gospel, it needed special guidance from God in a vision to tell him to go over instead into Macedonia. So God does, at times, give special guidance and special revelations. The Christian world today is full of stories of people who have genuinely been led by God in unusual ways. Ways that they would never have arrived at unless God had intervened with special guidance. Many people now in full-time ministry, missionary work, evangelistic work, or pastoral work have testified to a special 'call' from God to this kind of ministry. Without this special 'call' they would never have arrived at the conclusion on their own that this is what they were to do. Sometimes Christians will sense that they must speak a word of encouragement to someone, or pray for someone, and when they obey this guidance, it turns out to be providential that they did. They would never have been able to arrive at this action on the basis of general revelation or wisdom. They needed the special guidance and direction from God.

"There will undoubtedly be some occasions when general revelation is not specific enough to give us the particular guidance that we need at this moment. Wisdom too is limited, in that sometimes God, in His superior wisdom, would guide us to do things that do not seem wise to us under the circumstances. God can and will instruct us to do things that we, in our own limited and finite understanding, would never have understood ourselves. God can and does, on these occasions, provide a special guidance and direction, but a number of things need to be said about it. First, it is special and occasional. We must not expect it to happen all the time. When Moses waved his staff over the Red Sea and it divided, that does not mean that every time we go to the Red Sea and wave a staff over it, it will divide. It only happened once, to meet a special situation. Because Gideon with three hundred men defeated the Midianites does not mean that every time Israel went into battle they only needed to come up with three hundred men. It only happened once. These were special revelations to meet special needs. Christians sometimes do not understand this and wonder why God doesn't do 'Moses miracles' or 'Gideon miracles' all the time. The truth is that He does these things much more than we give Him credit for, but they are not repetitions of what happened to Gideon or Moses, they are unique manifestations of God for a special individual and to meet special situations. These special things are happening today, to many Christians.

"Sometimes, Christians will be thrilled because God spoke to them in a very clear and vivid way and gave them clear guidance about some issue in their life. They then expect that this special revelation should be repeated again and again and cannot understand why God does not speak to them again in the same way or as vividly as He did on that occasion. They want the thrill and clarity of that one special occasion to be applied to many situations, and they forget that God's creativity is infinite. He can do things in many different ways. We must not expect a repeat performance, but we must look and expect God to work and speak in many different ways.

"Second, these special guidances from God come mostly to those who are already living, to the best of their wisdom and knowledge, in the will of God. It was because Paul was obeying God in taking the Christian message to others and was fulfilling God's will by working as a missionary, that he received the special message to go into Macedonia instead of Asian Minor. If he had been disobedient and careless about God's will and was living back in Tarsus pursuing his own career and interests, in bland disobedience to God's call, it is not likely that the Macedonian call would have got through to him with any meaning. Philip was already operating as an effective evangelist in Samaria when he got the special guidance to go to the Ethiopian eunuch. If Philip was back in Jerusalem selfishly pursuing his own interests and looking after his own wealth and betterment, it is not likely that he would have heard any call to go to the Ethiopian eunuch. Special guidances are usually given to those who are faithfully and carefully and enthusiastically pursuing what they know to be the will of God right now. Special revelations are not normally given to those who have little interest in doing God's will and are full of their own interests and values. Special revelations are given mostly to those who will listen to them and interpret them correctly.

"That is why Jesus said that the wise man is the one who 'hears these words of mine and doeth them.' Spiritual wisdom is listening to God and responding to what you hear. When this is the attitude of your spirit and this is the atmosphere of your heart, then it is much more likely that you will be in a position to hear what God is saying and interpret it correctly. It is strange how God seems to be able to speak to some people continually and regularly, while others never seem to hear the voice of God. Usually those who hear the voice of God are those who have learned to listen and respond. They have the sensitivity of spirit and awareness of heart to pick up the voice of God in their inner being. Others pay little attention to God or what God is saying, until some crisis comes and then they suddenly, without experience or understanding, want God to talk to them and give them guidance. It often does not happen. Even if God does talk to them, they are so unfamiliar with how God does this sort of thing that they miss the message altogether.

"Listening and responding to God is a skill in prayer that is developed over time and experience. As your communion with Him becomes more real and vital, you will much more readily sense the nudging of His spirit and understand just what he is saying. This is a skill that you must develop if your prayer life is to be vital and healthy."

After this lengthy speech, the guide looked at Helen and smiled. Helen, however, did not smile back. This was clearly not what she had been wanting to hear. "So let me summarize what I have said," continued the guide. "It is essential that when you pray you pray in the center of God's will. How do you know what is God's will? Largely God's will is already revealed to us in the general revelation. We already know much of what God wants and what His priorities and value systems are for our lives. We need to be primarily seeking these things in prayer. Beyond the general revelations, there are the matters that call for simple spiritual wisdom. God expects us to deal with many of the issues of life ourselves and not call on Him to make every decision for us. To help us to do this, He will give us wisdom so that we can better understand his will and His values and make wise decisions on many of the issues that come before us in life. Lastly, there may be occasions when it is necessary for God to give us special revelations, and particular guidance. This He will do, but we must be in the pathway of His will and sensitive to the inner voice of His spirit, to pick up the guidance that he is giving."

I found all of this explanation very helpful and covered nearly all of the situations in life. Helen, however, did not seem so happy about it. She insisted, "But there are still some things that I encounter and I do not know at the time I am praying whether it is God's will or not. How do I pray then?"

"I have pointed out," said the guide patiently, "that it is a major responsibility for us to try to find out what is God's will. If, however, you insist on praying about something and you do not know whether it is God's will or not, then remember the statement that summarizes the essence of prayer: **prayer is learning to receive what God wants to give.** If you insist on praying without knowing whether God wants to give it or not, then the proper way to pray is a prayer of submission. When you pray like this, I would explain your uncertainty to God. I would pray something like this, 'Father I am not sure what you want to give in this situation, so I ask that whatever your will is, that it will be done, and I will gratefully submit to it. You give what you want to give to me, and I will receive it thankfully.' This, however, is not really a very satisfactory way to pray, it is more of a gamble than an investment, but at least you are not trying to get out of God something He does not want to give, but you are trusting in His love and goodwill that what He wants to give will be the right thing for you, so you ask, in trust, that in this circumstance He will give you what He wants to give. You are not in conflict with Him. You are still trusting in His goodwill and love, and you can be sure that God will respond by giving you what He really wants to give."

Helen had no more questions, and this seemed to end our session with the guide. We thanked him for his instruction and made our way back to our living quarters in the School of Prayer. We were all very thoughtful on the way. We had learned a lot and had many things to think about.

"Still," Helen burst out, "along the way there are many things I want to pray about, and I don't know what God's will is in these matters."

I replied, "I learned a lot there, Helen, perhaps you are just being stubborn and don't want to learn any more about prayer than you already know. Perhaps you don't want to venture into new territory in prayer but want to cling to your old ways of doing it, even though you now know that it is immature and retarding your growth in prayer." This response did not please Helen, and we spent the rest of the journey back to our living quarters in unhappy silence.

JOURNAL: *My first day in the City of Prayer has been tremendously full. I am not sure I can absorb all that I have experienced.*

*I understand better now what the essence of prayer is—**learning to receive what God wants to give.** I want to focus my prayer life on understanding what*

God wants to give, and then opening my heart to the wonderful gifts that He want me to have. My problem is not in the richness that God wants to impart, but in my ability and willingness to receive it.

I understand that the people living in the City of Prayer are learning to carry with them into their everyday life the Spirit and atmosphere of prayer, so that it affects all that they do. For me this will take a great deal of discipline and application, but I am determined to ask God to help me develop this atmosphere of life where I "practice the presence of God."

My experience in the Circle of God's Will was amazing. It makes me want to be sure I live my whole life in the center of God's will.

The discussion on God's will and wisdom was very helpful to me. I realize now that it is always wise to obey God. It is always unwise to disobey Him.

I am concerned about my friend Helen, who did not respond well to the discussion on the will of God. I will pray for her.

Tomorrow will be the second day here. It should be a great day.

TOPICS FOR DISCUSSION—CHAPTER TWELVE

1. Discuss the impression the pilgrims had as they walked through the streets of the City of Prayer:

    - Is this realistic?
    - Is this possible in the midst of a busy life?

2. What is the symbolic significance of the Circle of God's Will?

    - Discuss the different reactions of those who stood in the center of the circle.
    - Have you ever had a similarly type of experience of consciously being in the center of God's will?
    - How did your heart respond to this experience?

3. Discuss the statement "There is no experience more fulfilling to the human heart than to consciously be in the center of God's will."
4. What are the two main reasons why some people have difficulty accepting the will of God?
5. What are the implications of the concept that "prayer is not a gamble, it is an investment?"
6. Discuss the statement "God does not propose to make every single decision for us but expects us to develop maturity and responsibility in making choices that reflect His value system and priorities."

CHAPTER THIRTEEN

THE HALL OF CELEBRATION

After a good and refreshing night's sleep, our group met for breakfast and discussed the plans for the day. We all agreed that we should visit the Hall of Celebration. It sounded like a pleasant place, and after the heavy day we had had yesterday, we thought it would give us a lighter and easier experience. Once we had agreed to go the Celebration Hall, however, our agreement fell apart on the issue of how we were to get there. John and Alvin were adamant that our instructions were that we should go to the Central Cathedral and begin the journey at the Circle of God's Will. Helen, however, whose good night's sleep had not resolved her difficulties about the issues of God's will, argued that it was quite unnecessary to go the Central Cathedral. It was out of our way, and we should be able to find the Hall of Celebration quite easily without going to all the trouble and effort of first beginning at the Circle of God's Will.

"The guide was quite plain on this matter," said Alvin. "He said that until we are familiar with the city, we should begin any exploration by going to the Circle of God's Will. That is the reference point, and that is where we should begin."

"Right," said John. "And if we attempt to find our way, and omit that step, he said we are likely to get lost. I know it seems a little out of our way, and it is going to take some extra time to get there, but I am for starting at the Circle of God's Will, just as our guides instructed us to do."

"Well," said Helen with some heat in her voice, "I think it is a waste of time. I did not appreciate the discussion we had yesterday about the will of God. I am still unsettled about it, and I don't want to go back there and bring it all up again. I am not convinced that we have to go there. I think I can get to the Celebration Hall without going through the Circle of God's Will. It will be easier and shorter not to have to make that side journey. Besides, we were there only yesterday, why do we need to do it again?" She turned to me and asked, "What do you think?"

I had been listening to their dispute and asking myself the same question. I tended to agree with Helen, that going all of the way back to the Circle of God's Will seemed like an unnecessary addition to our journey. I thought it would be good sense to cut out that extra effort and just go straight to the Celebration Hall. The warnings of the guide that we are likely to get lost along the way if we neglect to do this seemed exaggerated. They were probably being unnecessarily careful with us. We were intelligent adults. We could find our way. We did not need to go back and start again at the Circle of God's Will. So, since everyone was waiting on my response to Helen's question, I said, "I tend to agree with Helen, I think we could get there more quickly and enjoy it longer, if we did not take the time to go back to the circle. I think we should find our own way there." Since there was not going to be an agreement between us, we decided to go our separate ways. John and Alvin would go the long way, back to the Circle of God's Will. Helen and I would set out to find our own way.

There was a map of the city on the wall of the classroom. Helen and I checked the location of the Celebration Hall on the map and then with a strong sense of confidence, we moved out into the streets of the city to find our way to the hall. We were quite convinced we could find our own way, and since we were not going to the bother of starting at the Circle of God's Will, we thought, rather smugly, that we would get there before John and Alvin. After all, we had consulted with the map. And if we did get lost, we could always ask someone how to get there. The people of the city were friendly and helpful; they would help us if we got confused. In this state of contented self-assurance, Helen and I made our way through the city. We seemed to be making good progress until we came to a cross roads. Helen said, "I think we go to the left here."

I said, "No, I think we should go to the right." We stopped to consider the situation, but Helen seemed so confident about where she was that I decided to give in to her direction and we went to the left.

After a while, Helen, looking a little uncertain and scratching her head, said, "You may have been correct. I do not think this is the right way. It is rather confusing. Let's cut through this street here and see if we can get back on to the right track." Since this seemed to be a very personal issue with Helen, and she was determined to prove that her opinion was the right one, I decided I would follow her guidance as she certainly did not seem to be in a mood to have someone contradict her.

We cut off down the side street that she indicated, but after a while it, became obvious that this was not the way to go. I ventured the opinion "I think we are lost."

"Not at all," said Helen. "We will find the way, just give me some time and have a little patience. Look, this road here is a main road and should lead us somewhere, let's go down there." And not waiting for an answer she headed down the road. I reluctantly followed. The road did not lead us where we wanted to go. We were clearly lost. Helen, however, had her jaw set stubbornly. She was determined to find the way. Her pride was at stake.

It was getting hot, and I was getting tired. We were wandering about in confusion. At one point I recognized some of the buildings. "Helen," I said, "we have been here before. We are going around in circles." She was not quite ready to admit that, but I could see that even her tough stubbornness was beginning to soften. "I am going to ask someone," I said. "This is silly. It's obvious we don't know where we are or where we are going." With that I stopped a man on the street and asked if he knew of the Hall of Celebration.

He immediately smiled and said, "Oh yes! I certainly know where it is. I go there often."

I tried to smile back and be pleasant. "Could you tell us how to get there?"

"Certainly," said the man. He pointed to the spire of the Central Cathedral, which was quite far away from where we were but could still be seen. "Do you see the spire of the Central Cathedral? Go there and start from the Circle of God's Will, and you will find the Celebration Hall quite easily."

This was certainly not what we wanted to hear. I thanked him for his help, and we went on our way without paying attention to his guidance.

"I am not going away back there now," said Helen. And I had to confess it seemed a long way from where we were. So we wandered about some more. We looked here and there. We tried this way and that, getting more and more confused, discouraged, and tired.

Finally I said, "I am going to ask someone else. Maybe they can tell us how to get there without going back to the Circle of God's Will." This, however, proved to be just as frustrating. The response to the questions was just the same.

"Yes," he said. And pointing again to the steeple of the Central Cathedral said, "You go to the Central Cathedral and to the Circle of God's Will, and you will find it quite easily from there."

"That's exactly what the last one said," mumbled Helen moodily. "I think they are all programmed to say the same thing."

I asked someone else and got exactly the same answer. "Go to the Central Cathedral and start from the Circle of God's Will and you will find it quite easily."

"You are not going to get any more out of that lot," grumped Helen.

"Well, this is hopeless," I said. "We made a mistake here by not going to the Circle of God's Will to start with. Our guides warned us that this would happen. We should have listened to them and not set out on our own, thinking we could do it by ourselves without reference to the will of God."

Helen was not ready to admit to a mistake but had to confess that the day had been wasted and that we had better get back to our accommodations and get some rest and refreshment. So feeling very disappointed, frustrated, and weary, we made our way back to the School of Prayer.

John and Alvin had not yet returned when we got there, but while Helen and I tried to rally our spirits and refresh ourselves after our tiresome and frustrating experience, John and Alvin entered the room. They were radiant. John, bursting with energy and a great smile on his face, cried with enthusiasm, "Wasn't that fantastic? I have never been so blessed in my life. It was wonderful" This exuberance did not fit with how Helen and I were feeling.

Alvin, whose face also seemed to be aglow with an inner joy, was a little more aware than John of the moody atmosphere that hung over Helen and me. He could see that we were not happy. He understood the reason. "You did not find the Celebration Hall?"

"No, we didn't," said Helen with a frustrated edge on her voice. "We looked and looked to the point of exhaustion and could not find it."

"Didn't find it?" cried John incredulously. "Oh you poor people, you do not know what you have missed. I would not have missed that for anything." John's enthusiasm only added to the discontent that Helen and I were feeling. He then poured fuel on the fire when he thoughtlessly carried on, "And it was so easy to find. Anybody could have got there."

Helen exploded, "Good for you, John. Good for you. I am glad you enjoyed it. We poor souls, however, missed it, so we cannot share in your enthusiasm." John, realizing that his cloud nine joyousness was having an adverse effect, quietly apologized and sat down with Alvin to hear our story.

We told them of the frustrating day we had had. About our searching but never finding. About the people who guided us but all they told us was to go to the Circle of God's Will, which we should have done in the first place. Our failure to do so not only caused us a great deal of grief and frustration but also robbed us of what was evidently a wonderful experience in prayer. Alvin and John listened carefully and understood our disappointment. After we had told our story, we felt a little less stressed at having been able to tell it to a sympathetic and understanding audience.

When we were finished, Alvin said thoughtfully. There is certainly a lesson in this for all of us. In prayer it is essential that we be careful about praying in the will of God. We must not be careless or shallow about this. It may at times seem like a lot of effort for us to try to be sure we are in the center of God's will, but it is worth the effort."

"Yes," I responded. "Both Helen and I thought we did not need to do this. We were sure we would find the way on our own. It seemed so simple and easy, and in our estimation it was quite unnecessary to go the Circle of God's Will and start from there. We were sure we knew the way. We were confident we could get there on our own. We proceeded without reference to God's will. Such a precaution, we thought, was unnecessary. How desperately wrong we were. I deeply regret that our foolishness has caused us to miss a great blessing and given us a great deal of disappointment and frustration."

"Well, we all know now," said John, "that when it comes to finding our way about in prayer, we need to start at the Circle of God's Will. Not to do this is only going to cause us frustration and grief." We all nodded in agreement with this, except Helen, who sat in depressed silence throughout this whole conversation.

Eventually I said to John and Alvin. "Tell us now about your experience. What was the Hall of Celebration like? Explain it to us."

John immediately caught fire with enthusiasm, and Alvin let him do the talking. "The hall is easy to find from the Circle of God's Will. It is a large hall, because a lot of people use it. It is a busy place because people from all over the City of Prayer often congregate there. It is not a one-time experience for them. It is part of their lives. They are frequent visitors. I know that I want to go again and again and again and experience it."

Alvin interrupted. "What John just said is important. You missed it today, but that does not mean you have missed it forever. The hall is there, you can go anytime. You and Helen still have opportunity to visit and experience it for yourself. Apparently the people in the City of Prayer go there regularly." This statement by Alvin greatly encouraged me. I realized that my mistake could be remedied and I would not forever miss out on this blessing.

John continued his description. "The building is quite large. It is brightly painted in happy colors. There are many windows, so a lot of bright light gets into the hall. It is obviously designed as a place of rejoicing and happiness and uplift. When Alvin and I first entered the building, I was surprised by the amount of noise. The noise was not offensive but was created by happy people singing, shouting, and praising God. Most of the people were singing. They sang with gusto and enthusiasm. Some of them raised their hands as they sang. Others waved their arms in sheer delight. Many of them were clapping their hands. There were even some who were dancing. At first it was rather overwhelming.

These people were happy and were praising God and lifting their voices in praise and worship. Their faces shone with inner happiness. I felt the urge to join them, and so I too began to sing and praise God. It was a wonderful experience. While I personally sensed the joy, I found that joining in with so many others seemed to multiply the feeling. Being part of such a great number seemed to lift me up to the very edge of heaven. I felt I was part a great congregation that was singing with one heart and one voice to the glory of God. It is hard to explain. Being part of that group of fellow worshipers made my own worship even more vivid and real. I felt my heart lift up to heaven. I have often sung the verse of the hymn:

> Oh that with yonder sacred throng,
> We at His feet may fall
> And join the everlasting song,
> And crown him, Lord of all.[1]

"But with that experience in the Hall of Celebration I do not think I have ever felt so close to being part of that throng. These were God's people. They were people of prayer. They lived in His presence and lived in the atmosphere of prayer, and I tell you they know how to rejoice. They know how to experience the real joy and wonder of the Lord. They love His presence. They have taught their hearts to praise. Their spirits are filled with thanksgiving. To me this will be one of the greatest features of living in the City of Prayer and will flow from regularly being in the presence of God. Your spirit is lifted on high before Him. It is joy. It is praise. It is thanksgiving."

John, being young and energetic, continued, "After a while I noticed that there was a group over in one corner of the Celebration Hall that was on their feet and they were dancing. This appealed to me, so I went over and joined this group. They danced in jubilation. They expressed worship and joy in a beautiful way, and I immediately melted into this group. Please, Philip! Please, Helen! Do not miss this."

Alvin had listened to John and enjoyed his description of the activities in the Hall of Celebration. Now he spoke up and said. "I too felt the joy of that great crowd. I too felt it was a privilege for me to join with them and raise my voice in praise to our Heavenly Father. There was so much joy and enthusiasm it was easy to be caught up in the spirit and become part of that great throng singing and praising God with all of their hearts. People of prayer know how to do this better than anyone else. They know how to sense His presence and to rejoice in His greatness. This is part of their lifestyle. This is the habit of their sprit, to commune with God and to talk with God and to let their spirit rise free in His presence.

"I too, like John, noticed after a while that there was a group of people who were sitting quietly in one section of the Celebration Hall. At first I thought that their quietness meant that they were not participating in the group's rejoicing. But as I looked closer, I could see that these people too were lost in praise and adoration toward God. But their method of expressing it was different. They were not noisy and exuberant at this time but quietly let their spirits rise in inner adoration and wonder. I could see their faces were lit up with a glow of ecstasy. Their spirit shone through in their eyes. Just as John was drawn to the dancers, I was drawn to this group. I quietly joined them. I seemed to rise into the very presence of God. He was near and my spirit was in touch with Him. What joy! What wonder! There was no need for noise. No need for singing. Just quietly to bask in the glory of His presence filled my soul with a delight that is not easily described. While I have this experience in my own private prayer time, I found that being in the presence of others who were people of prayer increased the intensity and richness of the blessing. Being with people who knew how to experience the presence of God and enjoy their contact with Him increased my own joy. I was part of the group, even though the group was quiet. We were lost in the wonder and glory of Christ, His presence seemed to fill my whole soul. His glory possessed my mind. I felt as if I was at the very gate of Heaven."

Helen and I listened to these descriptions, trusting that our friends were not exaggerating. After a period of quietness, I asked, "So the people in the City of Prayer experience this celebration spirit regularly?"

"Yes," replied Alvin. "But let me tell you a few things about the Hall of Celebration so that you understand it better. First, this is a community event. The people of prayer do in fact spend a good portion of time in private prayer. No doubt, in their private prayers, they experience moments of very joyful and thrilling interaction with God that brings worship and praise to their hearts. The elated praise of the Celebration Hall is not solitary, however, it is a community experience. You are joining with others in praise and thanksgiving. The very presence of others of like mind and like spirit adds a richness and intensity to the experience. The sense of being part of a fellowship that is communally in touch with God is an encouraging and nurturing experience. It can only strengthen your own faith to see others experience what you are experiencing. I am sure that many who are wrestling with doubts or facing disappointments go into the Celebration Hall and come out revived and refreshed and with a new courage and purpose. They have drawn strength, not only from the presence of God but from the presence of others who believe in God. It is wholesome to feel that you belong, that you are part of a group, that others believe what you believe and experience what you experience.

"Second, the experience in the Celebration Hall broadens your understanding of how God works in the lives and hearts of His people. The way people respond to being filled with the spirit of joyful praise is quite different. Some like to sing and shout. Some like to quietly let the Spirit flow through them. Some like to clap and wave their hands as an expression of happiness. Others express their joy by quietly and gently weeping. The experience generates excitement and energy in some, like our friend John here, and they want to express their energy in dancing and exuberance. In others, the joy increases their deep sense of the inner dwelling of God, and they rest in a spirit of peace and well-being. God moves differently in different people and in different personalities. Part of the spirit of fellowship and unity comes in the mutual willingness to accept what God is doing in the hearts and lives of others, and that they are responding in a different way, but in a way that is in keeping with their personalities and God's Spirit. The unity comes from all doing the same thing, and having the same purpose, even though we are doing it in different ways and expressing it differently. There is a maturing and broadening of the mind taking place when we learn to accept that others are responding to the blessings of God in ways that are appropriate to them. But although the expression is different, the basic experience is equally valid and real. The exuberant boisterousness of some is no more spiritual than the quiet worship of others. The quiet worship is not necessarily deeper and more authentic than the exuberance of others. Respect and acceptance for all is part of the unity and richness of the groups' experience. What is important is not how you express it, but that you authentically experience the presence of God in praise and worship and that you have a place where you can express this in community with comfort and acceptance.

"Third, the fact that the Celebration Hall is such a prominent and well-used feature in the City of Prayer indicates that for people of prayer, this is a common and welcomed experience. Joy is not a rarity here. The pleasure and satisfaction in God's presence is an oft-experienced reality. The peace and well-being of being in unity with God is a feature of prayer that enriches and satisfies the soul. For the people of prayer in this city, prayer is much more than a barren formality, or a dry duty that must be performed. It is more than a necessity that must be practiced if you are going to be a spiritual person. It is even more than the childish magic making that some seem to think it is. For the people of prayer, prayer is a path to reality. It is a soul-satisfying fellowship and communion with God that brings joy and peace and love into the soul. They are **learning to receive what God wants to give,** and what God wants to give is Himself, with all of His peace and love and joy. The more you experience God in prayer, then the more your heart will be filled with these emotions. The spiritual delight is well described by the song writer who wrote,

> Jesus is the Joy of Living:
> He's the King of Life to me—
> Unto Him my all I'm giving,
> His forever more to be.
> I will do what He commands me:
> Anywhere He leads I'll go,
> Jesus is the Joy of Living:
> He's the dearest friend I know."[2]

After this dissertation by Alvin, I determined that I must make a visit to the Hall of Celebration an essential part of my exploration of the City of Prayer. I did, however, have one comment to make. "All of this sounds wonderful, and I will look forward to my visit to the Hall of Celebration. I come, however, from a religious tradition where there was not a lot of physical demonstration, like clapping hands or dancing. Is all of that demonstration appropriate?"

Alvin responded, "I certainly think that we must be careful to make sure that our physical expressions are done in response to genuine spiritual experiences. When the experiences are real, and the feelings are authentic, then we applaud the clapping and dancing and hand waving. But we must be careful that we do not begin to do these things in an effort to produce the feelings, or to work up the spiritual experience."

"Yes," I said. "If physical demonstrations are indulged in when they are not an expression of real spiritual experience, then they are empty and spurious. When they are an expression of authentic spiritual experience, then they are good. When they are used to try to produce the experience, or when they are just an outward show for which there is no corresponding inner experience, then they are sham and frivolous."

After this, we discussed what our plans for the next day should be. After hearing the report from John and Alvin about the Hall of Celebration, I was anxious to go there but did not want to break up the group again. Helen too said she would look forward to going to the Celebration Hall, but she was also most anxious to experience the Quiet Room. So it was decided that we should keep the group together and Helen and I would accompany John and Alvin to the Quiet Room and reserve our visit to the Hall of Celebration some other, more convenient time. I noticed that Helen in particular seemed pleased about this decision. And John, with a smile on his face and a twinkle in his eye, said, "And since it is located in the Central Cathedral, then you two," looking at Helen and myself, "are not likely to get lost."

THE JOURNAL: I feel humbled and reproved after the experience of the day. Helen and I thought we could take a shortcut. We couldn't. Clearly this matter of being in the will of God is important to the whole success of prayer. I cannot, I must not, neglect this, or become careless about it. O Lord, help me to better understand your will.

TOPICS FOR DISCUSSION—CHAPTER THIRTEEN

1. Helen was having difficulty with the Center of God's Will. What do you think was the source of her difficulty?
2. After listening to Philip's and Helen's story about getting lost, Alvin said, "There is certainly a lesson in this for all of us."

    - What do you think the lesson was?

3. The Hall of Celebration indicates that joyful celebration is an important part of the life of prayer, yet each person wanted to express the celebration differently.

    - Is celebration an important part of your prayer life?
    - What do you have to celebrate about?
    - What form does your celebration take?
    - Do you celebrate better in a group setting or alone?

4. The spirit of celebration often expresses itself in outward physical ways. Comment on Philip's statement "If physical demonstrations are indulged in when they are not an expression of real spiritual experience, then they are empty and spurious."
5. In his journal comments for the day Philip writes "Helen and I thought we could take a shortcut. We couldn't."

    - Are you tempted to take shortcuts in prayer?
    - If so, what are they?
    - Have you ever been successful when you attempted to take a shortcut?

CHAPTER FOURTEEN

THE QUIET ROOM

We set out in the morning with full anticipation. Since the Quiet Room was located in the Central Cathedral, we had no fear of losing our way. When we reached the Central Cathedral, we took time to affirm ourselves in the Circle of God's Will and then made our way to the Quiet Room. The Quiet Room was located upstairs away from the activities of the cathedral. There were no outside windows, but a large skylight at the center of the ceiling softly diffused light around the area. The walls were painted in a subdued color. It was constructed to minimize all distractions. It was furnished with comfortable but not easy chairs. Its main feature was that it contained a number of partitioned-off booths. Each booth was furnished with a chair, a small table, and a kneeling rug on the floor. The booths were designed to give a measure of privacy.

As we carefully walked around the Quiet Room, we could see that there were a number of people there, each one in his or her solitary booth. As we passed by, we could see into some of the booths. Most of the people that we could see sat with their eyes closed, but from the look of concentration on their faces, you understood that they were not asleep, but in serious, focused, absorbed attention. Some did not use the chair to sit on but were kneeling on the chair in an attitude of prayer. Some, I also noticed, were quietly reading from the Bible or some other book. A few remained standing, but did so with their eyes closed and with the same look of absorbed concentration.

We stood quietly and observed this room. There was no noise at all and hardly any movement. The Quiet Room seemed to exude an atmosphere of deep and serious contemplation. John, however, obviously did not sense this. He whispered to us. "Not much happening here. Why are they all just sitting there doing nothing?"

Helen, who had not contributed much to the group since her discomfort with the center of God's will, objected to John's assessment. "Can't you sense it?" she asked. "They are in deep communion with God. Their mind and spirit are absorbed in Him."

"Well, maybe," responded John doubtfully, "but they could all be asleep for all I know. Prayer should have a little more obvious system and pattern to it than this."

"How do you know that there is no system to it? Just because they are quiet and not saying or doing anything does not mean there is no system or discipline to what they are doing."

"Well," said John, his voice getting louder, "They could be sitting there daydreaming for all I know."

At this a lady came over to us and signaled for us to be quiet. She beckoned us to follow her, and she led us into a small side room. After we had all entered the room, she quietly closed the door. She turned and looked at us and asked, "I gather this is your first visit to the Quiet Room?"

"Yes!" replied Helen. "We are new to the City of Prayer, and we are just beginning to explore its major features. Our teacher told us we should visit the Quiet Room."

"Good," answered the lady. "My name is Elizabeth. I am here to help you and explain to you the nature of the Quiet Room."

"I am glad to hear that, "said John. "I don't think I want to sit around here all day doing nothing."

"I can assure you that those people in there are not 'doing nothing.' They are participating in a very intense and disciplined form of prayer. Many would call it 'contemplative prayer.' I expect, as your prayer life matures and strengthens, you will spend more time in this form of prayer than any other. Many of the masters of prayer spend most of their prayer time in this kind of communion with God. Certainly, they worked hard to cultivate it.

"Remember that the essence of prayer you were taught was **prayer is learning to receive what God wants to give.** And while God, in His love and generosity, wants to give us many things, what He wants to give us more than anything else is Himself. He wants this, because He knows that in experiencing Him and His love and joy and peace, we will be experiencing life at its best. It is in contact and communion with Him that our soul finds its home and its fulfillment. Contemplative prayer is an effort to discipline our soul, to lay aside all other interests and focus only on Him. It seeks to supersede all other concerns and give total attention to our communion with Him.

"In this type of prayer, the objective is not to get things from God or to present our requests to Him, the objective is to simply let our spirit make contact with Him, rest in His presence, absorb His Spirit, let His love flow over us, let our spirit rise to Him in adoration and worship. This intimate connection between our soul and our Savior is a feast for our spirit. We are filled with the reality and wonder of God. We are awed in the presence of His greatness and power. We are humbled by His majesty. We are focused on Him. He is the center of our concentrated attention. We are doing this in a way that involves our whole being. Our bodies must be disciplined into quietness. Our mind must be disciplined into stillness. Even our spirits must cease demanding, and let the desire for Him and His presence become dominant. In our hearts we cultivate a 'hunger and thirst' after Him. We are not seeking to fulfill our own desires, wishes, or wants, we are seeking to lose ourselves in Him. Selfish desires and personal ambitions must fade in the wonder and glory of His presence. Success in contemplative prayer comes when our sprit is in touch with Him. When we lose ourselves in Him. When we rest and abide in His presence. When our soul is lost in wonder, love, and praise. When He fills our horizon and we bask in His grace and goodness. In contemplative prayer you seek to enjoy His presence and find quiet rest in communion with him.

"This type of praying reflects a maturing experience with God. When we are in this kind of fellowship with Him, what we say is not so important. What we are sensing and experiencing is important. In this kind of connection with God, we let our spirits rise to him. Any words seem inadequate. When we are resting in His presence like this, it is more important that we listen than that we talk. Here we can understand the values of God, sense His direction. Here our soul is open and receptive to His outpouring of love and grace, and we receive it as a thirsty land receives water."

We were all listening to this statement from Elizabeth with good attention. We understood that we were being introduced to a whole new realm of spiritual experience in prayer. Helen, however, seemed completely engrossed in what Elizabeth was saying. "Yes," she said, "I think I understand what you are saying. I think I have experienced this in some ways. I did not know what to call it, or whether I should pursue it or encourage it, but I am sure I have experienced it in some ways."

"I am sure you have," answered Elizabeth. "Most people who reach the City of Prayer have some experience with this kind of prayer and have made some excursions into it. Nearly all have had times of great spiritual blessing when they have experienced this. Now, however, we want to encourage you, not to see it as an occasional event, or a special but rare treat in prayer. We want to encourage you to cultivate this and develop your skill in it so that it becomes a vital and essential part of your prayer life. We want it to become the habit of your soul and the daily bread of your spirit. It is more than an occasional banquet of spiritual good things, but the normal, rich, and satisfying diet of the soul. It should be participated in regularly and experienced normally in our daily lives."

"Right," said Helen. "Show us how to do it. Where do we start?"

Elizabeth smiled at Helen's eagerness. I was also pleased to see that Helen had set aside her difficulties with the Circle of God's Will. John was the one who seemed uncertain about what Elizabeth was saying. "What you say sounds very nice," said John, "but when I saw these people in the Quiet Room, I thought it looked very like impractical, sleepy, daydreaming."

Elizabeth laughed. "When you get into it, John, you will find out that it is anything but 'impractical, sleepy, daydreaming.' I think it is the human spirit seeking out communion with God without going through the usual channels of human words, vocabulary, and thought processes. The spirit tries to bypass these things and have direct interaction with God. So in some ways, we try to lay aside the activity of the body and the mind in order to give precedence to the spirit. God, of course, who is spirit, is perfectly at home with this form of communication. To us, however, it is like entering a whole new realm of existence. We have, by habit, all the years of our lives, operated and communicated by means of words, speech, and thought. So when it comes to communion with God, we assume we should follow the same pattern. Contemplative prayer is a way of teaching us that we can find communion with God in a more direct way—spirit to spirit. It allows our spirit to rise into God's presence, and sit there, and do nothing but enjoy and absorb His presence. The spirit, beyond words, rests in the quietness of His peace and in the awareness of His nearness. It sees being in touch with God, not as a means to an end, to get God to act on our behalf, but rather it is an end in itself. It is enough just to be in His presence and to quietly soak in His Spirit.

"In fact this type of prayer is often a matter of listening to God, sensing His moving, becoming aware of His desires and accepting His love and grace. There is a story I heard about Mother Teresa, I have never been able to confirm its authenticity, but it certainly could be a genuine expression of her great heart. Mother Teresa was being interviewed by a member of the press. The questions got around to Mother Teresa's prayer life. The questioner asked, 'What do you say to God when you pray?' Mother Teresa answered, 'Not much, mostly I listen.' 'You mean you mostly listen to what God is saying to you?' continued the questioner. 'Yes,' Mother Teresa agreed. Not satisfied, the questioner persisted. 'Then what does God say to you?' Mother Teresa answered, 'Not much, mostly He listens.' Because of the obvious confusion that her answer had caused, she added, 'If that does not make sense to you, young man, then there is not much I can do for you.' The story, whether apocryphal or not, captures the spirit of contemplative prayer. 'Mostly I listen,' 'Mostly He listens' does not make sense until you enter the realm where the spirit, unencumbered, is in touch with the Spirit of God and the two are interacting. It is beyond words. It is even beyond thought processes. It is the spirit in direct interaction with God. In trying to describe this experience, a medieval writer wrote a book on the subject that has become a classic in spiritual writings, but he chose to call the book *The Cloud of Unknowing*.[1] That very name indicates the inexpressible experience that we are trying to reach out for in this type of prayer.

"Since this kind of experience is so outside of our usual channels of interaction and communication, it is a skill that must be developed. It is a habit that must be cultivated. For some of us"—Elizabeth looked at John with a smile—"it will be more difficult than others. But once you begin to experience this type of unity with God, you will find it is something that you will desire more and more. Once your spirit has tasted it, you will develop an appetite for it. There are some pointers that I can give you that will help you as you begin this kind of praying, but remember this is not so much a matter of methods or systems with the guarantee that if you follow the right system you will be successful. Systems and methods help, but the real inspiration is to understand that this is a matter of atmosphere, awareness, culture, and sensitivity. Thomas Merton in his book *Contemplative Prayer* says, 'From these texts we see that in meditation we should not look for a "method" or "system," but cultivate an "attitude," an "outlook": faith, openness, attention, reverence, expectation, supplication, trust, joy.'[2]

"Let me give you some simple pointers to get you started. The purpose is to let your whole being be focused on God and absorbed in Him. This calls for a high level of concentration. To do this you first need to eliminate, as far as you can, all distractions. That is why we call this place the Quiet Room. It minimizes distractions. No television, no telephones, no radios, no people walking about or talking to you or to each other. It is quiet. You need to find some place in your home or life that is free from distractions, and the threat of distractions. In the Quiet Room, each person has their own little cubicle. This ensures a measure of privacy and aloneness. This kind of praying is done alone. It is a solitary exercise. Some parts of the spiritual life are best done in community with others. For this kind of praying, however, we advise quiet aloneness. In our busy hectic culture, this is not always easy to ensure, but each of us can find some place for quiet aloneness. That is why in the City of Prayer, we provide this Quiet Room, and as you can see, many avail themselves of its facilities.

"Concentration is also helped by quietening physical activity. That is why so many are seated or kneeling. It is hard to gain the proper concentration while you are engaged in some physical activity that needs attention and care. So lay aside all activity and sit in a comfortable chair where you can be at ease, but not so comfortable that you fall asleep. Physical discomfort becomes a distraction. Most people will close their eyes, because when there are things to see, they tend to attract our attention. When you close your eyes, you shut out the world, and you can begin to look inward and become aware of the movings of your soul. It also helps to be surrounded, if possible, with some of the aids to devotion. It is a great benefit, if you are able, to have a special room or place that we associate with our devotions. A cross, a picture, a Bible, even a candle, helps create an atmosphere of devotion and encourages us to lay aside all distraction and focus on God.

"Once we have taken care of the physical distractions as best we can, we next must take care of the inner distractions. The distractions of our thought life and our emotional life. We must seek to lay aside the common thoughts of the day that crowd in upon us. Our worries, schedules, plans, disagreements need to be laid aside. We know these thoughts and issues must be dealt with, and we can promise ourselves that we will pay attention to them when the time comes but not at the moment. We do not want them to invade our prayer time. Right now, we want to focus on God and on getting in touch with Him. So accept the demands of your mind and acknowledge the thoughts, but lay them aside and fix your attention on Him. Think of His glory, His greatness, His love. Set your mind on Him. Center your attention on Him. This is the time when all else is laid aside so that you can communicate with Him. Some find it helps to use their imagination here. For example, you could imagine you are walking across a flat table-land. You are walking toward a bright light that is God. Imagine as you walk toward God you consciously shed off all of your concerns, worries, and interests. One by one you drop them and leave them behind until there is nothing left. You are bare and empty, and only aware of the encompassing light and presence of God. There you rest.

"Others find that it helps settle their mind and emotions if they first take time for some spiritual reading. They read from the Bible or some other spiritually encouraging book or writings. This gathers your attention on to spiritual matters. It helps focus your mind and spirit on spiritual issues. Then you focus inward to your own spirit. Become aware of it. Set it free. Let it rise to the heavens into His presence. Let your spirit express itself and move into His presence. Sense His nearness. Touch His love. Absorb His spirit and enjoy His joy. Let your spirit find peace and joy in His presence. Now you are in touch with Him, and you need to continue to center your spirit on Him.

"This is a beautiful experience. In this state of spiritual awareness, you can hear Him. Enjoy Him. Worship Him. Adore Him. Drink in His grace. Here you blossom in His presence and rejoice in His wonder. Here your spirit reaches out to touch Him in love and humility. Your soul is open to His presence and feasting on His greatness. This is the home of the soul, and the experience of God that is the yearning of every human heart. Do not hurry here. Hold this experience. Do not feel you must rush on to something more productive and practical. At first you might find it difficult to maintain this attitude for any length of time, but as time goes on, and you learn how beautiful, fruitful, and satisfying this experience is, you will be able to cultivate the skill of staying in this contact longer and longer. For many, much of their prayer time is spent in this quiet receiving from God the blessing of His presence and letting His love and grace wash over them. This is not an empty waste of time, this is not to be seen as part of the journey into prayer that must be passed through in order to get on with the real business of praying. This is the destination. This is the real business.

"What I suggest," Elizabeth continued, "is that you all go into the Quiet Room and try to practice this type of centering prayer for a short period of time, and then come back in here and we will talk about how you got on."

We agreed to do this. So Elizabeth instructed us; "Find a quiet cubicle of your own in the Quiet Room. Settle down comfortably in the chair. Take time to gather yourself together. It might help you to read a portion from the scriptures. Psalm 23 or Psalm 46 are good scriptures to start with. Some find it helpful to quietly sing over in their mind the words of a worship hymn such as

> Holy, holy, holy! Lord God almighty!
> Early in the morning my song shall rise to Thee.
> Holy, holy, holy! Merciful and mighty!
> God in three persons, blessed Trinity![3]

"These quiet exercises help us transmit ourselves into a spiritual state of mind. They are aids to help us cultivate a receptive awareness of the state of our soul and our relationship with God. Then focus your attention on God. Let the eyes of your soul gaze upon Him. Let your soul rise to meet Him and enjoy His presence. Sense His nearness. Be aware of His presence. Humbly accept His contact. Let your soul feast on Him. This takes complete concentration and attention, but once you sense His presence and you become aware that your spirit is in touch with His spirit, then hold it there and enjoy it. And rejoice in it. Keep your mind and heart focused on Him. Let your spirit drink in His presence. Try to maintain this attitude. Try to stay in His presence. Keep the contact of your soul with Him solid. You may want to worship and adore Him. You may want to feast in the sense of His love. You may want to listen to His voice. You may want to move deeper and deeper in your interaction with Him. In whatever way you experience it, let the blessing flood your soul for a period of time. Then after a while, gradually withdraw and come back into this room and we will discuss the experience together."

Quietly we all found our own cubicle. I settled down in mine. I tried to remember the instructions. I sat down on the chair and settled my body down, by consciously letting it relax. I sat for a few minutes looking at a picture on the wall. It was a picture of Jesus praying in Gethsemane. I let my mind focus on this and tried to understand what this prayer meant for Jesus. Then, as Elizabeth had suggested, I opened the Bible at Psalm 46 and began to read "God is our refuge and our strength, an ever-present help in trouble." I focused on God and His reliability and strength. I thanked Him for His constant loving kindness. I felt in my heart the need to express my appreciation to Him, so I took time to say, 'Thank you!' As I went through these exercises, I began to sense that I was really in the presence of God. But I soon found I was having difficulty. There was something in me that was not content to remain quietly in His presence. I wanted to rush on and pursue other things with Him, rather than rest and enjoy what He was giving at the moment. His presence was real, and I did not want to waste this moment by doing nothing with it. There grew in me an impatience to use this time to pursue some spiritual objective or get on with some spiritual purpose. I tried to curb the impatience of my soul and discipline the desire to be moving on to something else. I tried to stay focused on Him and what I was experiencing of Him at this moment. Stay. Enjoy. Rest. Commune. This is not part of the journey, this is the destination. This was not a springboard to something else, this was the end in itself. I needed to simply let my soul enjoy Him. Fellowship with Him. I needed to stay focused on Him and let my soul rise more and more into His presence and sense His greatness. I had some success at this but still felt a constant struggle to be doing something more practical. I thought I must ask Elizabeth how I can learn to stay quiet and be content to simply rest in His presence.

After a while I decided that it was time to go back to the small room and find out how my companions had got on with their experience in contemplating prayer. John was already in the room when I got there, and Alvin arrived at the same time as I did. There was, however, no sign of Helen. We waited for some time, but Helen still did not appear. Finally Elizabeth said, "I will go and get her." Elizabeth left the room and soon returned with Helen at her side. I could see immediately that Helen had been having a good and satisfying experience. Her face was at rest, and she had a sparkle in her eyes that had been absent since her struggle with the issues of God's will at the Central Cathedral.

Elizabeth sat down and then looked at us all. "How did you all get on?"

I went first and described to the others the procedures I went through to try to focus my soul on God and to enter His presence. "I believe that I did indeed enter His presence, and I sensed His nearness, and my spirit seemed to be in touch with Him. It was enriching and beautiful. I could tell, however, I was very much a beginner in this, but I caught enough of it to realize that a whole new, unexplored continent of prayer experience and fellowship lay before me. I certainly see how I need to improve and cultivate this skill." I continued, "The thing I had the greatest problem with was being content, just to rest in His presence. It seemed that I was impatient. I felt like I needed to be doing something, or saying something, or asking for something. But just to be sitting there resting in His presence and contentedly enjoying the nearness of His Spirit, I found it hard to relax. What can I do to still my restless soul, so that it can be content in His presence?"

"There are one or two things that can help with this," said Elizabeth. "It is not an uncommon problem. We live in a world and in a culture which demands that we be in constant activity. In our society, activity is equated with effectiveness. Busyness is a sign of importance. Unless we are doing something, or moving on to the next stage, then we are not being productive people. As children of this culture, it is very difficult for us to imagine that quietly waiting in God's presence can be the most fruitful use of our time. We want to gulp down our meal so that we can get on with something else, or move on to the next course. Yet to taste, chew, and inwardly digest our meal is one of the healthiest and most rewarding things we can do. Just being sensitive to His nearness and taking time to let it sink in and soak down to the depth of our being is one of the great sources of spiritual health and vitality. Resting in His presence brings calmness, assurance, peace, joy, and confidence that enriches our souls. But we must take time to let it sink in. Our hearts need time to let it percolate into our being. A mighty cloudburst of rain washes the earth away and destroys the plants, but a soft, gentle, steady rain is absorbed into the soil and feeds and nourishes the plants enabling them to grow and flourish into sweet and strong fruitfulness.

"There is a beautiful verse in the book of Psalms that does not give the idea of great hurry and rush in God's presence. The Psalmist says, 'Lord, I look up to you, up to heaven, where you rule. As the servant depends on his master and the maid depends on her mistress, so we keep on looking to you, Lord our God, until you have mercy on us.' (Ps. 123:1-2). So, Philip"—here Elizabeth gave her full attention to me—"refuse to yield to the rush of your spirit at this time, but quieten it down and let it rest in His presence. Hurry and rush will rob you of the blessing that God has designed. And the more you do it, the easier it will become. As your spirit learns what a fruitful and blessed thing it is to stay quiet in the presence of God, it will develop the mature understanding that it is not only acceptable, but that it is necessary to spend time like this, interacting with your Heavenly Father. Remember what God said through the prophet Isaiah, 'This is what the Sovereign Lord, the Holy One of Israel says: "In repentance and rest is your salvation, in quietness and trust is your strength, but you would have none of it."' (Is. 30:15).

"I know you are right," I said. "In fact now I remember being impressed with a verse of scripture that I read before my prayers. It was from the passage you suggested, Psalm 46 and verse 10, it says, 'Be still and know that I am God.' There is a way of knowing God that only comes from us being still and quietly being in His presence."

Elizabeth smiled and nodded in agreement, then continued, "In addition to this, many have found the use of mantras to be very helpful in overcoming this impatience of the spirit. A mantra is a simple but meaningful statement that you repeat time after time. It is repeated so regularly that you do not have to think about it, but it does keep the mind focused on God. Probably the best known of the mantras is called the 'Jesus Prayer.' This mantra is often used in the Orthodox tradition, you simply repeat 'Lord Jesus Christ, have mercy on me.' It can be repeated continually, until, like your heartbeat, it carries on in your mind without conscious awareness. But it helps settle the mind on the things of God. Francis of Assisi spent uninterrupted hours in prayer, saying the same thing, 'My Lord and my God.' You can develop your own mantra. Something that helps you focus your mind, stops it from wandering, and quietens your spirit, so that your attention and heart are set on communion with your Lord. Whatever you do, Philip, understand that as you develop this skill, your fellowship will be enriched and your soul will flourish, and you will increasingly understand the value of simply waiting on God."

John was next to share his experience. He said, "I just don't seem to be able to get into this. I cannot seem to conquer the feeling that I am wasting my time. I keep feeling I should be doing something more practical, or praying in a more active way. There are so many needs in the world. There are so many people who need help. I keep thinking of all of the ministry and service I could be doing for the Lord. I need to be praying about all of these things and not simply sitting there and dreaming my hours away. I think I feel guilty that I am not doing something more productive with my prayer time. With this inner battle going on within me, I just did not seem to get very far with this contemplative prayer. I hate to say it, but I feel like I am wasting my time."

Elizabeth smiled at this but nodded her head again as if she understood John's feelings and that she had heard all of this before. She said, "John, I understand your enthusiasm to be involved in active and creative work for the Lord and for His Kingdom. This is good and must never be lost to you. Your personality and your energy keeps pushing you to be doing things that are useful and practical. This is to be applauded and developed. After all, the Lord Himself called us to be his servants and to do the work of the Kingdom on His behalf. Lazy, slothful servants are not rewarded. Unfruitful branches are cut off and burned. Serving with fruitfulness and effectiveness are an essential part of the Christian life and should be a natural outcome of our fellowship with God. It should, however, be noted that the emphasis in Christ's teaching about service is that the service should be fruitful. Lots of good activity is not necessarily good Christian service. Busyness in the affairs of the Kingdom should not be equated with effectiveness for the Kingdom.

"The apostle Peter learned this lesson very early on when he started to follow Jesus. Jesus came to Capernaum and lived in Peter's home. It was a very exciting and successful time. Many people were healed, demons were cast out, great crowds of people thronged to listen to Jesus. Peter's home was filled to capacity with people wanting to see and hear and watch Jesus. So Peter was quite dumbfounded when he got up the next morning and Jesus was nowhere to be found. Peter and others set out to search for Him. Peter was urgently aware that the whole town of Capernaum and many other people from surrounding areas were anxious to see Jesus. Peter thought that the obvious thing for Jesus to do was to capitalize on His popularity, get on with the work that He had been doing yesterday, so that even more people would be healed, more demons cast out, and this great crowd would hear the truth proclaimed. So why had Jesus disappeared? What could be more important than getting on with the work? Where was the Master when so many people were in need of Him? Eventually they found Jesus, out in the hills, all alone praying. Peter thought Jesus was missing the point. Didn't Jesus realize that this was the time to be getting on with the work? There were lots of needs, great spiritual hunger, many people to convince, so what was Jesus doing out here away from everybody and, of all things, praying. Such a waste of time, to be out here alone praying when there was so much work to be done. Mark's Gospel describes the incident in this way: 'Very early in the morning, while it was still dark, Jesus got up, left the house and went off to a solitary place, where he prayed. Simon and his companions went to look for him, and when they found him, they exclaimed "Everybody is looking for you!"' (Mark 1:35-36). Peter seemed to be saying to Jesus, just what you are saying to us John, 'What are you doing out here, wasting your time when so many people are looking for you, and so many things needs to be done?' Jesus, however, understood the reality of service in the Kingdom of God. The work is done in a spiritual realm. The effectiveness is found in the power of the Spirit. Christian service is more than just good Christian activity. To be effective, it must have the presence and power of the Spirit of God in it. Jesus understood, and we too must understand, John, that in order to be fruitful and effective for God in the work of the Kingdom, we need our own soul to be healthy and vital. We cannot effectively reach others when we ourselves are not in touch with God. If our own spirit is empty, then we cannot fill others. If we are drained of spiritual power in our own lives, then we cannot bring power to others. Fruitfulness in the Kingdom of God requires that the servant be closely in touch with the Master and the Master's wishes.

"Jesus made this plain when He was talking about the fruitful branches. The fruitful branches were the ones that were connected to Him and were abiding in Him. He stated the principle quite clearly when He said, 'Remain in me, and I will remain in you. No branch can bear fruit by itself; it must remain in the vine. Neither can you bear fruit unless you remain in me. I am the vine, you are the branches. If a man remains in me and I in him, he will bear much fruit: apart from me you can do nothing' (John 15:4-5). In a similar vein, when Jesus was ready to leave the earth and return to the Father, He left the responsibility of the continuing work of the Kingdom in the hands of the disciples. But when He was instructing them, He did not tell them, 'Now it's up to you, get to work, be active, the whole world has to be won, so you need to urgently get on with the preaching, healing, and winning.' Jesus knew the job was far beyond the power and skill of the disciples, no matter how enthused they were or how dedicated. His instruction to them was 'Do not leave Jerusalem, but wait for the gift my Father promised, which you have heard me speak about. For John Baptized with water, but in a few days you will be baptized with the Holy Spirit . . . . But you will receive power when the Holy Spirit comes on you: and you will be my witnesses in Jerusalem, and in all Judea and Samaria, and to the ends of the earth' (Acts 1:4-8). Spiritual service without spiritual power is ineffective."

Elizabeth continued to instruct John, "A car may be beautifully designed and well constructed. It may have all of the parts necessary for effective driving on the highways, but if it has no gas in its gas tank, it is not going to get very far. And it has to keep on filling its gas tank to keep on being useful. So it is in spiritual service, John, we must keep on filling our gas tanks. We do this by renewing the power and presence of God in our lives. And one of the essential ways that we do this is by prayer. Refreshing our own soul in His presence. Opening up our own hearts to the inflow and infilling of His Spirit. If we are empty, we have nothing to give. If we are out of touch, then our service may be active and busy, but it will lack ultimate power and reality in the Kingdom of God. An impatient driver in a great hurry to get somewhere may chaff at having to go into the gas station to fill up his car. He may be frustrated because it needs repair and maintenance, but if he neglects these things, then the car is going to be very limited in its future service. The great men and women of God have understood this balance John. They have served effectively and well, but they also took time to refresh and renew their own souls. They took time to be in touch with God. They took time to open their soul to the presence and filling of God's Spirit. This was the secret of their ongoing effectiveness for God. If they had neglected this, then they could have continued their activities. Momentum could have kept them going for a while, but the power and reality would gradually have been drained out of their service. They would be doing it on their own strength and their own power, and it would lack the effectiveness that only the Spirit of God can give.

"So, John," concluded Elizabeth, "it may seem to you that this is a waste of time, but like the maintenance of a car, if you neglect it, then the car will function less effectively and for a shorter period of time. Some of these people in the Quiet Room, who seem to be doing nothing, are in fact some of the most dynamic and effective people in the City of Prayer. Their lives and service are a great blessing to many people. But they are also the people who find it necessary to come into the Quiet Room most often. Do not fall into the trap, John, of thinking that busyness in the Lord's work is the same as effectiveness in the Kingdom. You need to take time to be in God's presence. You may have to do less, but you will do it more effectively."

It was now the turn for Alvin to explain his experience in the Quiet Room. "I enjoyed it," said Alvin. "But I think I need a little more form to it. I like to follow methods and procedures. I can't just sit there and hope something will happen. That is too loose for me. I need to have a disciplined path to follow and a track that is laid out for me to stay on. Intuitive, unplanned waiting on God tempts me to follow every little rabbit track that my mind suggests to me.

I need a better understanding about what is vital and important and what are just frivolous mind wanderings. I need a method for doing this. I need a guide to keep me straight. I cannot just rely on hoped-for inspiration and intuitiveness to lead me into the presence of God."

Elizabeth responded very quickly to this. "Yes! Many people are like you, Alvin. For them, this is unknown territory, and they need some guidance and direction. If you are going into a dark and unknown cave, it helps a lot if you have a guide rope to follow. Especially if the rope has been laid by people who have gone the route before you. The fact is that there are many methods or systems to help us move into the spirit of contemplative prayer. We have already mentioned the common methods that are used. There are the physical methods that help you to set aside the demands of the body and concentrate on spiritual things. You seek a quiet and solitary spot. You set it up so that there are sacred symbols around you, and it has the atmosphere of being sacred ground. You rest the body by sitting or kneeling. You close your eyes to shut out the world. All of these are simple methods. In order to bring your thoughts into the atmosphere of prayer, you can sing a song of praise. You read some spiritual reading. You repeat a mantra. These are methods to help your mind get focused. There are methods to help your spirit reach out and touch God. Focus on Him.

"There is also, however, an intuitive aspect to this type of praying. Often you must be guided by the direction your spirit leads you in. For example, Alvin, you could imagine that you are in His throne room and kneeling before Him. Imagine His power and greatness. As you continue to kneel in His presence, and as you focus your attention on Him, your spirit may want to express itself. Then let your spirit express itself and follow where your spirit leads. You may feel like praising Him. You may feel like bowing in humble adoration. You may want to express great faith in Him. You may want to call on His help in petitions. There is freedom here. There is freedom to let your spirit go in the direction that it wants. This is, in itself, a method of release and openness.

"These are all methods. Sometimes you do not need them. There are times when your spirit is anxious and hungry for God and seems to be ready to rise into His presence naturally and easily. These are good times. But there are other times when you need the help of a method, to systematically lay aside the affairs of the world and the concerns of the flesh. Your spirit needs the assistance of methods to help it focus and direct itself towards God. There will even be times when no matter how hard you try or what methods you use, they all seem ineffective in enabling you to reach out and touch God. But whatever the method you use, the important thing is to focus and concentrate and take time. Make it a habit, whether you feel like it or not. Do it, even though you are not in the spirit. It is the constant practice of being in His presence that will help you develop greater skill. It will become easier when the pathway is well trodden, the methods will improve with practice. You will find it becomes more natural, and your spirit learns how to be more ready for His presence. Also, Alvin, if you are focused on Him, then you are doing the main thing. This is not frivolous or trifling. Any thought that leads away from your concentration on Him should be denied and disciplined. When you are concentrating on Him, then you are doing what is most important."

We now turned our attention to Helen. "It was wonderful," she said. "It seemed that I could very quickly rise into the presence of God. I sensed His presence and felt my soul rest in Him. I felt like I was surrounded by His Spirit, and my thirsty soul was drinking in His grace and strength. When you came to get me, I was surprised that so much time had passed. I did not want to come out of the Quiet Room. I wanted to stay there. I find this very refreshing and fulfilling." Helen's joy and spirit were transparent, and we all saw that this was a very meaningful exercise for her.

Elizabeth then spoke to all of us. "You have now been introduced to the fellowship of the Quiet Room. You have learned some lessons about it. I want you all to go back in and take more time to develop this spiritual skill and become more proficient in utilizing this spiritual means of grace. For some of you it will be easier than others. Helen seems to quite naturally flow into it. Others will have to work at it and will find it more difficult to develop the focus, concentration, and discipline that are necessary. But all of you should do it. And in the City of Prayer make frequent and regular visits to the Quiet Room part of your life here. It is an important feature of the city. It is part of the prayer life. So I would go in again to the Quiet Room. Spend as long as you like, and then when you go home, discuss your experiences together."

We thanked Elizabeth for her guidance and helpfulness, and we all returned again to the Quiet Room. This time we were a little better informed and had a clearer understanding what our expectations should be.

After a while, John, Alvin, and I finished our time in the Quiet Room. We waited for Helen to come out, but she seemed to be still enthralled in her prayers. We decided then to go back to the accommodations in the School of

Prayer and leave Helen in the Quiet Room. We went home, and although we waited up for some time, there was still no sign of Helen. As we waited, John began to complain that he did not feel well and wanted to retire to bed. He did in fact look quite sick. John left us. Alvin and I waited for some time, but still Helen did not return.

"She must be having a great time," observed Alvin.

We finally decided to go to bed.

THE JOURNAL: *After the activities of this day, I took my Bible again and read the words from Psalm 46:10, "Be still and know that I am God." I feel that I have been introduced to a whole new world of fellowship with God today. I realize that I am not very good at it, but I determine with God's help to develop this ability in my spiritual life. It is strange how this type of prayer is difficult for some and easier for others. John seems to have great difficulty with it. While Alvin and I had some success, we will clearly have to work at it. Helen, on the other hand, seemed to grasp it and blossom in it right away. But then, Helen had a terrible struggle with the center of God's will. My understanding is that there are many aspects to prayer, and each personality finds some of these aspects natural and easy while other aspects are difficult. I wonder what aspect I will find most difficult.*

I will pray for my friend John, who seemed to be really sick tonight.

TOPICS FOR DISCUSSION—CHAPTER FOURTEEN

1. Try to explain the main objective of contemplative prayer.
2. Name some of the "pointers" that Elizabeth gave to help us enter into the spirit of contemplative prayer.
3. Each of the men had a particular difficulty that they had to deal with in trying to cultivate the spirit of contemplative prayer. Discuss the nature of each difficulty:

Philip—anxious to move on to something more practical.

John—"I am wasting my time. I should be doing something more active in my time with God."

Alvin—needed a system that had more form and body to it. He was uncomfortable just hoping for the spirit to come and intuitiveness to lead him into the presence of God.

CHAPTER FIFTEEN

THE BOOTH OF INTERCESSION

As we gathered together for breakfast the next morning, we became immediately concerned because John did not appear. After knocking on his bedroom door a number of times and calling his name without response, Alvin and I entered his bedroom. John was still in bed, but seemed to be in a delirious state. He was not conscious that we were there. His face was damp with sweat. His pillow and sheets were wet. We knew right away that something was seriously wrong with him. We called on George, the School of Prayer teacher. He took one look at John, laid his hand on his head. "He is burning up," he said. "We must call an ambulance and get him to the hospital right away."

Alvin and I stayed at John's bedside while the George called for an ambulance to come. Alvin and I felt quite helpless. "Let's pray," I suggested. Alvin agreed, and we bowed our heads and prayed for our friend and colleague whose health and energy had always been a stimulant and encouragement to us. We prayed that God would heal John of this sudden and unknown sickness, or that God would give the doctors and the medical staff wisdom and understanding as they treated him. I realized that in this emergency, I did not really know how to pray, or what kind of prayer was appropriate in the desperate situation. Alvin too seemed hesitant and uncertain about just how he ought to pray for John.

We had just finished our prayers when the ambulance people arrived, and quickly John was transported out of his bed and into the ambulance. We stood on the steps of the school and watched with great concern as John was driven off to the hospital. We went back to the dining room where Helen was just finishing her breakfast. When she heard the story of John's serious illness and quick transfer to the hospital, she joined us in deep concern over John. As we talked about John's condition, I asked the question, "I don't know how to pray about this. Should we pray for John's healing? Should we pray for the doctors and medical staff? Should we simply commit John to God and hope for the best? What should we do?"

We were discussing this when the teacher, George, joined us at the table, so we asked him what was the best thing to pray about under the circumstances? "I understand," he said, by way of reply, "that you were planning to go to the Intercession Booth today?"

"That is correct," I answered, "but I am not sure if we should go ahead with these plans or not, with John so deadly ill?"

"I would urge you to go there today," said George. "In fact I cannot think of anything you could do that would be better for you and for John than for you to spend time praying for him at the Intercession Booth."

We could see the sense in this suggestion. There was nothing we could do for John just sitting around in the school all day waiting for news. If we went to the hospital, there was nothing useful we could do there. But if we went to pray for John, this would give us something to do that may influence the outcome of his illness. So without delay we hurried off to find the Intercession Booth. "But in our hurry and anxiety, we must not bypass going to the Circle of God's Will," said Helen.

"Under the circumstances," I argued, "do we really need to do that?"

"You of all people should know the answer to that," scolded Helen. "Have you so quickly forgotten the day we experienced when we tried to find the Celebration Hall, and thought we could do it without first going to the Circle?"

I had to admit that she was right. I was also a little surprised at the change of attitude she exhibited. So in spite of the sense of urgency that I had to get to praying about John, we took time to go into the Central Cathedral and begin our journey from the Circle of God's Will. From there we found the Intercession Booth quite easily. When we arrived at the booth, I quickly conceded that I was glad we had taken the time to go first to the Center of God's Will.

The Intercession Booth was rather a plain building. It was obviously not built for comfort or ease. The furnishings were rather stark, and there were no decorations on the wall. The room was divided into individual booths where those involved in intercession and prayer could find privacy. There were also some sections designed for group prayers, where a number of people could gather and pray together for a single cause or person. As usual there was a teacher there who could guide us and direct us in our intercessory prayers.

When we explained to the teacher that we were stressed and burdened for our friend John and had an urgent need to pray for him, she suggested that we immediately go to one of the group rooms together and spend some time in prayer for John and then, once we had unburdened our hearts, come back and she would explain the functions and purposes of intercessory prayer. This instruction reflected the strong desires of our own hearts, and we readily agreed.

The teacher led us to one of the small group praying rooms. The only furnishings were a circle of chairs facing inward. Helen, Alvin, and I did not hesitate but immediately fell on our knees and began to pray for John. I prayed first. I asked God to heal John. I stated that He, God, had the power and that He had the ability to heal and I was asking Him to do that. Given His power and wisdom, I asked that by the time we got home after our day in the Intercession Booth that we would hear that John was healed and had recovered sufficiently to come home. I realized that I was asking for a miracle of healing but could see no reason why I should not ask for this. After all He is a God of power and has performed miracles in the past, and we really needed a miracle right now on John's behalf.

Helen prayed next. She was a little more moderate in her request. She prayed that God would bless John in the hospital and would give the doctors wisdom and skill in their treatment of John, and she prayed that God would give John a speedy recovery under their expert care. Alvin's prayer was even more generalized than Helen's. He prayed with equal intensity but committed John into God's hands and prayed that God's will would unfold here and that whatever His will was, that we would be given grace to accept it.

I was deeply troubled by these prayers of my friends. I thought they should have been a little more forthright in praying for John's healing. I felt that they lacked faith in the miracle power of God. If they were really having faith, then they would be asking for great Divine intervention and pleading for God's healing power in John's case. I kept my thoughts to myself, however, as we gathered back in the teacher's room for some instruction on intercessory prayer.

"Intercessory prayer is when you pray intensely on behalf of others," the teacher began. "Intercessory prayer is a very unselfish type of prayer. You pray deeply for the needs and concerns of others. One of the characteristics of intercessory prayer is its intensity. You carry a burden. You care deeply. You focus intently on the needs of others and present their needs to God. When James in his epistle claims that the 'effectual fervent prayer of a righteous man availed much' (James 5:16 KJV). He is talking about this intense, deeply caring petition on behalf of others.

"Moses prayed an intercessory prayer on behalf of the Israelites on Mount Sinai. While Moses had been up on the mount receiving the laws from God, the people had grown weary waiting for him and, with the approval of Aaron, made a golden idol and were worshiping it. When Moses came down from the mountain and found what was happening, he was distraught. He immediately turned to God in prayer and pleaded with God not to reject the disobedient people but to continue to accompany them and bless them in their journey into the promised land. So intense was Moses's feelings about the matter that he agonized before God, 'Oh, what a great sin these people have committed! They have made themselves gods of gold. But now please forgive their sin—but if not, then blot me out of the book you have written' (Exod. 32:31-32). You can sense from this statement the intensity of Moses's feelings about this petition—intense enough to ask that if God could not respond favorably to his petition on behalf of his people Israel, then He should blot Moses's name out of the book that He had written.

"The same intensity is reflected in Jesus's great prayer on behalf of the city of Jerusalem. As he stood overlooking the city he wept and prayed. 'O Jerusalem, Jerusalem, you who kill the prophets and stone those sent to you, how often I have longed to gather your children together, as a hen gathers her chicks under her wings, but you were not willing' (Matt. 23:37). Then who can match the incredible intensity of the apostle Paul as he prays for his own people of Israel. 'I speak the truth in Christ—I am not lying, my conscience confirms it in the Holy Spirit—I have great sorrow and unceasing anguish in my heart. For I could wish that I myself were cursed and cut off from Christ for the sake of my brothers, those of my own race, the people of Israel' (Rom. 9:1-3). This intense pouring out of the heart for others is a true and genuine expression of Christian love. It takes great love to be so deeply and passionately involved in the welfare of others.

"This unselfish intense prayer for others has remained a part of the Christian experience down through the ages. It is a burden accepted by the people of God on behalf of the needs of others. The needs can be for their spiritual redemption, a crises in their life, their spiritual or physical welfare. In fact some of God's people have made this type of praying an essential part of their ministry and work for God. They spend great amounts of time in concentrated prayer for others. Sometimes they will take upon themselves the welfare of others and will cry to God and wrestle with Him in spirit in order to bring His blessing and help upon those for whom they are praying. Some of the great servants of God who have achieved much for the Kingdom have been blessed by having intercessors as partners who will pray for them and hold them up before God in prayer. Many of these great people of God will openly confess that they attribute much of the power and effectiveness of their ministry to the prayers and intercessions of these faithful people. The work and ministry of intercession is a strong tool in the building of the Kingdom of God. The importance of this kind of ministry can be understood from Paul's statement in Romans 8:34, where he tells us that even now the 'Jesus who died—more than that, who was raised to life—is at the right hand of God and is also interceding for us.' The writer to the Hebrews confirms this continuing ministry of Jesus Christ when he says, 'Therefore he is able to save completely those who come to God through him because he always lives to intercede for them' (Heb. 7:25). Even now, at the right hand of God, our risen and conquering Savior is involved in this ministry of interceding on our behalf.

"Understand that an essential element in intercession is the intensity. There are many other types of prayer offered for others that do not have the depths of intensity or burden that true intercession has. Often, Christians will pray for one another and for others without the focused intensity of intercession. This is good and should not be discouraged. Christians will sometimes say, 'I will pray for you,' but they are not thinking in terms of extended, interceding, and passionate praying. Often we will say to each other when we are sick, or in need, or facing difficult situations, 'I will pray for you,' and we do. Prayer lists, prayer chains, prayer requests are often a part of the Christian fellowship. But these are more casual prayers. They are expressions of goodwill and thoughtfulness. It is good when you are sick, or when you are going through a difficult phase in your life, to have the assurance that your Christian brothers and sisters are remembering you in prayer. It gives you assurance and encouragement. This kind of faithful praying brings people to our minds that we otherwise might not think about. It reminds us of our obligations to one another and gives us a good vehicle to express our concern—we pray for each other. But these more casual, general prayers of goodwill and thoughtfulness are not the intensely focused and burdened passion of intercessory prayers. Both types of praying are good but really fulfill a different purpose.

"The difference between intercessory prayer and casual prayers of goodwill is illustrated in the way I water my lawn. My watering hose has an adjustable nozzle on it. If I adjust the nozzle, the water can come out as a gentle spray that covers a lot of territory and dampens it. Or I can adjust the nozzle and strong concentrated stream comes out of the hose that impacts a very small area but in a powerful way. The gentle spray is like the generalized prayers expressing goodwill and concern. The powerful jet stream is like the concentrated power of intercession. So the casual prayers of concern and support are good. They spread around a positive spirit of goodwill, mutual love, and support. There are, however, situations that arise in the Kingdom of God and in the lives of individuals that call for a much more concentrated and powerful effect than this. You adjust the nozzle and a jet stream of water comes pouring out that is directed to a specific area that needs inundated with water. This is the focused power of intercession.

"Jesus understood that there are some spiritual battles that call for intense and powerful praying that only intercession can satisfy. You remember the story in the life of Jesus, when he and some of the disciples came back down from the Mount of Transfiguration? There was a crowd waiting for them there. In the crowd was a father whose son was afflicted by a demon. He had asked Jesus's disciples to cast out the demon, but they had been unable to do so. The man placed the issue in the hands of Jesus, pleading that he do something for his badly tormented son. Jesus commanded this powerful demon to come out of the boy. The Bible describes the scene vividly. 'Jesus rebuked the evil spirit. "You deaf and mute spirit," he said, "I command you, come out of him and never enter him again." The spirit shrieked, convulsed him violently, and came out. The boy looked so much like a corpse that many said, "He's dead." But Jesus took him by the hand and lifted him to his feet, and he stood up. After Jesus had gone indoors, his disciples asked him privately, "Why couldn't we drive it out?" He replied, "This kind can come out only by prayer"' (Mark 9:25-29). Jesus seemed to be indicating that there were some battles in the Kingdom of God that were so intense, and the enemy was so fierce that casual prayers were not enough. Victory called for intense heartrending prayers in order for the spiritual victory to be won. This is the prayer of intercession. When the enemy comes in like a flood. When the roots of sin are deep in the human heart, when the devil is determined not to give up territory to God, then special, intense, prayers of faith are called for.

"Another feature about intercessory prayer, a feature that many find hard to accept, is that God has granted the person being prayed for the power of personal choice. In other words, in spite of the intense praying done by the intercessor, the person prayed for still has the right and the ability to reject whatever God is trying to do in their lives. Moses interceded for the people of Israel, yet in spite of Moses's great intercession, these same people continued to disobey God until, in disgust, God condemned that whole disobedient generation to die in the wilderness, and that group never entered the Promised Land. Jesus prayed for Jerusalem, yet very soon it was the people of Jerusalem that would cry for His crucifixion. The disobedient city itself would be destroyed by the Roman armies in 70 AD. Many a mother and father have given themselves to agonizing prayer for their child, only to find that their deeply loved child continues to make the choices that move him away from God and the Kingdom of God. In spite of Paul's deep agonizing prayer for the people of Israel, they continued largely to reject his message until finally in frustration he cried to the Jews, 'We had to speak the word of God to you first. Since you reject it and do not consider yourselves worthy of eternal life, we now turn to the Gentiles'" (Acts 13:46).

As I looked into the faces of my companions, I could tell that Alvin was having a difficult time with what the teacher was saying. "But," he interrupted, "if God is sovereign and His will is supreme, then what He wishes must come to pass. We know that He wishes and wills for people to be saved, so why would He then not answer a prayer for the salvation of the souls of our loved ones?"

"Yes!" replied the teacher. "God is sovereign, and in His sovereignty He willed to create a being in His own image. That is, a being who had moral and spiritual self-determination. A being who in the spiritual world could choose its own course and determine its own destiny. God, I am sure, realized the risks and dangers in this course of action, but in His judgment, the risks were worth it. He crowned His creation by creating a self-determining being that had its own choice in many moral and spiritual matters.

"This being, however, was free to make decisions and choose values and courses of action that were not necessarily in the will of God. It was not God's will that Adam and Eve should eat of the Tree of the Knowledge of Good and Evil, but contrary to God's will they did. God's original plan for Moses was that he would lead the Children of Israel into the Promised Land. But because of some of the decisions Moses made, God had to change His plans. His will was frustrated by Moses's decisions. We are told in the Bible that God is 'patient with you, not wanting anyone to perish, but every one to come to repentance' (2 Pet. 3:9.) So while it is not God's will and wish that anyone should perish but that all should come to repentance, that is not what happens. Not everyone repents, and so some, in spite of our prayers, will unfortunately perish. When Jesus preached, some believed and some didn't. Each made their own choice. When He called for repentance, some repented and some didn't. Each was responsible for their own choice. As morally free persons, we have the responsibility of making our own moral choices. This is a power and responsibility that God will not normally interfere with. So in spite of the earnest prayers said on their behalf, if a person chooses not to listen to the truth and the voice of God, they have been given this option, and God will not withdraw this power of free will or overrule their decision.

"God will not force people to choose salvation. He will not coerce people into a way of life that they do not willingly choose. He will not force people to follow Him if they choose to go another way. He certainly could do that. He has the power, but in His graciousness and wisdom, He has granted to us the responsibility of making moral choices for ourselves. So even if you pray passionately for someone, and you should, you must understand that the ultimate choice and responsibility lies with the person, and in spite of your prayers, they may choose a pathway in life that is not what you wanted or for what you prayed. This is a hard saying, for we want to think that we have the power, under God, to make people do what is right and what we think is best for them, but in actual fact, while we can certainly influence them, we do not have the power to force them into moral decisions that we think they ought to make. Even God has opted not to exercise this power."

The teacher paused here, because she knew that we would have some questions and objections. Alvin went first. "But I thought if you prayed fervently and in faith for someone, God would answer your prayers. You are saying that in spite of my fervent and believing prayers, the person may still choose to go away from God and make choices that are wrong for them?"

"What I am saying, Alvin, is that God has granted to each of us the ultimate responsibility for the state, condition, and destiny of our own soul. That is a responsibility that is placed even on the person that you are praying for so fervently. The responsibility of ultimate choice is up to the person, not you, or even God. You also said, Alvin, that God would not necessarily answer your prayers when you pray for a person. But of course God will answer your prayers. In response to you prayers, He will speak to that person. He will soften their heart. He will bring influences to bear upon them. He will bring people into their lives. He will change their circumstances so that they might be more open to the word of truth. The Holy Spirit, in response to your prayers, will convict them of sin and make them more aware of spiritual things. All of this can happen in response to your prayers. You must pray for them, and keep on praying for them. You do not know but that the influences that are brought to bear upon them in response to your prayers may be the very thing that makes the difference. Your prayers allow God to work in their lives. Also, God, in response to your prayers, may guide you into some action that you can do for them, that will help God convey His love and concern for them. But God will not force them to make choices against their will. God will not coerce them into moral and spiritual choices that are contrary to their own will. But certainly, you must continue to pray for them. It is your prayers that help release the power of the Holy Spirit in their lives and gets the spiritual influences working in their hearts."

"But if you are not sure what decision they are going to make, and there is no guarantee of the outcome, is it worth our effort to pray for them?" asked Helen.

"Certainly it is," replied the teacher instantly. "Because you and I are involved in a spiritual warfare. The devil and the forces of evil are very active in the world. Always the purpose of evil is to turn people away from God and endorse choices and ways of life that are contrary to the will and choice of God. The forces of evil are continually acting in the lives of people, and with their active influence, people are continually making choices that lead them away from God. If evil were the only force and influence in people's life and there was no contrary force to combat it and oppose its purposes, then, evil would come in like a flood and overwhelm the whole of the human race, and there would be nothing to stop it, or direct people back to God. But evil is not the only influence in the world. God is here, and He has influence as well. The work and ministry of the Holy Spirit is present in the world. He is constantly seeking for ways to remind people of their spiritual condition. He seeks for ways to speak to them, to influence them, to make them more aware of spiritual things. He will convict of sin, He will create a sense of guilt when they do wrong. He will agitate their consciences when they consciously disobey God. He makes them aware of God and their souls. He is constantly at work trying to convince them of His love for them. Because of His activity, in their hearts, the power of sin is often restrained, frustrated, and defeated.

"Jesus explained to His disciples about the work and ministry of the Holy Spirit. In promising the disciples the presence and power of the Holy Spirit, Jesus outlined the great work that He would do. He said, 'When He comes, he will convict the world of guilt in regard to sin and righteousness and judgment: in regard to sin, because men do not believe in me; in regard to righteousness, because I am going to the Father, where you can see me no longer: and in regard to judgment, because the prince of this world now stands condemned' (John 16:8-11). So there is a continuous warfare going on for the allegiance and affections of the human heart."

Looking directly at Helen, the teacher continued, "You and I, Helen, are involved in that warfare. We are soldiers in the conflict. Our prayers and our cooperation with the Holy Spirit is the very thing that can make the difference in the lives of many people. It is inexcusable, Helen, for us to stay on the sidelines of the battle and simply observe. It is irresponsible for us to withdraw from the conflict and simply say, 'Well, there is nothing meaningful that we can do. I cannot influence the outcome. Whatever God is going to do He will do, and I don't make any difference.' Of course you make a difference. You work and cooperate with the Holy Spirit. Your prayers bring spiritual power and influence to bear that would not be there otherwise, or else it would be much weaker. You are a soldier in the Lord's army, and you need to get in there and bear a burden and cooperate with the Holy Spirit and assist Him in what He is doing. And what He is doing is pointing people to Jesus Christ and urging them to believe in Him. But He gives them a fair choice and will not force them against their will to become Christians, but will influence them so that they have every opportunity to make the right decisions."

"But I thought that God was going to win the battle?" cried Helen.

"God will ultimately win the war against evil," said the teacher, "but within the war, there are many battles, and the outcome of these battles are not up to God so much as up to us and the choices we make and our willingness or unwillingness to cooperate with the Holy Spirit. While the ultimate and eternal war will be won by God, there are many battles within the war that will not be won. You know that from your own life. Sometimes you are tempted, and you do not resist the temptation. That is a battle lost. It may not change your direction in life or your commitment to follow the Lord, but it is still a defeat. So in the lives of others. Some are won to the Lord, and some are not. Some listen to the voice of God, and some resist. I am afraid that not all battles are won for the Lord."

Helen seemed to understand this, so the teacher advanced her statements and said, "One reason why prayers of intercession can be so intense and agonizing is the very uncertainty of the outcome. In intercessory prayer, we often struggle in the uncertain world of human free will and moral choice, and because the outcome is still in doubt, we pray with more urgency and intensity than we would if we knew the outcome was a forgone conclusion."

It was my turn to ask a question, and I wanted to ask about prayers for healing. I said, "When we were praying for our friend John that God would heal Him, we all prayed in a different way. I prayed that God would perform a real miracle and heal John, so that when we see him later on today he would be better, having been cured by God's healing power. Helen, on the other hand, prayed that the doctors would be given skill and wisdom to correctly diagnose John's trouble and be able to give him the proper treatment that would cause him to recover. Alvin prayed that whatever God's will was that it be done and that we be given grace to accept it. Which prayer was the correct prayer?"

As I suspected, the teacher compromised and said, "In some ways and in some situations each one of these prayers is quite acceptable."

I was not happy with this, and I pursued the matter. "But doesn't God heal? Didn't Jesus heal people? Didn't the apostles heal people? Are there not people who are healed today in answer to prayer?"

"Philip," the teacher said thoughtfully, "I will try to answer your questions about the prayer for healing, but I must tell you that there are some things I do not know and some questions for which I have no answer. There are mysteries about healing that I, at least, do not understand. Let's take it one step at a time. First, yes! Healing has been a feature of the Christian ministry down through the centuries. Sometimes it was more prominent than at other times, but it has always been there to a greater or lesser degree. Yes! Jesus healed many people. The apostles also had cases of healing, but not so extensive as Jesus. Yes! People are still healed today. The Christian churches circulate many stories of people who have been healed. There are those today who claim to have special gifts of healing. Many wonderful stories surround these people and their ministry. So that is the first point. Yes! Healing has taken place and still does take place.

"Second, while it is clear that healing has happened in the work and ministry of the Christian church from the time of Jesus until now, it is equally evident that not everyone was healed. Even in the ministry of Jesus, while he healed many people of leprosy, there were still, no doubt, lepers in Israel when Jesus died. He did not get to heal all of them. While He cast out many demons, there were, no doubt, still some people troubled with demon possession when Jesus died. He did not get to cast out all of them. He even raised some people from the dead, but clearly that cannot be the expectation for everybody. So while healing happens, it is clear that we must not expect universal unending healing for all ailments. The Bible tells us that 'Man is destined to die once, and after that to face judgment' (Heb. 9:27). We all anticipate that one day we are going to die. But when we die, it is because something in our body breaks down or wears out. We are not promised that God will go on healing and renewing our present bodies indefinitely. Healing must stop in order to let us die. To claim universal, unending healing is not realistic. So the question that is hard to answer is when should we expect healing to happen and when should we not expect it?

"It is interesting to me to note that Jesus when he went to the Pool of Bethesda in Jerusalem encountered many sick people there. The traditional story about the pool of Bethesda was that it had strange healing powers. On occasion the water in the pool would be stirred up, and the superstition developed that whoever was able to get into the water first after it stirred would be healed. Jesus went to visit this pool. In his Gospel, John tells the story, 'Here a great number of disabled people used to lie—the blind, the lame, and the paralyzed. One who was there had been an invalid for thirty-eight years. When Jesus saw him lying there, and learned that he had been in this condition for a long time, he asked him, "Do you want to get well?"' (John 53-6). The story goes on and tells how Jesus dealt with this man and brought about his wonderful healing. But my question is 'Why did Jesus pick out this man from amongst all of the other sick and ill people that were around him?' He did not heal everybody at the pool. Why not? He did heal this man. Why Him? Healing certainly happened in Jesus day, but not to everybody.

"Another interesting story is the occasion that happened after the disciples were filled with the Holy Spirit on the day of Pentecost. Peter and John were going up to the temple at the time for prayers. Around the temple were many poor beggars who hoped to capitalize on the generosity of those who were going to the temple to pray and worship. Yet one of these beggars, a lame man, was singled out for healing. The story is found in Acts chapter 3 verses 3-8, 'When he saw Peter and John about to enter, he asked them for money. Peter looked straight at him, as did John. Then Peter said, "Look at us!" So the man gave them his attention expecting to get something from them. Then Peter said, "Silver or gold I do not have, but what I have I give you. In the name of Jesus Christ of Nazareth, walk." Taking him by the right hand, he helped him up, and instantly the man's feet and ankles became strong. He jumped to his feet and began to walk. Then he went with them into the temple courts, walking and jumping and praising God.' This was a wonderful demonstration of the healing power of God, but the question comes up again, out of all of the lame and sick beggars in the streets of Jerusalem, why him? So it is clear that not everyone was healed and we ought not to proclaim that everyone should be healed. This is a false expectation and raises false hopes in the minds and life of many sick and ill people."

The teacher shook her head sadly. "I have no clear answer to these questions that I raise. While I rejoice greatly with those who are healed, it seems to me that in my personal experience I have had to try to bring new courage and hope to sick people who have become discouraged and disillusioned because they were not healed. I have found it a cruel pain in the lives of many good people who have had their hopes raised that they would be healed and then were plunged into discouragement, depression, and doubt because the healing never came."

"But is that because they did not have faith?" I asked.

"Well, that brings me to the third step here, and that is to ask why some are healed and some are not? I have no clear answer to that question. It would be easy and simple for us to say, 'If you have faith, God will heal you. If you are not healed, it is because you do not have enough faith.' Certainly Jesus made it clear that the element of faith was an important ingredient in receiving divine healing. He often told those who sought Him for healing, "According to your faith be it unto you." Sometimes when a healing had successfully been accomplished, he would say to the person, "Your faith has healed you." We are told that He could do very little in His own hometown of Nazareth because of their unbelief. James tells us in His epistle that if we are sick, we should call for the elders of the church and have them anoint us with oil, and he says, 'The prayer offered in faith will make the sick person well; the Lord will raise him up' (James 5:15). The presence of faith seems to be an essential ingredient to successful divine healing. Perhaps some of us would feel a little more at home with the father whose son was possessed with a demon. When he came to Jesus to ask for help, he said to Jesus, "But if you can do anything take pity on us and help us" "If you can?" said Jesus. "Everything is possible for him who believes." Immediately the boy's father exclaimed, "I do believe: help me overcome my unbelief!" This desperate father seemed to have a mixture of faith and unbelief. I think many of us can understand this feeling. But even when there is a mixture of belief and unbelief, it was sufficient for the boy to be healed. So some measure of faith seems to be essential for successful miraculous healing to take place.

"I am not sure, however, that we can say with equal certainty, that when healing does not take place, it is because there is a lack of faith. If this were the case, then some of God's choicest and most faithful servants apparently lacked faith. The apostle Paul was not healed of the 'thorn in the flesh.' Timothy was not healed of his easily upset stomach. In the history of the church, many of the great men of God have been afflicted by physical illness that apparently hampered their ministry. For some it even caused them to die prematurely. Can we say with casual blandness that these men and women did not have faith? Even in an atmosphere where healing faith is encouraged, such as the meetings and conventions conducted by those who claim to have the gifts of healing. In this very charged atmosphere, there are many stories of remarkable healings, and we rejoice in this. But the fact of the matter is that even in this atmosphere, most of the sick go home unhealed. Can we say that those who were healed had faith, while those who were not healed did not have faith? I am sorry, Philip, but I have no definitive answer to my own questions. I do not know why some are healed and some are not. All I know is that sometimes healing takes place and sometimes it does not, and there is an element of mystery here for which I have no answer."

"So," I said, "my friend Alvin was correct when he prayed for John that 'God's will be done.'"

"Certainly a better understanding of the full will of God would help us pray more intelligently for those who are sick. There are other options than the option of divine healing. There are other paths that God may want us to follow than just the path of miraculous healing. Sometimes a period of sickness lays us aside, and we have time to interact with God in a way that would never have happened if we had remained healthy and active. There are times when sickness can teach us lessons that are to be learned that we would not have learned without the pain of sickness. And if we learn the lessons, we emerge richer and better persons. Then the lessons of care and patience need to be learned by those who have to look after the sick. Sometimes it may simply be that our time to die has come. There is a mystery here, and I do not pretend to understand it all. So it is very appropriate when we are not sure whether healing is the proper thing, to ask, as Alvin did, that God guide us and direct us in the best way to handle this sickness. Paul got guidance from God about his thorn in the flesh, and when he got the guidance, he ceased to pray for healing. Timothy got some advice on how to handle his delicate stomach. It seems that Jesus was guided to that particular man at the Bethesda pool. Peter and John were led to heal that special beggar at the gate of the temple. It does appear that the Holy Spirit can led and direct the healing for some. He has a wisdom and insight I do not have, but I can call on Him for guidance."

"Why then should we pray for healing if we do not know whether we will receive it or not?"

"Because we are instructed to pray about it. The God of mercy will either heal us or give us grace and guidance on how to handle the sickness victoriously. If we are prepared to listen, He will also guide us in the proper prayer to make in this situation. Also, an attitude of positive faith will help us in our recovery from the sickness much more than an atmosphere of questioning doubt."

I continued insistently, "Then the prayer that Helen prayed, that the doctors and the medical staff would be given wisdom and insight in dealing with John's illness was also correct?"

"Keep in mind, Phillip, that back in the days of Jesus, medical science was extremely primitive, and largely superstitious. People who got sick in those days did not have the medical knowledge and expertise that our physicians have today. They did not have hospitals. There were not available to them all of the drugs and medicines that we take for granted. The fact is that many of the people who came to Jesus for healing would not have needed to do that if they were living in our culture and society today. It is only good sense for us to make use of the advanced medical knowledge of our day. While there are some truly remarkable stories of people today who have been healed when medical science seemed unable to help them, there are also some tragic stories of those who refused help from the medical world because they believed God could heal them or their loved ones. In the days of Jesus, people had few options if they wanted healing. They had to turn to God for His help and trust for Divine intervention. Today we have many other options, and I think it is only wise for us to avail ourselves of them. It is appropriate for us to pray that the doctors will be given wisdom and understanding so that they can deal with our sickness and guide us on the right path to recovery."

This discussion on healing was not very satisfying to me. I felt that I had many unanswered questions. My only comfort was that there did not seem to be any answers available to the questions. I concluded, as best I could, that we should certainly pray for healing when we are sick. We should not jump to easy judgments on ourselves and others about lack of faith if healing does not happen the way we think it should and at the time we think it should. We should also avail ourselves of all of the scientific medical help that we can get and be thankful that we are living in a day and age when this knowledge is available to us. It is damaging to raise false hopes that everybody should be healed under all circumstances. Sometimes, I understood, that when healing does not happen, there may be other richer and more fulfilling paths for us to follow. In the end I also concluded that I would somehow have to learn to live with an unanswered mystery here.

"I suggest now," said the teacher, "that you return to your private intercession booths and pray alone. But remember this is the place where you learn the prayers of intercession, so I urge you to focus on the real needs of other people and concentrate your prayers on their needs. Become deeply involved with them and feel in your heart the pain and suffering that they feel. Love them as God loves them. Let the compassion of God's Spirit flow through you to them. Then present them to God along with your well-defined petition. Intercede to God on their behalf. Pray that they will receive what God wants to give them in this situation."

We separated each to our own private intercession booth. I had no difficulty in knowing who I wanted to intercede for—my good friend John and his sudden and severe illness. I was not clear, however, in knowing just how I should go about praying for him, or even what I should pray for. Should I pray for his healing? Should I pray for the doctors and medical staff? Should I pray that general prayer that God's will be done? I was uncertain. I did know, however, that I had a strong sense of burden and longing for John, so that is where I started my prayer of intercession. I simply expressed to God the desires of my heart for John. I said, "God, I have a deep longing in my heart for my friend John in this time of his need. My heart aches for him. I place him and his need before you. I pray, I plead with you to reach out and touch him at this time. I want John to receive just what you want to give him. I am not sure just what you want to give, but I believe you will give him just what you want him to receive." This prayer I felt I could trust in and believe that God would do whatever it was He wanted to do for John. It seemed to me as I prayed that my heart would break for John. My whole soul throbbed with passion for his welfare. I continued in this way of intercession for a long while. The pain in my heart grew greater. My longing for John stretched and expanded within my soul. I pleaded with God on John's behalf. It seemed beyond language. It even seemed beyond understanding. I only knew that I was in touch with God, and my spirit was crying to Him on behalf of John.

While I labored under a very deep and heavy burden for John, and while my spirit was in great pain for him, it seemed like it was an exquisite pain. It was pain for others. It was a redemptive pain. It was a pain I voluntarily assumed on behalf of others. It was not a spiritual cross that was laid on me whether I wanted it or not, but rather it was a cross I took up willingly and readily on behalf of others. It was a pain with a purpose and an objective, and so seemed be an expression of the Spirit of God within me. What I was feeling was just what God wanted me to feel. I was in touch. I was in the flow of the Spirit. Words seemed incapable of expressing the feeling, but the intensity was great. Suddenly, the scripture came to my mind. I took the Bible and looked it up in Romans 8:26-27, "In the same way, the Spirit helps us in our weakness. We do not know what we ought to pray for, but the Spirit himself intercedes for us with groans that words cannot express. And he who searches our hearts knows the mind of the Spirit, because the Spirit intercedes for the saints in accordance with God's will." This seemed to describe what I was experiencing. The spirit was praying through me. My soul was expressing the heart and mind of God. I did not understand it all, but I knew that a great spiritual happening was taking place. The Holy Spirit had laid on my heart a burden for John. And I was open to this action of the Spirit.

My pleading and intercession continued for quite some time until I began to experience an inner relief. I felt the burden begin to lift, and a beautiful sense of peace flooded my soul. I felt at rest and satisfied. I had an assurance that God had heard my prayers and that I had properly responded to what the Holy Spirit wanted of me. It was a beautiful sense of oneness with the desires and will of God. My pleading changed to thankfulness. I thanked God that He had heard me. I praised Him for His goodness. The assurance of the Spirit flooded my soul, and I was satisfied that I had done what God wanted me to do.

I realized that I had been involved in this spirit of intercession for quite some time, and I wondered how my companions were getting on. I left my private intercession booth and found them waiting for me. I think they had been waiting for quite some time. I was so sure that God had used me in this work of intercession for John that I wanted to go to the hospital and visit him before we returned to our accommodations at the School of Prayer. My companions agreed. After thanking the teacher at the Intercession Booth, we made our way to the hospital.

On the way to the hospital, I tried to explain to my companions just what I had experienced in the Intercession Booth. Language failed me. But I was delighted to find out that they too had experienced similar spiritual burdens that they could not always explain or describe. They agreed that it seemed like the Holy Spirit possessed them and expressed in their spirit the cares and burdens of the heart of God. We were speaking God's language. We were experiencing God's passion. We were feeling God's pain. How do you describe an exquisite pain? Alvin stated it well when he referred to the ambitions of the apostle Paul when the great apostle stated, "I want to know Christ and the power of his resurrection and the fellowship of sharing in his sufferings, becoming like him in his death" (Phil. 3:10). I felt I had shared in the sufferings of Christ. I felt I had willingly drank deep of the same cup that He drank, and while it was a heavy cross to bear, it was also a joy to know that I could share this with Him. I realized that great work could be done for the Kingdom of God through this ministry of intercession. I wanted to be used of God in this way. My heart seemed at home in this kind of praying.

When we reached the hospital and made our way up to John's room, I was filled with great anticipation to see if there were any outward results from our time of intercession. It was a great joy to enter the room and see that John had significantly recovered and was in fact anxious now to leave the hospital and come back with us. When we questioned him about his recovery, he indicated that it was in the afternoon, about the same time that we were praying, that his fever began to break. He felt his strength return and his body revive. We rejoiced with him and shared our experience of intercession. We all rejoiced together. The doctors agreed that John had had a remarkable recovery, but they were not yet ready to let him leave the hospital. He would have to stay another night so that they could continue to observe him, but if he was strong enough in the morning, they would let him go home.

As Alvin, Helen, and I made our way home, I was deeply impressed with the power and effectiveness of intercessory praying. It seemed to me that in my intercession, I shared in the heart and the Spirit of God in a way that I had never done before. I realized that I wanted to experience more of this and that this was a real ministry that I could perform. My heart leapt at the thought of becoming an intercessor. I wanted to be used of God in this way. My heart felt at home in this kind of praying.

THE JOURNAL: Today was life changing. I will never be the same again. I sense in my heart that the ministry of intercession is for me. I have been helped and blessed by all that I have learned about prayer since I came on this journey and entered this city, but today was different. It was special. I have learned that prayer has many aspects to it, but I know in my heart that this particular type of prayer is where my ministry and work really belongs. My spirit feels fulfilled when I love people with the love of God. When I can carry their burdens, enter into their pain, feel their loneliness, experience for myself their sin and separation from God. I am not sure whether this might be considered as a "call from God," but I know in my spirit that God wants His love for people to be expressed in my heart through intercessions for them. He wants me to identify with them and pray for them in Jesus's name. This is to be an important part of my spiritual work. This is what He wants me to do for the Kingdom. And I respond by saying, "Yes." It is like He is saying to me, "You can do this, Philip. You have the gifts and abilities to do this very well. I need you to do this with me. Will you do it Philip?" And I say, "Yes."

I do not expect that my companions will sense the same obligations to intercede that I do. They will specialize in some other aspect of prayer. But this I must follow. I must learn, improve, and serve my Lord as an intercessor to the best of my abilities. It was wonderful to see how John recovered so amazingly. I believe God can work through me to bring about other victories in other people, in many varied and surprising ways, through the power of prayer. I have found my ministry.

TOPICS FOR DISCUSSION—CHAPTER FIFETEEN

1. When Philip, Helen, and Alvin prayed for John's healing, they all prayed differently. Describe the three different prayers for healing. Which type of prayer do you think was correct?
2. Discuss the essence of intercession—an intense, specific, unselfish prayer on behalf of others.
3. Discuss the difference between intense intercession and general prayers of good will.
4. Discuss the issue of intense intercessory prayer and the moral free will of the person for whom you prayed.
5. Given the free will of others, how does God respond to our intercessory prayers of faith.
6. Discuss the sensitive issue as to why some are healed and some are not. Is there a definitive answer to this question?
7. Philip, in his time of intercession, felt deeply burdened for John and 'wrestled in the spirit' for his healing:

    - Have you ever felt this specific kind of burden for others?
    - Have you prayed with intense faith?
    - Philip felt called to this type of prayer ministry. Are we all called to pray like this?

CHAPTER SIXTEEN

THE PALACE OF THE KING

When we gathered for breakfast the next morning, we discussed our plans for the day. We all agreed that these days of exploration in the City of Prayer had been exciting and enlightening. We were anxious to continue to explore and experience the great features of the city. They were new to us, and we were enjoying fresh initiatives with God that we had never had before. These experiences, however, seemed to create within us an even greater hunger and desire for more. I know that I was sensing in my own soul a deeper desire for the presence of God and for a greater understanding of His will than I had ever had before. I was encouraged to remember Jesus's statement in the Sermon on the Mount, "Blessed are those who hunger and thirst after righteousness for they shall be filled" (Matt. 5:8). I certainly knew what spiritual hunger was. But it is exciting to be hungry when you know that there is a good meal coming. Hunger that is going to be satisfied is an exciting thing. Hunger that will never be satisfied is a frustration and pain.

As we discussed our plans, we agreed that the first thing we had to do was wait and see if John got out of the hospital. If he did, we would then inquire if he wanted to join us in our day's activities. We did not have long to wait. We had just finished breakfast when John walked in. John had been released early and had been given a clean bill of health. He had made his way immediately to the School of Prayer and joined us around the breakfast table. We welcomed him with great enthusiasm. He informed us that in spite of his sudden illness two days ago, he was now feeling fit and well and was ready and anxious to continue his explorations of the City of Prayer.

It was decided that since Helen and I, through our own folly, had missed out on the visit to the Celebration Hall, we would go there. John, on the other hand, because of his illness, had not been with us in the Intercession Booth, so he would go there. Alvin, who had some trouble getting into the spirit and reality of the Quiet Room, would go back there and try to understand its meaning and experience its atmosphere in a more satisfying way. We first went together to the Circle of God's Will so that we could all start our exploration from the center of God's will and then be separated to go our various ways. We would meet again in the evening and share our experiences.

Once again, it proved to be an enriching and satisfying day for all of us. John came back enthused about the Intercession Booth. He was coming to a clearer understanding that prayer not only had its joys, it also had its burdens. Alvin was beginning to grasp the meaning and wonder of the Quiet Room. Helen and I certainly enjoyed to the full the worship and enthusiastic happiness of the Celebration Hall. It had been a good day.

"The only place left for us to explore from the list our teacher, George, gave us, is the Palace of the King," I said. "Why don't we all go there tomorrow?" Everyone approved of this suggestion with eager anticipation. "Of all of the places we have visited in the City of Prayer, this seems to be the most important," I said.

"Can you imagine what it will be like to be in the Throne Room of the King?" asked Helen dreamily. "I imagine it will be overpowering with His majesty and grandeur. To see the King in all His splendor, surrounded by all of his greatness, is hard to conceive." Nobody could add anything to this because we knew that we were entering a realm that was beyond anything we had known before.

The next morning, we informed George of our plans. He was pleased and encouraged us to pursue them. "Remember, when you get to the Palace of the King, you will want to spend some time in the palace garden. This will be a beautiful experience for you. You will never have experienced such rich beauty as you will see in the Garden of the King. The time in the garden will prepare you to enter the Throne Room. When your time comes to enter the Throne Room, you cannot do it together. Each one must enter this room by themselves. It will be reduced simply to you and God."

"What is the Throne Room like?" asked Helen. "Is it beautiful? Is it filled with treasures and lavish art and decorations, fit for a great king?"

George smiled but would not make any comment. The only thing he said was "I think you will be surprised."

We had learned by now to always start at the Circle of God's Will, which represented the center of His will. Experience had told us that any enterprise in prayer that did not start from the center of God's will was not going to flourish. After we had reaffirmed ourselves of His will, we found the journey to the Palace of the King easy, and we had no difficulty finding the palace and its gardens.

The palace was situated in very extensive grounds and surrounded by a high strong wall. There were attendants on duty at the main gate to the palace grounds. When we told them, however, that our purpose was to seek access to the Throne Room, they very quickly let us through and pointed us to a small guest house located near to the main gate. "Go in there and you will find someone who will explain the gardens to you and will guide you to the Throne Room of the King."

In response to our knocking at the door of the guest house, a very pleasant young man opened the door. Without hesitation, he welcomed us in and introduced himself as David. "If you wish, I will help you and guide you in your visit to the Throne Room. First, I will take you to the palace gardens. It is important that you spend some time in the gardens. They are beautiful, and you will enjoy them. What they do is express the spirit and personality of the King Himself. The beauty and fruitfulness of the gardens reflect the beauty and fruitfulness of the King. In the gardens, you will begin to absorb the atmosphere of the palace and the King. They are peaceful and filled with color. You will see they are groomed and tended to with loving care. You will find that all of the plants seem to flourish with great ripeness and flower with great beauty. I want you to sense it, drink it in, and absorb the atmosphere into your own spirit, until the quietness and fruitfulness of the garden begin to express what is happening in your own heart. This will not happen unless you take time to let the spirit of the garden affect and influence your own spirit. You will be seeking an audience with the King in his Throne Room. If this is to be a successful meeting, there will need to be a bonding of His Spirit with yours. The garden will prepare you for that.

"You remember the apostle Paul wrote about this in his epistle to the Galatians. He listed a number of the attitudes of spirit that were contrary to the Spirit of the King, and he said that the people who reflect these bad attitudes would not get into His presence. He then listed the good fruits of the Spirit. Those who do enter the presence of the King and enjoy His fellowship are people who have absorbed into their being the attitudes and atmosphere of the fruits of the Spirit. Paul said, 'The acts of the sinful nature are obvious: sexual immortality, impurity and debauchery; idolatry and witchcraft; hatred, discord, jealousy, fits of rage, selfish ambition, dissensions, factions and every drunkenness, orgies, and the like. I warn you, as I did before that those who live like this will not inherit the kingdom of God. But the fruit of the Spirit is love, joy, peace, patience, kindness, goodness faithfulness, gentleness and self control' (Gal. 5:19-23). In the garden, you will absorb the fruits of the spirit. Your spirit will begin to drink in the warm love, the deep joy, the great gentleness that is the Spirit of the Lord. You must let these things flow into your soul and become the atmosphere of your heart. They are the fruit of the Spirit. They are the natural result of being in the presence of the King. Let them flow into your heart until they become the dominating condition of your life. Then you will be rich in spirit and pure in heart and ready for the Throne Room of the King."

"Oh yes," cried Helen. "Let's go. I just cannot wait." Her enthusiasm was catching, and we all were anxious to get going on this great experience.

"I will take you to the garden," said David. "I suggest you take time to explore it and see its beauty for yourself. It would be better if you each did this on your own. Some will want to linger over some sections of the garden while others will be more absorbed with other parts. This is a personal and singular journey. We are all different in personality, and so we will respond to the garden differently. After a while, I will come and take each of you on your own to the Throne Room of the King. After you have been in the Throne Room, you can come back here to the guest house and wait until all of you have visited the Throne Room."

David led us along a pathway that led to the garden. On the way, he instructed us, "You will find the garden is very appealing to look at. In fact all of the senses will be stimulated in the garden. The perfume of the flowers, the singing of the birds, and the laughter of the water will appeal to your senses as well as the color, beauty, and variety of the flowers and shrubs. But the important thing is to not only appreciate the garden with your senses. Let it sink into your soul. Let its appeal go beyond what you see and sense. Give your soul a feast. Let it flow into your spirit and bring freshness and inspiration to the functions of your heart. Let the spirit of love, and joy, and peace flood your personality until the fruit of the spirit comes to ripe fullness in your own spirit."

We reached the gate of the garden, and David left us there, saying, "I will let each one of you take time to explore the garden on your own. Take time. Linger over the parts that seem to speak to you the most, then I will come to take you each one individually, to the Throne Room of the King."

As I meandered alone through the many pathways of the garden, I realized that this was not a wild garden. A great deal of effort and time had been spent planning, organizing, and maintaining it. While the plants and trees were clearly rich and healthy in blossom and color, they were that way because they had been carefully attended to, nourished, and pruned. The garden was beautiful, but someone had cultivated it and maintained it, so that its beauty was disciplined and organized. As I thought about this, I realized that it was also true about the growth of the fruits of the Spirit in my own heart. To develop and flourish, they needed attention, pruning, cultivation, and faithful nourishment.

I came to one part of the garden where a clear stream gurgled over some rocks. At this spot, there was a beautiful bower with a comfortable seat. I sat down and listened to the brook singing. The seat was surrounded by a lattice work to which a large vine had entwined itself, forming a gorgeous wall and ceiling to the bower. The vine had an abundance of deep purple flowers that gave off a gentle aroma. This was an unusually peaceful and relaxing spot, and I decided to spend some of my time here. As I sat quietly in the seat and began to drink in the sounds, sights, and atmosphere of the garden, I seemed to float away from my body. I became more and more aware of the existence of my spirit. I sensed the peace of the garden beginning to flow into my soul. I felt great waves of love and grace roll over me. My heart seemed to sing with joy. A great and unfathomable peace enveloped me. I was absorbing the fruit of the Spirit. I was being overcome by the atmosphere of the King. His spirit of love and grace seemed to dominate me and take possession of my heart. This was what David meant when he spoke about drinking in the fruit of the Spirit. This was resting in His presence and letting His grace flow over me. My heart was full. My soul rejoiced. I felt the wonder of loving God as I had never felt it before. The channels of my heart were wide open. He was flowing into me and filling me. And His presence was awe inspiring. I do not know how long I was in this state of receiving the inflow of the fruits of the Spirit into my being, but I know I was surprised when David arrived to take me to the Throne Room of the King.

David smiled at me. "I can see that the fruit of the garden has possessed your soul and that you are alive with the atmosphere of the King. That is good, for I am now going to take you to the Throne Room of the King." My heart was so full that I had no comment to make in response to David. But I did wonder to myself that if the garden of the King is so beautiful, what will his throne room be like? If I felt so enriched by the atmosphere of the garden, what will I feel when I stand before His throne and kneel in His presence? I will be overwhelmed.

My mind was so taken up with these thoughts, and I was so full of anticipation mingled with a little awe, I paid little attention as David led me into the large palace building. In the hallway of the building, there was a set of large, heavy, wooden doors. David led me to these doors. "These are the doors that take you to the Throne Room of the King. I will open the doors. You walk through, and you will be in the Throne Room. I will close the doors behind you."

I was trembling now with excitement and anticipation. I had no idea what splendors and wonders waited for me behind those doors. To be alone in the presence of the King seemed unspeakable. To stand in reverence before His throne would be overpowering. David opened the doors, and with awe, I hesitatingly entered the Throne Room of the King. I heard the doors close behind me, and I knew that I was alone. I was speechless. I was struck dumb. In all of the things I had tried to imagine what the Throne Room would be like, I had never imagined this. Throughout all of the conversations that I had had with my friends about what would be in the Throne Room of the King, no one had come even close to describing what I saw now. It was empty, stark, and bare. The wooden floors had no covering to relieve their plainness. The walls were painted a simple brown and had no pictures or decoration to enhance their bareness. There was no furniture. No paintings or ornaments. No color or design. And most of all, in the Throne Room of the King, there were no thrones. How could this possibly be? In the middle of the floor, there was a small prayer mat. On the mat lay a Bible that was open. In the ceiling above the prayer mat was a skylight. From the skylight some outside sunshine shone in and illuminated the prayer mat. Beyond these simple things, the so-called Throne Room of the King was barren, empty, and featureless.

In my first astonished reaction of unbelief, I said to myself, *There must be some mistake. David has brought me to the wrong room.* Then I thought, *This is not the Throne Room, there must be another door that leads me from this room into the Throne Room proper.* In desperation I looked around, but there was no other door than the one through which I had entered. *I must go out and talk to David,* I thought. *He has made a mistake or failed to explain something to me. This empty space, devoid of everything, including thrones, cannot be the Throne Room of the King.*

I turned and opened the doors that were behind me. David was still in the hallway. "There must be a mistake," I said. "That is not the Throne Room of the King."

David slowly shook his head. "There has been no mistake, Philip. This is indeed the Throne Room of the King."

"But there is no throne in there. How can it be a throne room if there is no throne? And where is the King. He is not in there either?"

"Philip, tell me what you saw in there?"

"Well, that's just it," I responded. "There was nothing in there. Absolutely nothing! It was bare and empty except for a little prayer mat under the skylight with a Bible open on it."

"What else was in there Philip?"

"Nothing! I was in there alone."

David laid a hand on my shoulder and said carefully, "Philip, you were in there. And when you are in there, think carefully Philip, when you are in there, then there is a throne and there is a king. Now what I suggest is that you go back into the Throne Room. Change the level of your expectations, and go and kneel on the prayer mat and read the Bible. You will find that the Bible has been marked, and important passages that you need to read have been underlined. Read these passages and you will begin to understand what the Throne Room of the King is all about."

Chastened and humbled, but still mystified, I entered the Throne Room again. Nothing had changed. It was still empty but for the prayer mat and the Bible. But I too was in here. And I realized that my presence had some significance. I quietly went over to the prayer mat and knelt in prayer. I noticed that the Bible was open and part of the printing had been underlined. I picked it up and read the verses that were underlined. They were from John's Gospel chapter 14 verses 20-24. They are taken from the last dissertation of Jesus to the disciples before his crucifixion. He said, "On that day you will realize that I am in my Father, and you are in me, and I am in you. Whoever has my commands and obeys them, he is the one who loves me. He who loves me will be loved by my Father, and I too will love him and show myself to him. Then Judas [not Judas Iscariot] said, 'But Lord, how do you intend to show yourself to us and not to the world?' Jesus replied, 'If anyone loves me he will obey my teaching. My Father will love him and we will come to him and make our home with him. He who does not love me will not obey my teaching. These words you hear are not my own: they belong to the Father who sent me.'"

As I read these verses, the truth gradually but powerfully began to dawn on me. God wants to live within me. The Kingdom of God is within me. God's kingdom is wherever God rules. How well does God rule in my heart and life? Am I obeying Him? The throne is really my heart. But who is on the throne? Whose will is done in my life? Who sits on the throne of authority in my heart? Does God sit there in unquestioned authority? Do I want to share the throne with Him? Do I resist His kingship and authority in parts of my life? Is He Lord of all, or am I withholding some aspects of my life and "rights" from Him?

Here, as I knelt on this simple prayer mat, in the Throne Room of the King, I realized that the throne was my own heart and my own will. Did the rule and authority of God extend to all of my life?

I turned again to the Bible and saw there were other markers that guided me to other portions of the scripture. I opened the Bible to the place where the next marker indicated. The verse that was underlined was Romans 12:1, which said "Therefore, I urge you, brothers, in view of God's mercy, to offer your bodies as living sacrifices, holy and pleasing to God—this is your spiritual act of worship." What God, the King, is calling for is an act of supreme commitment to Him and to His will and His rule. He wants to be the King of my heart. He wants to rule all of my life. He wants to sit on the throne of my being. I began to sing the hymn:

All to Jesus I surrender;
All to Him I freely give.
I will ever love and trust Him,
In His presence daily live.

I surrender all.
I surrender all.
All to Thee my blessed Savior,
I surrender all.[1]

The next Bible verse that I turned to was the well-known verse where Jesus responded to the question, "Of all of the commandments, which one is the most important?" His response was. "'Hear, O Israel, the Lord our God, the Lord is one. Love the Lord your God with all your heart and with all your soul and with all your mind and with all your strength.' The second is this: 'Love your neighbor as yourself.' There is no commandment greater than these" (Mark 12:29-31). As I meditated on these words of Jesus, the word that seemed to burn itself in my mind was the word *all.* I realized that I could not love God with all of my heart if I resisted His will in some ways. I could not love him with all of my mind, soul, and strength if I was withholding some parts of these from Him. All meant all. King meant King. Lord meant Lord. Who was going to sit on the throne of my heart? Did I want to reserve some of the authority and rule for myself? Did I want to maintain the right to have occasions when I would sit on the throne and be the authority? There were certainly many times when I was ready to have God sit on the throne, but I was not sure that I wanted Him there all of the time. I really wanted to reserve the right to say no sometimes. But I also realized that if the Kingdom of God was to come in its fullness to my life, then God must be king of the kingdom. Not half the king. Not a kinghood shared with me, but king of all.

As I continued in prayer, I realized that the issue I was facing in the Throne Room of the King was one of complete commitment and trust. In my mind I remembered the times I had visited the Circle of His Will in the Central Cathedral. These had been precious times when being in the center of God's will had thrilled my heart. But what I was looking at now was not a visit or an occasional experience but a life lived in the center of His will. Not partial commitment. Not reserved obedience. Not conditional trust, but complete commitment. I thought about driving a car. My heart and spirit were like a car. I owned the car, it was my car, so I was the driver. I was willing to be generous with Jesus about the use of the car. I was willing to oblige Him and often take Him anywhere he wanted to go. I was ready to put myself to considerable inconvenience and cost in order to use the car for His needs and wishes. But until now I had still retained the right to be the driver. I had ultimate authority. I could reserve the right to say no to Him if I wished. I did not think that that no would happen very often, but I did want to reserve the right to say it. After all it was my car, and I was the driver. I could use the car for my own business and wishes whenever I wanted. But here in the Throne Room of the King, what was being called for was for me to say, "Here is the car. I give it to you. You take it, it is yours. I give up my right to it, and let you have complete control. You be the driver. You decide what must be done with it. It is yours and is available to do your will." Then I would depend upon the generosity and love of Jesus, rather than have Him depend upon my generosity. Faith told me that the car would be put to much better use if it was under His control, rather than mine.

As I struggled with this concept of complete commitment in the Throne room of the King, I realized with joy that I was willing for this to happen. I was willing to get off the throne of my heart and invite Him to sit there. He would be king. He would have the authority. His will would be done. As I knelt in prayer, I found I could say with all sincerity, "Your kingdom come in my life. All of Your will be done in me." I willingly yielded the throne of my life to Him. In my imagination I could see myself stepping off the throne and inviting Him to sit there. And He came. He sat on the throne, and He brought with Him his wonderful presence and majesty.

I realized that this was a decisive moment, and I felt immediate changes begin to happen in my heart. When I yielded my all to him and said, "Thy will be done." I felt my heart being invaded by a wonderful sense of His presence.

He was in control of my heart in all His fullness. I was aware of His Divine presence as I had never been aware of it before. There was a sense of communion with Him and unity with Him. I was flooded with His presence and nearness. He possessed the throne room of my heart. He had come to make his home in me. The scripture was now fulfilled in my life: "If anyone loves me, he will obey my teaching. My Father will love him, and we will come to him and make our home with him" (John 14:23). I felt as if He now had a true home in my heart, and had moved in and taken possession. I was living in Him, and He was living in me.

I remembered what Jesus had promised to his disciples on that last evening he had with them in the upper room before His death. He promised them, "I will ask the Father, and he will give you another counselor, to be with you forever—the Spirit of truth. The world cannot accept him, because it neither sees him nor knows him, but you know him, for he lives with you and will be in you. I will not leave you as orphans; I will come to you." (John 14:16-18). I felt the Spirit had come, and my heart was filled with His abiding presence. I belonged to Him; He belonged to me. We were united. Together. We were one. It was a wonderful experience, and I sensed it was there to stay as long as I let Jesus sit on the throne of my heart. I was reminded of the chorus that we sometimes sang asking the vital questions:

> Is your all on the alter of sacrifice laid?
> Your Heart does the Spirit control?
> You can only be blest and have peace and sweet rest,
> As you yield Him your body and soul.[2]

I understood now what the Throne Room was all about. I was the throne room, and He was now the King on the throne of my heart. The oneness and unity was very real. There was now no division of will or wishes. I wanted what He wanted. I wished what He wished. I could now understand the wonderful promise He had given about prayer when He said, "If you remain in me and my words remain in you, ask whatever you wish, and it will be given you" (John 15:7). This was understandable when what I wished was what He wished. The expression of prayer as **learning to receive what God wants to give** made perfect sense now since there was a unity of heart, and I only wanted what God wanted, and I only wanted to receive what God wanted to give.

With a great sense of fullness and peace, I rose from the prayer mat and left the empty room but carried with me the Kingdom of God in my heart and His presence on the throne of my life. When I left the room, I could see that

David was still waiting for me. He seemed to sense right away that I had made a vital spiritual discovery. He smiled, took my hand, and said, "So you found the throne room did you?"

"Yes," I replied, "and guess who is sitting upon the throne?"

David laughed and gave me a brotherly hug for joy. "And you will carry this presence around with you. Be sure that you keep refreshing His Lordship and renewing His control of your life day by day. This is a daily commitment and a constant recognition. Be sure you keep it alive and renewed each day. Come and I will take you back to the gatehouse, and you can wait there for your friends. They too must visit the Throne Room of the King."

"Can I tell them what happened to me and explain to them about what the Throne Room is all about?" I asked. "They will be as surprised and shocked as I was when they enter the Throne Room of the King. I should warn them about it and explain its nature to them."

"No. This is something they must discover for themselves. It will be much more valuable to them when they see and discover the light for themselves."

With that David led the way back to the gatehouse and told me to wait here, or go into the garden and enjoy it until he returned with my friends. I was impatient to hear what my companions experienced in the Throne Room but decided that I might as well enjoy the beauties of the garden while I waited. This second experience in the garden was even more fulfilling than it had been before. It seemed to shine with an even greater glory than before. The atmosphere and fruit of the Spirit seemed to flow into me in greater abundance, until my heart overflowed with the love, and peace, and joy of the Lord. As I absorbed this wonderful atmosphere, time seemed to stand still, and I was surprised when David returned with Helen. I could tell from the sparkle in her eye and the glow of joy on her face that she too had discovered the realities of the Throne Room. While Helen and I shared our mutual experience of complete commitment to the Lord and having Him sit on the throne room of our hearts, David returned first with Alvin and then finally with John. All of us had discovered the meaning and the purpose of the Throne Room. We were all filled with the same presence of the Spirit. We had all been surprised at our first entrance to the Throne Room but had, because of the guidance given to us by the scriptures there, finally understood the lesson that we were supposed to learn. All of us had gladly accepted it, except for Alvin, who had had a deep struggle making his complete commitment to the Lord. But even Alvin had finally taken the step and was now filled with the wonderful sense of His presence.

As we made our way back to our accommodations in the School of Prayer, we were rather quiet. We preferred to let the experience of the Throne Room take root in our hearts and settle in our spirit. Just before we reached home, however, I said to my companions, "We have now explored the main features of the City of Prayer. We have been to the Central Cathedral and the Circle of God's Will. We have been to the Celebration Hall, the Quiet Room, and the Intercession Booth. Today we visited the Palace of the King with its Gardens and Throne Room. All of these we were told are essential and important features of life in the City of Prayer. We have been in the city for a number of days now, and we understand better what it is about and how life is conducted here. We must now decide if we wish to stay and make the City of Prayer our home. Why don't we take the night to think and pray about it, and then, if we are ready, we can discuss our decisions tomorrow morning at breakfast?" To this everyone agreed, and we each went to our own room to think and to pray about whether or not we should make the City of Prayer our home.

THE JOURNAL: I have made great leaps and bounds in my spiritual experience in the last few days. I already know in my heart that I want to stay here. I want to make this place my home. I want to live in this city so that I can carry the atmosphere of prayer with me into my everyday life, and live with the spirit of prayer always within easy reach.

I reread the scriptures that had been outlined in the Throne Room. As I meditate upon them, I am even more aware of the presence of the Lord in my heart and I gladly confirm Him on the throne of my life and endorse Him as Lord of my life. This is something I will do regularly.

TOPICS FOR DISCUSSION—CHAPTER SIXTEEN

1. The Garden was not wild and unruly but well tended and maintained:

    - What do you think this means to the growth of the fruit of the Spirit in your life?

2. The Throne Room of the King was a great surprise to Philip:

    - Was it a surprise to you?
      What did you think it would be like?

3. In the Throne room, Philip realized, "The throne is in my heart."

    - Discuss what this means.
    - What does it take to let Jesus sit on the throne?
    - What were the results of letting Jesus sit on the throne?

CHAPTER SEVENTEEN

A DAY IN THE LIFE OF THE CITY OF PRAYER

When I went down for breakfast the next morning, I knew that my mind was made up—I wanted to stay in the City of Prayer. I was, however, anxious to know what my companions were going to do. I had formed a deep affection for each one of them, and I would sense a great loss if any of them decided not to stay. I was surprised to see that the teacher, George, was also at the breakfast table along with my three other friends. They were in deep conversation but made room for me when I arrived.

Helen smiled as I was sitting down and told me, "George has something important to say to us."

George looked at me and, in order to bring me up to date on their conversation, said, "I understand from what your friends are saying that you are going to decide today whether to stay in the City of Prayer or not." I nodded my agreement. George continued, "This is a very important decision, and I want to do all I can to help you make a choice that will be correct and satisfying for you." Looking at all of us George said, "You have all done well. You have made the journey to the city. You have explored the main features of the city, and you are now ready to decide whether or not you want to stay here. There is, however, one other suggestion that I want to make to you before you determine your final decision. I would like each of you to agree to spend one day with a family in the City of Prayer. You will observe how that family goes about the business of living their day-by-day lives in the spirit of prayer. You will spend time with them as they live through what should be a normal day in the life of the City of Prayer. We have been at great pains to emphasize to you that this is just a normal city. The citizens are normal people. The difference is that the people in the city seek to bring the spirit of prayer into their everyday lives. Prayer is a constant influence in what they do and how they react. They endeavor to make the atmosphere of prayer and the presence of God so predominant that it colors the whole picture of how they go about their lives. While you have experienced some of the outstanding features of the city, I now want you to see how this works out in the everyday lives of normal people. After you have spent a day with them, then you will be better informed as to whether or not you would like to stay here.

"I think it is important that you understand that the City of Prayer is, more than anything else, something that you carry in your heart. It is living your life in the spirit of prayer. The spirit of the City of Prayer is more than a place it is a way of life. You have all experienced now the great features of the city—the Central Cathedral, the Quiet Room, the Intercession Booths, the Hall of Celebration, the Garden of the King, and the Throne Room. By practicing and maintaining these features of prayer and letting them sink into your heart and spirit, they become strong characteristics of what makes up the spirit and atmosphere of your life. The City of Prayer is largely a spiritual experience that makes prayer influential in the living of your life and in all aspects of that life. You carry these features in your heart and maintain their spirit as you go through each day. To experience the City of Prayer in your heart means that you will live with the spirit of prayer influencing all aspects of life."

I was not sure that it was necessary for me to take this last step as I had already made up my mind, but I had tried to always follow the guidance and advice of my teachers throughout the journey and in the explorations of the city, and they had always given me good advice, so I would agree to this but responded rather doubtfully, "Thank you for this. I think it would be interesting, and it certainly would not do us any harm."

This halfhearted endorsement was not quite what George was hoping for. After a little thought, he said, "You must understand that you have had some very wonderful and exceptional experiences in prayer. But somehow, you must learn to bring these great experiences down to the level of practical everyday living. In the City of Prayer, you cannot spend all of your time rotating around the great features such as, the Central Cathedral, the Celebration Hall, and the Quiet Room. You should certainly visit them and make use of them, but you cannot spend all of your time doing this and still live the normal life of the city. You will have to get a job and a house. You will need to spend time looking after yourself and entertaining your friends. The average people in the City of Prayer do not spend all of their time, even if they want to, visiting the great features of the city, they have to live a normal life. Since they cannot withdraw from life and spend all of their time praying, they seek to bring the atmosphere and practice of prayer into their everyday lives. They want to adopt attitudes that reflect the Spirit of God. This is prayer made practical. This is life in the City of Prayer. You have to see this in action and take note of how it works in the midst of the distractions of making a living and the stresses of family life."

After this speech from George, I felt somewhat reprimanded. So with a little more enthusiasm, I said, "I understand, and I think it is important." I looked at my companions, and they too seemed satisfied that this last step had to be taken, and we would delay our decision time until after we had spent a day in the life of the city.

Sensing our agreement, George said, "I will need to make arrangements for each of you to be the guests of a family. I suggest that you take this day to rest and relax, and then this evening I will introduce each of you to the family that you will be staying with. You will stay with them overnight and accompany one of the members of the family through their day tomorrow, and then I will return and get you tomorrow evening. When we are all back here, you can then discuss together whether you want to stay in the City of Prayer or not."

We all thanked George for his interest in us, and looked forward to a quiet and restful day. I spent most of the day in my own room, reviewing and evaluating the experiences in prayer that I had had since leaving the Viewing Platform up until now. I felt thankful for the progress that had been made and for the help that I had received from so many people bringing me to this point in my journey into prayer. I felt as if my inner life with God had been transformed. Now I was anxious to let these influences affect how I lived my daily life.

It was rather late, about nine o'clock in the evening, when George knocked on my door and asked me to accompany him to my host family. We drove in George's car. As he drove, George gave me some background about the family I would be staying with. "You will be living with Jim and Nancy Parker," he said. "Jim and Nancy have two children, a boy, Bill, who is about sixteen years old, and a girl, Rena, who is about fourteen. Both Jim and Nancy have jobs. Jim is a bank manager, and Nancy works in an art store. Their son Bill is a fine boy and greatly interested in basketball, he is on the high school basketball team. Rena is in the early teenage years and is a bit of a problem to them right now. It is not clear what direction Rena will take in life. At the moment she does not know herself and is a little rebellious. Jim and Nancy are a great couple and an excellent example of how to live with the spirit of the City of Prayer in your heart. You will accompany Jim through his whole day tomorrow. I want you to observe him and ask any questions that you wish. I will come and pick you up tomorrow evening about this time."

We drove to a middle-income, suburban area of the city and drew up in front of a home situated toward the end of a row of houses. I smiled when I saw a basketball net fixed over the garage door. "This is where the Parkers live," said George. "I think you will enjoy staying with them." Jim welcomed us at the door and warmly invited us into his home. He introduced us to his family. His wife Nancy was a pretty and energetic lady who welcomed me with enthusiasm. The son Bill was tall and thin, *A basketball player*, I thought. Bill was open and friendly and seemed quite relaxed to have me there. Rena, however, seemed a little more reticent but was polite. She was dressed in a rather exaggerated way with her hair in a strange unspeakable style. Both children soon excused themselves as they had homework to do. George, after the introductions were complete, also took his departure, leaving me alone with Jim and Nancy. Since it was now quite late, Nancy suggested some refreshments before we retired for the night.

The three of us adults gathered informally around the kitchen table for coffee and sweets. I felt very much at home and comfortable with Jim and Nancy. We were soon talking together without inhibitions. "How long have you lived in the City of Prayer?" I asked.

"We have been here for over ten years now," Jim responded.

"And how do you like it," I asked.

"Oh, we enjoy it," said Jim. "We had a little bit of a struggle to start with getting into the way of life and culture of the city, but we have adjusted our habits and developed a pattern of life that accommodates the spirit of the city."

I pressed on with my questions. "Do you think you will ever leave the city?"

Nancy jumped into the conversation. "Oh, no!" she said. "This is our home now. We love it here. We would not want any other way of life."

"How do the children fit into this kind of life?" was my next question.

"Bill is a free, relaxed fellow. He has made the adjustment very well. He enters into the lifestyle without a problem. He does well at school and loves sports. We have no problems with Bill. Rena is going through the common turmoil of girls her age. She is more of a problem to us, and we are not at all sure how things will turn out with Rena."

"Do you think your children will decide to live here?

"That will be their decision. Bill could easily fit in here. At the moment Rena would have her difficulties."

Jim drained his coffee cup and said, "My instructions from George are to let you accompany me throughout the day tomorrow and to answer any questions that you may have. I consider it a privilege to do this. I hope the experience encourages you to become a citizen here. I will not do anything different tomorrow than what is usual in the daily run of things. I get up at six in the morning. I have my time of prayer and devotions until seven. After that I go for a walk, come back, and get showered and dressed for the day. If you could plan to accompany me on the walk and then be with me throughout the day, I will attempt to make it as ordinary a day as possible." I thanked Nancy and Jim for their kindness and hospitality and retired to bed for the night, wondering what tomorrow might bring.

I was up early the next morning, and after having my own time of prayer, I was ready to join Jim in his morning walk. He walked briskly and did not say much. He seemed deep in thought, until our way led us into some parkland. "I come here every morning," said Jim. "I enjoy being surrounded by nature. The quietness and beauty of the place helps me be thankful to God for the world He has made."

I had a question that was on my mind but did not want to interrupt Jim's thoughts, so I said nothing. He still seemed to be in an attitude of prayer. It was as if he was continuing his prayer time while he walked. The walk was long and fast, and I was not used to this, so I was somewhat glad to arrive back at the house again.

Jim excused himself to go and shower and get dressed for work. I also went to my room and got ready for the activity of the day. All of the family was ready for breakfast by the time I got down to the kitchen. As we gathered around the table, Jim asked Bill to give thanks for the meal. After breakfast was finished and before the family scattered for the day, it was the practice for a member of the family to pray and ask the Lord to go with all of them that day. This morning Nancy did the honors.

Nancy had to take Bill and Rena to school and then would go directly to her work in the art store. Jim took the other car and drove us to his bank. I sat in the front of the car with Jim. As we drove to the bank, Jim mentioned to me that he really enjoyed classical and sacred music. "At Christmastime," he said, "it has become traditional for Nancy and me to go and enjoy a performance of Handles' Messiah in one of the large concert halls in the city." He then switched on the car stereo system and played some quiet, sacred music.

As we were driving along, I found listening to the music very relaxing and soothing. While enjoying the music, I started to think what had already taken place that morning in Jim's life. He gets up at 6:00 a.m. He has an hour of prayer. He goes for a long and fast walk into the parkland and enjoys being surrounded by nature, thanking the Lord for all that is around him. He then gets dressed and ready for his day's work. He has breakfast and prayer with the family, and now he is on his way to work, listening to this quiet and sacred music. I was very impressed by what I had already seen, and the day was only beginning. I turned to Jim and asked him about his regular morning schedule. "The day is still young, Jim, and so far I am very impressed. Is this your normal morning schedule?"

Jim smiled. "Yes, Philip, this is my daily practice. In the early hours of the day, before work starts, my mind is relatively free to go where it wants to go. I make it my habit to use these hours to focus on God and let my spirit be aware of His presence. I do this through prayer. I do this as I walk. I do this as I communicate with my family. Some days it is easier than others. Sometimes I struggle to make contact with Him, while on other days it seems to happen naturally without any effort. But easy or difficult, I have learned to make it the habit of my life. The whole tone and atmosphere of the day is usually set in these early hours. I do not want to miss it. Now the timetable changes at the weekends when I am not working. But for workdays, I try to discipline myself to follow the schedule you have observed this morning. It gives me time to contact God and let Him speak to me when He wants. It is not always easy to carry this spirit with me all day into the work atmosphere, but I will try. You will see for yourself and determine how well I do this as you observe the day unfold."

Jim's bank was in the downtown section of the city and seemed like a busy major center for business. Some of the staff had already arrived at the office, and when we entered, Jim greeted them and introduced me to them. He then went into his office to begin the day's work.

The day started with him opening his mail and then his e-mail. His secretary came in to get her instructions for the day. She brought with her a number of reports that Jim had to examine and sign. He gave full attention to these responsibilities. Now and then the telephone rang, and he always answered courteously. He had two interviews that morning. One interview was with a prospective employee. The other interview was with a businessman who was looking for a significant loan from the bank. Since the interviews were private matters, I could not stay in the office while this was going on, but Jim indicated to me that even in the midst of these conversations, he tried to stay aware of the inner presence of God with him. "These interviews are very important to the people involved, and may change their whole life, so I attempt always to treat them with respect and be wise and sensitive in what I am doing. Often, I am able to breathe a short prayer for these people, both before and after the interview."

The morning passed quickly. I had no doubt that Jim was engrossed in his work and his mind was absorbed in all that he had to do. Yet even when his whole attention was focused on his duties, he never seemed out of spirit or in discord in any way. Although he had many responsibilities and dealt with difficult situations, he maintained a peaceful confidence in his own demeanor. *This*, I thought to myself, *is a man of God at work.*

When lunchtime came, Jim suggested we get out of the bank and eat lunch at a nearby restaurant. "This," he said with a laugh, "is not normal. Usually for lunch I eat a quick sandwich in the office, but in honor of your presence we will today eat out. When I eat in the office, it also gives me a little time to disengage from the affairs of the bank and relax by focusing my mind on other things. I enjoy thinking about the family and some of the good times we have had together. In fact I keep some photographs of happy family vacations in my desk drawer, and it relaxes me to take them out and look at them. I also like, at this time, to think again of my fellowship with God. In fact, I try to make it a habit throughout the day to remind myself of His presence and say a quick prayer to Him."

As we ate lunch, I asked Jim a few questions. "I am impressed with your way of life Jim. In spite of the pressures you are under, you seem to be able to maintain a spirit that is calm and confident. Do you ever get discouraged or weary with this kind of intense spiritual life?"

"In the big picture and the overall experience of the prayer life, the answer is no. But if you mean are there days when I get discouraged or weary, then certainly, yes, there are. But the big picture of my life here is that I would not want to live any other way. This is satisfying, fulfilling, and helps me to live life in every dimension, not just the physical life, or the mental life, but a full orbed and balanced life that includes life in the spirit and fellowship with God. There are elements of joy, and peace and contact with God that I would not want to change for anything else in the world. When the apostle Paul talks about 'Christ living in you,' I think he meant that we should live and be conscious of the Spirit of Christ in us. It is 'living in the Spirit.' I try to do that. My prayer life is a vital part of this style of living. I am learning better all the time how to live and be aware of God's presence in me."

"Are you still making progress in prayer, or do you feel like you have learned enough and don't need to grow any more?

"Oh, by no means. Always in prayer there are new challenges, new demands on my faith. Sometimes I feel that I have a long way to go in this matter of praying. In fellowship with God there are always new things coming up. God is remarkably fresh. He is always leading us into new and exciting paths that we have never gone before. Without exploring new territory, the walk with God would get mundane and boring. But for those who are open and seeking, then new and exciting things are constantly being revealed, and old truths are continually being refreshed and renewed. For those of us who are growing in grace, monotony and lack of exciting discovery is just not an issue."

As the meal concluded, Jim said, "I have an important meeting of the bank board scheduled for this afternoon. I would like to return to the office and give myself ample time to prepare for it. When I have a meeting like this, I also like to have time to pray prior to the arrival of the board members. If you don't mind, I would like a little private time, and then I will check with the board members to see if they would object to you sitting in and observing the meeting." I appreciated his willingness to accommodate me and was more than willing to accompany him back to the bank so that he could prepare for his meeting.

The plan was that the meeting would be held in the bank boardroom. It was a well-appointed room. The walls were wood paneled with a deep dark wood. The furnishings were rich with matching color. Comfortable executive chairs were arranged around a large mahogany table. I looked around the room while Jim was in his office preparing for the meeting that he had to chair. I thought it was a very comfortable room for board meetings to be held.

The meeting took most of the afternoon. Although some difficult issues were dealt with, and there were strong views expressed about some of the items on the agenda, I noticed that Jim's quiet and confident spirit seemed to keep the atmosphere respectful and positive. I had never been in a meeting where these levels of important decisions were being made, but I had attended meetings of much less importance and saw great tensions and divisions emerge. I was very impressed with the quality and professionalism with which Jim guided this group of people to make significant conclusions. I felt that this skill was not only an expression of his own abilities but also reflected his spiritual strength and character. His life of prayer was present and important, even though not prominently displayed to the group.

After the meeting was over, Jim indicated that he was tired and ready to go home. As we drove to Jim's home, I mentioned to him that I was impressed at the way he had chaired the meeting. I asked, "Does your prayer life help you handle these situations?"

"I find that when my own spirit is at peace, and I am at rest within myself, then those differences of opinion do not upset me. It is easier to keep harmony between people when your own heart is in harmony with itself and with God.

In this job, difficult decisions must be made. It can become quite stressful sometimes, especially if there are strong differences of opinion. To be able to sense the presence of God in the midst of all of this brings confidence and assurance that helps you guide things to a proper conclusion."

"When you pray before a meeting, what do you pray for?"

"I pray for wisdom, so that I can handle the issues and the people well and with respect."

""Do you pray for guidance so that the correct decisions will be made."

"Not much. Decisions that come up in meetings like that have to be made quickly. I find that if I am going to do God's will, then I need time to give the issue some thought and prayer. I need to let God guide my spirit and my thinking. This takes time. I don't have that luxury of time in some of these meetings, so I pray more for wisdom than for guidance. I pray for understanding more than for power and authority to get my own way."

"Do you think then, that God's will is always done in these meetings since you have prayed about them?'

"Absolutely not. I would not dare blame God for some of the decisions that the bank has made."

I thought about this for a while and then asked, "What about board meetings in the church. We pray about these decisions before we start. Do you think God's will is always done in the decisions that the church makes?"

Jim smiled at this question. "I would hope that churches making decisions would be a little more alert to the will of God than a bank board meeting, but even there, I am afraid, God's will is not always done."

Jim was the last of the family to arrive home after the day's activities. Nancy was busy preparing the supper. We were, apparently, in a little bit of a rush because Bill had to go to a basketball practice. I noted that around the table there was a free flow of conversation. Each member of the family outlined some of the important things that had happened to them that day. There was courtesy and consideration shown to each other.

"Nancy has to take Bill to his basketball game," said Jim. "Rena wants to go around to her friend's house so that they can do their homework together. Why don't you come with me as I drive Rena to her friend's house?"

After we had dropped Rena off and were on the way home, Jim said, "As you can see we are a busy family. With two teenagers who are involved in a number of sports and clubs, and with Nancy involved in some church activities, in addition to the time she spends giving free art lessons to some young people who are really very gifted but can't afford to take lessons elsewhere, our evenings are often rather hectic. When I get some free time at home, I like to spend some of it talking with Nancy and doing some personal reading. I don't watch much TV. I like to watch some sports, the news, and a few other programs. Before retiring for the night I always give thanks for the day, commit myself afresh to God, and write in my journal."

"I expect that George will call for me not long after we get home," I said. "This day has been really helpful to me in many ways. I appreciate your kindness and your hospitality. I also thank you for being honest in answering my questions. You have been encouraging, and yet at the same time, you have given me something to strive for when I move into the city permanently."

We were not long back in the Parkers' home when George arrived to take me back to the School of Prayer. "Well, how did you get on?" asked George as we drove home.

"I am glad that you suggested that we do this before we make up our minds about staying in the City of Prayer. It really gave me an insight into the life of a busy and responsible man, who, nevertheless, is able to carry into his life the spirit of prayer and the atmosphere of God. In spite of the pressures and the distractions, he is able to maintain his connection with God and keep his spiritual awareness alive. It is encouraging to see and observe that one can go through a busy day and not forget all about God and your soul. While we all believe that Christ lives in us, Jim lives as if he was aware of Christ's presence with him all the time. It was a great encouragement."

"I gather," George said, "from your comments that your decision is to stay on in the City of Prayer?"

"Yes," I said. "I will be interested to know what my companions have decided."

"Well, we will find out shortly," responded George as he drove into the parking lot of the School of Prayer.

I thought that the session of decision making may be long and involved. Actually it was short and sweet. Like me, I found that all of my companions had already made up their minds. We all wanted to stay in the City of Prayer. This was a matter for great rejoicing for us. Without coaching, we stood and hugged each other and congratulated each other. Then we stood in a circle with our hands together and thanked God. I looked around at the faces of those three people that I had grown to love and admire, and rejoiced that we had made this journey together and had decided to stay in the city. I said, "When I have settled down, I feel especially called to focus much of my attention on intercession. That is the aspect of prayer and service that I think God is calling me to."

Alvin said, "I know I will have to find myself a job, but I also want to give as much of my time as possible to teaching and helping others understand this life of prayer. I want to be a guide and a teacher."

"And I," said John, "while I will stay in the city, I will spend time out of the city contacting others to come here and encouraging them to make the journey into prayer that we have made."

"What I am looking forward to," said Helen "is to spend time in the Quiet Room. I just want to get closer and closer to God."

With a happy and joyful spirit I looked around into the happy faces of those my friends and companions and said, "You know **I think we are learning to receive what God wanted to give us.**

THE JOURNAL: I have learned today what life in the City of Prayer is like:

1. *It is a normal life lived by normal people.*
2. *They do, however, value prayer very much and make sure that there is good and sufficient time left in their busy schedule to pray.*
3. *There is a strong sense of discipline required, so that they do not allow themselves to become neglectful or careless about their attention to prayer.*
4. *Their main purpose in prayer is to carry the spirit and atmosphere of prayer into their everyday life. They practice the presence of God. They live in the spirit.*
5. *There is a sense of progress here. No one feels that they have "arrived." All recognize that there is still much to learn. They continue to "hunger and thirst after righteousness."*

TOPICS FOR DISCUSSION—CHAPTER SEVENTEEN

1. Discuss the meaning of George's words, "The City of Prayer is, more than anything else, something you carry in your heart. It is living your life in the spirit of prayer."

2. Consider the first hours of Jim's day before he arrived at work:

   - Compare them with the first hours of your day.
   - Are there adjustments you could make to improve the early hours of your day
   - Is there any advice you could give Jim that would improve these hours?

3. Jim prayed for wisdom in decision making rather than for guidance. Discuss the meaning of this concept.
4. They all decided to stay in the City of Prayer:

   - What would it mean for you to live in the City of Prayer?
   - Do you live in the City of Prayer?

POSTSCRIPT

I have lived in the City of Prayer now for ten years. I was able to get a job in Jim's bank, and I am making good progress there. Helen and I got married, and we have two little boys. They are the delight of our lives. While these things are happening, I am still pursuing my calling to be an intercessor, and I rejoice that I have experienced many wonderful answers to prayer. Helen works in the library but frequently visits the Quiet Room. This brings her great joy and satisfaction. Alvin was able to get a job, but his real love is to devote as much time as he can to teaching in the Second School of Prayer and helping many to work their way through some of the questions and problems that they have regarding the life of prayer. His work and ministry there is deeply appreciated. John, my special friend, is employed in the central office of a mission society. This satisfies his desire to "be doing something for the Lord." While he enjoys this work he also gives time as a kind of "prayer missionary" encouraging people who live outside the city to make the journey into prayer and join us in the City of Prayer. Many are now here because of the efforts of John. We all see each other frequently. We are still close friends and give encouragement to each other. This friendship was particularly valuable to Helen and me when we went through the grief of losing our first child. We have made it a habit now, when we get together, to ask one another the simple question, "**ARE YOU LEARNING TO RECEIVE WHAT GOD WANTS TO GIVE?**"

APPENDIX ONE

Books suggested to Philip for early reading.

R. A. Torrey, *How to Pray* (Old Tappan, New Jersey: Spire Books, Fleming H. Revell, 1973).

Philip Yancey, *Prayer, Does It Make any Difference?* (Grand Rapids: Zondervan, 2006).

Richard J. Foster, *Prayer, Finding the Heart's True Home* (San Francisco: HarperCollins, 1992).

Hank Hanegraaff, *The Prayer of Jesus (Nashville: W. Publishing Group, 2001).*

CHAPTER NOTES

Chapter 5

1. Bernard of Clairvaux, *Worship in Song* (Kansas City: Lillenas Publishing Company, 1972), 110.
2. Isaac Watts, *Sing to the Lord* (Kansas City: Lillenas Publishing Company, 1993), 271.
3. Mary Brown, Ibid., 538

Chapter 6

1. Adelaide A. Pollard, *Worship in Song* (Kansas City: Lillenas Publishing Company, 1993), 480.

Chapter 7

1. J. Edwin Orr, *Worship in Song* (Kansas City: Lillenas Publishing Company, 1993,),516.
2. Albert Arsborn, Ibid., 526.
3. William Barclay, *Daily Celebration: Volume Two* (Waco, Texas: Word Books, 1976), 89.
4. Robert Burns, *Burns' Poetical Works* (Glasgow: Collins) 370.

Chapter 10

1. Thomas A. Kempis, *Imitation of Christ* (Nashville: Thomas Nelson Publishers, 1999), 37.
2. Brother Lawrence, *The Practice of the Presence of God* (Westwood, New Jersey: Fleming H. Revell Company), 55.
3. Charles R. Swindoll, *Intimacy with the Almighty* (Dallas: Word Books, 1996), 39.

4. Bernard of Clairvaux, *Worship in Song* (Kansas City: Lillenas Publishing company, 1972), 110.

Chapter 11

1. Charles Wesley, *Sing to the Lord* (Kansas City: Lillenas Publishing Company, 1993), 434.
2. Henri Nouwen, *Spiritual Direction* (New York: Harper Collins, 2006), 5.

Chapter 12

1. Thomas Ken, *Sing to the Lord (*Kansas City: Lillenas Publising Company, 1993). 7.

Chapter 13

1. Edward Perronet, *Worship in Song* (Kansas City: Lillenas Publishing Company, 1972), 11.
2. Alfred H. Ackley, Ibid., 398.

Chapter 14

1. Unknown, *The Cloud of Unknowing* (New York: Doubleday, 1973).
2. Thomas Merton, *Contemplative Prayer (New York: Image books, 1996), 34.*
3. Reginald Heber, *Sing to the Lord* (Kansas City: Lillenas Publishing Company, 1993), 2.

Chapter 16

1. Judson W. Van De Vemer, *Sing to the Lord (*Kansas City: Lillenas Publishing Company, 1993), 486.
2. Elisha A. Hoffman, Ibid., 351.

CPSIA information can be obtained at www.ICGtesting.com
Printed in the USA
LVOW12s1327130714

393975LV00001B/52/P

9 781453 531037